THE COMPLETE GUIDE TO SINGLE STOCK FUTURES

What They Are and How to Trade Them

THE COMPLETE GUIDE TO SINGLE STOCK FUTURES

What They Are and How to Trade Them

RUSSELL WASENDORF, SR.
with **ELIZABETH THOMPSON**

McGraw-Hill

New York   Chicago   San Francisco   Lisbon   London   Madrid
Mexico City   Milan   New Delhi   San Juan   Seoul
Singapore   Sydney   Toronto

The *McGraw·Hill* Companies

Library of Congress Cataloging-in-Publication Data

Wasendorf, Russell R., 1948-
    The complete guide to single stock futures : what they are and how to
    trade them / by Russell Wasendorf ; with Elizabeth Thompson.
        p.   cm.
    ISBN 0-07-143413-5 (alk. paper)
    1. Single stock futures.   2. Futures market.   I. Thompson, Elizabeth.
    II. Title.

    HG6041 .W37   2003
    332.63'228—dc22   2003016377

1 2 3 4 5 6 7 8 9 0 DOC/DOC 0 9 8 7 6 5 4 3

ISBN 0-07-143413-5

This publication is designed to provide accurate and authoritative information in regard to the subject matter covered. It is sold with the understanding that neither the author nor the publisher is engaged in rendering legal, accounting, futures/securities trading, or other professional service. If legal advice or other expert assistance is required, the services of a competent professional person should be sought.

—From a Declaration of Principles jointly adopted by a Committee of the American Bar Association and a Committee of Publishers.

This book was printed on recycled, acid-free paper containing a minimum of 50% recycled, de-inked fiber.

McGraw-Hill books are available at special quantity discounts to use as premiums and sales promotions, or for use in corporate training programs. For more information, please write to the Director of Special Sales, McGraw-Hill Professional, Two Penn Plaza, New York, NY 10121-2298. Or contact your local bookstore.

Dedicated to Connie.

Thanks again!

Contents

CHAPTER 14

Other Means of Analysis: Looking Beyond the Chart Lines   237

CHAPTER 15

Find Your Trading Style and Your Electronic Trading System   257

CHAPTER 16

Get a Hold of Yourself: Trading Well Under Stress   275

THE COMPLETE GUIDE TO SINGLE STOCK FUTURES

What They Are and How to Trade Them

Preface: Why Single Stock Futures?

Single stock futures may be the greatest trading tool since stock index futures were launched in 1982. If used by educated traders, they will be one of the most useful trading tools U.S. markets have seen in a long time. They will have multiple uses for both institutional and retail investors—as I hope to show you in this book.

Single stock futures are the first truly hybrid product, blending the benefits of stocks and futures. This trading innovation has caused legislators, regulators, and, of course, traders to take notice. There is no reason to be out of the loop in learning about this new product. So, we'll ask the most basic question: What are single stock futures?

WHAT ARE SINGLE STOCK FUTURES?

Single stock futures are futures contracts based on individual stocks, such as AOL or Microsoft. These contracts are agreements between two investors to buy or sell, at a future date, a specific quantity of shares or of the component securities of a narrow-based index at a certain price. The uses of these new products will be threefold: speculation, hedging, and risk management. (We'll discuss these uses in detail later.)

WHY LEARN ABOUT SINGLE STOCK FUTURES?

Single stock futures offer many advantages over trading stocks, and thus they are going to revolutionize stock trading in the United States and throughout the world.

Single stock futures are capital-efficient. You can trade on 20 percent margin, whereas for stocks you must put up at least 50 percent margin. This offers greater leverage and exposure to the underlying stock.

They will also be easier to trade than stocks, as there is no uptick rule. To short stocks, you must wait until the stock goes up, according to securities law. To short single stock futures, you will not have to wait for an uptick in the stock.

They will be marked to the market closing price every day.

They will create tighter spreads. For example, at MEFF, the Spanish exchange for single stock futures, contracts trade at a spread of 2 to 3 Euro cents versus a spread of 10 cents for the underlying stock.

They will have better price transparency.

Single stock futures trades will be executed quickly, as these futures will be predominantly traded electronically. NQLX, for example, will be a wholly electronic market, as will OneChicago. (These two exchanges have already been approved to trade single stock futures.)

They will be cheaper. No certificates will change hands until settlement, whereas in regular stock trading, the transfer of certificates between safekeeping accounts results in fees that are passed on to investors. In addition, there are no borrowing costs on short sales or margin accounts, whereas broker/dealers charge interest for short sales of stock and margined transactions. Also, no prospectus is required for them; there are fewer legal documents and, thus, fewer fees. Again, with regular stock trading, the cost of the legal documents would be passed on to you in fees.

Single stock futures are also cheaper than their closest trading relative: the synthetic short future (which we'll discuss in Chapter 8). To create a synthetic short future, you must sell a call and buy a put; thus you will be charged for two transactions.

WHY NOW?

For more than 18 years, single stock futures were banned because the regulatory agencies that oversee the futures and securities industries, the Commodity Futures Trading Commission (CFTC) and the Securities and Exchange Commission (SEC), could not iron out their differences and develop suitable regulation for this investment tool.

The purpose of this book, then, is to give you a brief history of and education about the securities and futures markets and the development of the regulation of these markets and single stock futures, and finally to show you how to trade these new products.

CHAPTER 1

Stocks, Futures, and Stock Futures

Perhaps you've traded futures. Or perhaps you've traded stocks—or both. Now traders and investors have the opportunity to hedge risk or to speculate with a new tool that was years in the making—single stock futures. For two decades, American investors were denied the opportunity to trade futures on individual stocks. But an act of Congress in late 2000 changed all that. After several years of regulatory hand-wringing, U.S. single stock futures made their debut in November 2002.

You probably already have some good insights into how the markets work and are looking for some in-depth information on how this tool could work for you. But first, let's take a look at how the stock and futures markets in the United States and their regulatory bodies developed. This will bring us to the creation of single stock futures.

THE STOCK MARKET

"Everyone has the brainpower to follow the stock market. If you made it through fifth grade math, you can do it."

—Peter Lynch, former manager of
Fidelity Magellan Fund

Economic Functions of Stocks and How They Trade

What exactly is a stock, anyway? When you buy a stock, you are actually buying a piece of a company. Stocks represent an investor's ownership in a com-

3

pany. The investor gives the company money in return for the right to a share of the profits of the company, which can come in the form of dividends. Stocks provide a way for companies to raise capital in order to expand their business and a way for investors to potentially build their wealth.

There are two types of stock: common stock and preferred stock. Anyone can purchase common stock, and holders of this type of stock can receive dividends based on how profitable the company is.

Corporations, on the other hand, usually purchase preferred stock. Preferred stock gives the shareholder special rights, such as a greater claim to the company's assets in case of bankruptcy. They also receive dividends at a fixed rate, which protects them when the market slides but limits them if the stock shoots up.

Investors buy stock, or "go long," when they expect the stock's price to rise. Conversely, when investors believe that the price of a company's stock is likely to fall, they can make a profit on declining prices by "shorting" that particular issue. In order to go short, however, the investor must borrow stock from a brokerage house. At some point in the future, the investor will buy back the shares and the trade will close.

A Brief History of the Stock Market in the United States

The roots of the stock markets in the United States can be traced back to England. The first stock certificates changed hands in the late seventeenth century, during the Age of Reason. The East India Company and the Hudson Bay Company were the first companies to offer stock certificates in exchange for an investment in their company.

But where there is money being made, there must be a watchful eye. It didn't take long for Parliament to realize that this industry needed to be overseen, so in 1697 Parliament developed a licensing system for brokers. Following that, more rules were put in place over the years, and the London Stock Exchange was organized in 1773.

In the United States, the first formal exchange system emerged 20 years later, in New York. Its centerpiece was an agreement among 24 brokers in Corre's Hotel. The growth of the Industrial Revolution over the next century provided plenty of fodder for interested investors. The development of steamboats in 1807 and steam engines for trains in 1829, the construction of the first land telegraph line in 1844, and the invention of tickers in 1866 and telephones in 1878 all drew investment dollars into the U.S. stock market.

Despite the inventive whirl of the nineteenth century, the market endured seven panics prior to the Great Depression, yet very few major regulations were developed during this time. However, there were at least two. In 1846, the government created a subtreasury system to watch over public funds in response to the collapse of the United States Bank in 1836.

The second of these major regulatory innovations didn't come until 1913, when the Federal Reserve Act was passed. After the panic of 1907, the government created the Monetary Commission to research the market. It was that commission's work that led to the Federal Reserve Act of 1913.

Shortly after the creation of the Federal Reserve, the United States was given the opportunity to exercise its financial might during World War I. It became a major creditor to the Allies, and the United States enjoyed an economic boom until 1929.

However, in 1929, after a bull market lasting more than a decade, a frenzy of buying created a bubble in stock prices. On that historic "Black Tuesday," October 29, 1929, panic selling hit the New York Stock Exchange, unleashing a major collapse in stock prices.

What caused the crash? Many point to widespread margin buying as a key factor. As stock prices were rising to their peak in 1929, many investors were buying stocks on credit, and banks were willingly giving out loans. Despite warnings from the Federal Reserve, Charles Mitchell, the president of National City Bank, opened the bank's coffers and lent freely to speculators.

The massive borrowing and lending probably would not have occurred if there had been solid regulatory structures in place. After the crash, however, it did not take long for the government to organize regulations to whip the securities industry in shape.

Seven Laws That Govern the Securities Industry

The framework for today's securities industry regulations emerged in the years following the Great Crash. The first key piece of legislation was the Securities Act of 1933. When Congress enacted this law, the Dow had plunged 89 percent from its 1929 peak. This act, also known as the "truth in securities law," requires companies to supply financial information and other significant information to investors and also prohibits fraud in securities trading.

Regulation didn't stop there. Over the next 7 years, Congress passed several more acts to regulate the industry, which had seemingly spun so out of control. In 1934, it passed the Securities Exchange Act, the statutory mandate for the Securities and Exchange Commission (SEC). This act gives the SEC the authority to regulate, register, and oversee brokerage firms, transfer agencies, and clearing agencies, as well as self-regulatory agencies. Through this act, the SEC also maintains disciplinary powers.

Just 1 year later, Congress passed the Public Utility Holding Company Act of 1935. This act subjects "interstate holding companies engaged, through subsidiaries, in the electric utility business or in the retail distribution of natural or manufactured gas" to government regulation.

Congress gave securities regulation a rest for a few years before passing the Trust Indenture Act of 1939. This act governs debt securities and says that bonds, debentures, and notes may be registered under the Securities Act. However, they may not be offered for public sale unless the trust indenture, a formal agreement between the issuer of bonds and the bondholders, meets the standards of this act.

The following year, Congress passed the Investment Company Act and the Investment Advisers Act. The Investment Company Act regulates the organization of companies whose services consist primarily of investing and trading securities and whose securities are publicly offered. The Investment Advisers Act, with certain exceptions, requires investment advisers to register with the SEC and adhere to SEC regulations.

For more than six decades, these six laws have governed the way in which securities are traded in the United States. However, after a wake of corporate scandals in 2001 Congress was once again called upon to enact new regulation. In July 2002 President Bush signed into law the Sarbanes-Oxley Act. The Act, crafted primarily to protect investors from fraud, created the Public Company Accounting Oversight Board (PCAOB) to oversee the activities of the auditing profession. It also mandated reforms to improve corporate responsibility, financial disclosures and prevent fraud.

In the 70 years since the SEC was created, the commission has had help in enforcing those rules from self-regulatory agencies such as the National Association of Securities Dealers (NASD). Each has enforced the laws and developed new ones as the market has matured.

THE FUTURES MARKET

The Economic Function of Futures and How They Trade

The futures market has several inherent differences from the stock market. When you buy a company's stock, as mentioned earlier, you are actually purchasing a share of ownership in that company. However, when you go long or short a futures contract, you are entering into a contract to buy or sell the underlying instrument in the future at a predetermined price. The way you make money in futures is similar way to the way you make money in stocks. If you are long a futures contract and the price rises, you make money. If you are short a futures contract and the price falls, you make money.

What benefits do the futures markets provide to the economy and the free-market system? The futures markets allow for an efficient form of price discovery; they permit hedging by commercial users, which results in lower prices for consumers; and "they act as a focal point for the collection and dissemination of statistics and key market information."

Futures contracts have only one buyer and one seller at any moment in time, who agree on a price. These contracts can be traded electronically or in the pits on the floors of the exchanges, depending on the available platforms.

All specifications except for the number of contracts to be bought or sold are standardized. All the terms under which the commodity is to be transferred are established by the commodity futures exchange on which it trades. The futures contract specifies

- The commodity to be delivered
- The quantity of this commodity
- The quality of the commodity
- The delivery point (or cash settlement)
- The delivery date
- The *ticker symbol,* a shorthand way of identifying the contract and the exchange on which it trades (e.g., ED is Eurodollars on the Chicago Mercantile Exchange)
- The *trading unit,* or the size of the contract (e.g., the trading unit for ED is $1,000,000)
- The *tick* or *minimum price fluctuation*—the size of the smallest price movement for the contract
- *Trading hours*—the time during which the commodity will be traded (these differ from commodity to commodity)
- The *daily price limit*—the maximum range of high and low prices during one trading session

When you buy a futures contract, you agree to be contingently liable for accepting delivery of a specific amount of a specific commodity at a specific time in the future at a specific price. Every futures contract is carefully defined in terms of size, quality, quantity, delivery location, and delivery date. When you buy a contract, you are considered to be long the commodity—it "be-longs" to you. You own it at a given price.

When you sell a futures contract, you contingently agree to deliver a specific amount of a specific commodity at a specific time in the future at a specific price and location. If you are a seller of a futures contract, you are short—you are currently "short" of the commodity. Generally, though, most speculators liquidate their trades well ahead of expiration, so delivery is not an issue.

Brief History of the Futures Market in the United States

The futures markets in the United States developed in Chicago in the early 1800s. The agricultural action around Chicago gave rise to the need for buyers and sellers to develop an efficient system for marketing their goods. During the harvest, a time when there were surpluses, grain users pressed for low prices, often forcing farmers to accept ridiculously low offers.

Grain merchants stockpiled as much grain as they could afford at the low harvest prices, but storage facilities were limited. As the year progressed, the supply of stored grain shrank, and users were forced to bid aggressively for the remaining supply that was still stored on farms. Violent price swings from harvest lows to late-season highs drove the grain industry to search out an alternative marketing method—forward contracts.

The early contracts were tailored to a particular buyer and seller. They specifically stated the price, quality, quantity, delivery date, and location of each delivery. Farmers knew in advance the price that they would receive for their grain at the future date. The users also had the comfort of knowing that they would have grain when they needed it.

Once the farmer signed a forward contract, he had locked in a price, thus eliminating the risk of a price decline. But one last risk remained for the farmer: A drought or crop spoilage might prevent him from producing enough grain to fulfill the contract. In this case, he would be forced to buy grain on the open market to satisfy the commitment.

The user was similarly bound by the contract, but in this case the danger was more likely to be price. If the grain price declined unexpectedly, the user would still have to pay the higher contract price. These contracts have stood time's test well. Even today, many farmers fix prices before delivery through forward contracts.

As forward contracts became more common, speculators appeared on the scene. They hoped to make a profit by assuming temporary long or short positions in forward contracts. The speculator hoped to profit by reselling (or rebuying) the forward contract at a higher (lower) price. Eventually, developing these contracts individually became cumbersome, inefficient, and restrictive.

This led to the creation of the Chicago Board of Trade in 1848. The existence of a centralized marketplace highlighted the need for stream-lined trading procedures. Over time, these forward contracts acquired specific standards and became similar to modern futures contracts—one of the most flexible pricing mechanisms in the history of commerce.

Regulation of the Futures Industry

Regulation of the futures industry is not nearly as detailed as that of the securities industry (which is why it took so long for single stock futures, a hybrid instrument, to become legal, as we'll see later).

It should come as no surprise that major regulation governing the futures industry came into being at the same time that Congress was passing laws to regulate the securities industry. In 1936, the Commodity Exchange Authority was created by the Commodity Exchange Act, which replaced the Grain Futures Act of 1922.

As the futures business grew following World War II, the government saw the need to rework the system of futures regulation, and so, in 1974, the Commodity Exchange Authority was replaced by the Commodity Futures Trading Commission (CFTC). The commission was charged with overseeing the entire futures industry; its job is to protect market participants from manipulation, abusive trading practices, and fraud. The Commodity Exchange Act sets the standards in futures trading, from what constitutes fraud to how firms are to conduct business and keep records.

The CFTC is also aided in regulation by self-regulatory agencies such as the National Futures Association (NFA), the counterpart to the securities industry's NASD.

FINANCIAL FUTURES

Financial futures have also proved to be useful tools for price discovery and for hedging risk. Foreign currency futures and stock index futures are the predecessors of single stock futures. It's important to understand how these hybrid instruments developed in order to understand their usefulness to the markets.

Foreign Currency Futures

Trading in foreign currency futures got a boost in the early 1970s, following President Nixon's 1971 announcement that the United States would no longer be tied to the gold standard. Prior to that time, the 1944 Bretton Woods Agreement had set the U.S. price of gold at $35 an ounce, and the values of other nations' currencies were also fixed in relation to gold and thus to the U.S. dollar. The Smithsonian Agreement, enacted in December 1971 by the finance ministers of the world's major industrialized countries, attempted to keep currency fluctuations to a minimum by restricting trade to within a certain band.

However, that agreement collapsed in 1973, opening the door to the free float of currencies. Currency futures, which began trading on the International Monetary Market (IMM), a division of the Chicago Mercantile Exchange (CME), in May 1972, gained momentum as volatility in the world currency markets increased.

Stock Index Futures

With the success of foreign currency futures, it's no surprise that exchanges, firms, institutions, speculators, and investors alike were ready for another sophisticated trading tool, the stock index future.

How did the development of this tool come about? The first stock index futures contract was the Value Line Index, based on 30 industrial stocks, which was offered by the Kansas City Board of Trade (KCBT) in 1982. The CME followed suit quickly, opening trading on the S&P 500 index just 2 months after the KCBT.

These new products increased the overall volume of the market and have proved their effectiveness even amidst market slides such as the stock market crash of 1987. New indexes are constantly being created by markets here and abroad. For example, in 1999, when the Euro became a regional currency for 11 countries, markets rushed to create continental indexes, and some of them still flourish.

THE SHAD-JOHNSON ACCORD: AN AGREEMENT BETWEEN THE REGULATORY BODIES

But who had jurisdiction over futures on stocks? As stock index futures began to develop in the 1970s, a debate between the CFTC and the SEC as to which agency would oversee these new hybrid products ensued.

The result of the debate was the 1982 Shad-Johnson Accord (named after the commissions' chairmen), which placed a temporary ban on single stock futures and futures on narrow-based stock indexes (known collectively as security futures) until the commissions could iron out their differences. The accord also gave sole jurisdiction over broad-based stock index futures to the CFTC. Broad-based indexes were defined as meeting one of two sets of criteria.

Criteria A:

- There are 10 or more securities.
- No single component constitutes more than 30 percent of the weighting.
- The five largest components by weight collectively constitute no more than 60 percent of the weighting.
- The bottom quartile of component stocks has a combined average daily trading volume of more than $50 million, or $30 million if the index includes at least 15 securities.

Criteria B:

- There are nine or more securities.
- No component constitutes more than 30 percent of the weighting.
- Each component is a large stock (defined as one of the top 500 stocks in terms of both market capitalization and average daily trading volume).

Any index that does not conform to these standards is considered narrow-based and, as such, falls under the joint jurisdiction of the CFTC and the SEC.

HOW SECURITY FUTURES DIFFER FROM THE UNDERLYING SECURITY

For those who are used to buying and selling stocks, there are some differences to be aware of when trading single stock futures. When you buy stock, you own a fractional interest in that company and are guaranteed certain rights as a partial owner. For example, when you own stock, you may be able to vote on matters affecting the company, to receive dividends from the company's profits, and to receive certain corporate disclosures and reports.

However, if you buy a single stock futures contract, you have no special rights with regard to the company; your rights and obligations are limited to those specified in your contract. So, if you buy a December GM single stock futures contract, you are agreeing only to take delivery of 100 shares of GM. Once you receive those shares, you may be entitled to certain shareholder privileges, but the security futures contract alone does not give you those privileges.

Another difference between trading single stock futures and trading the underlying stocks is that futures contracts are "marked to market" on a daily basis. When trading closes each day, your account will be credited for any profit and debited for any loss, using the contract price established at the end of the day for settlement purposes (the *daily settlement price*). When you own securities, you receive a statement of profit and loss when you liquidate your position and each quarter.

In futures trading, your profits and losses are calculated daily. You may be required to deposit additional funds into your account if you are long and the price of your security futures contract decreases. Similarly, if you are short a security futures contract and the price increases, you may have to deposit additional funds. This is an important distinction between securities and futures. Depending on market fluctuation, you may even have to deposit additional funds into your account for several days in a row if the price of your contract continues to rise or fall.

The last main difference is that security futures contracts expire on a specific date. Thus, if you have not liquidated your security futures contract before it expires, you must settle it upon expiration. If you have gone long a single stock futures contract and have not offset it prior to expiration, you must take delivery of those securities. If you have shorted a single stock futures contract and have not offset it prior to expiration, you must make delivery. The owner of the underlying stock, on the other hand, can hold a long position for an extended period of time, with no expiration, in the hope that the price will finally go up.

COMPONENTS OF A SECURITY FUTURES CONTRACT

What are the key components of a security futures contract? Size, price quotation, expiration date, and tick value. Each component may vary by exchange, even if the contract covers the same security, so you may want to talk your broker or the exchange about contract specifications.

Each security futures contract has a set size, determined by the regulated exchange on which the contract trades. For example, a security futures contract for a single stock may be based on 100 shares of that stock; in that case, the value of the contract would be the price per share times 100. It's entirely possible that an exchange might, at some point, increase the contract size because of user demand.

The expiration date of security futures contracts is also determined by the regulated exchange. For example, if you have entered into a contract that expires the third Friday the month, you may liquidate your position or settle your contract as we discussed in the previous section.

Price quotations for security futures contracts are usually based on quotations on the underlying security; thus, if a security is quoted in dollars and cents per share, the futures contract on that security would also be quoted in dollars and cents per share.

The last main component of a security futures contract is the *tick*, which is the minimum price fluctuation allowed for that contract. This means that if a particular security futures contract has a tick size of 1 cent, you can buy the contract at $52.21 or $52.22 but not at $52.215. Like all other components, this component may differ from exchange to exchange.

HOW THEY WILL BE TRADED

To start trading single stock futures, you must deposit funds, usually at least 20 percent of the current market value of the contract, with your brokerage firm, in either a securities or a futures account.

If you have an open position, either long or short, you close it by entering an opposite position. For example, if you were long one December GM single stock futures contract, you would offset, or close, your position by selling one December GM single stock futures contract. Generally, futures contracts are closed prior to expiration, and so holders are not obligated to either receive or deliver the stock.

As we discussed previously, whether your position is long or short, if you do not liquidate it prior to expiration, you must settle it through physical delivery. With physical delivery, if you are long the contract, you must pay the final settlement price set by the regulated exchange or the clearing organization and take delivery of the underlying shares. Conversely, if you are short the contract, you must deliver the underlying shares in exchange for the final settlement price.

At this writing, non-U.S. exchanges may specify cash settlements. In this case, if you were long a security futures contract, you would pay the value of the shares. If you were short, you would receive an amount of cash determined by the exchange or clearing firm. This amount is usually based on the value of the shares at the end of trading on expiration day. Once this transaction is complete, neither party has any further obligations under the contract.

The Commodity Futures Modernization Act

The passage of the Commodity Futures Modernization Act (CFMA) on December 21, 2000, ended the ban on single stock futures and paved the way for the development of this new tool, which is trading today.

What sparked the movement to lift of the ban? Within the United States, an official statement by the President's Working Group in 1999 made the case for regulatory change. This group, which consisted of representatives from the Federal Reserve, the Treasury, the SEC, and the CFTC, declared that single stock futures could be a useful risk management tool and that the ban should be repealed.

Competition from abroad also lit a fire beneath U.S. legislators. In September 2000, 4 months before the United States repealed the ban, the London International Financial Futures and Options Exchange (LIFFE, now Euronext.liffe) announced that it planned to offer 15 single stock futures on its trading platform.

However, the legalization of single stock futures in the United States was slowed by regulatory disagreements between the CFTC and the SEC. When Congress expanded the definition of a commodity 30 years ago, it opened the door to a regulatory turf war in the United States, something that other countries have not had. In many other areas, such as Hong Kong, the same financial regulators oversee both securities and futures markets. Exchanges in the U.K. were able to launch single stock futures before the Financial Services Authority (FSA), which oversees the whole of the U.K.'s financial markets, was developed. Universal stock futures, the U.K. version of single stock futures, began trading on January 29, 2001, while the FSA was not active until December 1, 2001.

THE SEC AND THE CFTC COME TOGETHER

While the CFMA actually legalized the trading of single stock futures in 2000, there was a long regulatory road to walk before these instruments were allowed to hit the screens and begin trading. The CFMA actually made provisions for many different things, including providing legal certainty for over-the-counter derivatives markets, reauthorizing the CFTC for 5 years, clarifying the Treasury Amendment exclusion in the Commodity Exchange Act, giving the CFTC jurisdiction over retail foreign exchange trading and repealing the Shad-Johnson Accord ban on single stock futures.

We are going to focus on the repeal of the Shad-Johnson Accord, as it applies directly to single stock futures. The CFMA mandated that the CFTC and the SEC work together to flesh out rules on how single stock futures would be traded and granted the two agencies shared jurisdiction over single stock futures trading. Working together was no small feat for these agencies, considering the differences in the two industries' philosophies.

In short, futures regulation starts with the premise that if you protect the integrity of the market, then you will ultimately protect the investor. In the securities industry, the premise is that if you protect the investor, then you will have market integrity. In addition to the philosophical differences, each commission wants what is best for its industry. Futures industry professionals have advocated single stock futures for years because they believe these instruments will bring more business to their industry. On the flip side, securities professionals fear that single stock futures will draw business away from them. To create parity between the industries, the commissions had to review several areas of difference and develop solutions.

Areas of Difference between CFTC and SEC Regulations

In order to appreciate the difficulties that these two bodies have overcome through their regulatory compromises, it is useful to look at the disparities in their views. The CFTC and the SEC had different ideas on several key issues affecting the regulation of single stock futures. These included margin requirements, tax treatment for short- and long-term trades, shorting on an uptick, insider trading restrictions, and restricted-stock rules. Here's how each of those issues has been resolved.

Margin Requirements

When you buy a stock, you are required to deposit at least 50 percent of the value of that stock; this is considered a "down payment" toward ownership. This differs from margin requirements in the futures industry, which are generally much lower—anywhere from 2 to 20 percent of the value of the contract. Furthermore, in the futures industry, the margin is not considered a down payment; instead it is considered a "performance bond." If the traditional futures margins had applied to single stock futures contracts, futures brokers would have had an obvious advantage in soliciting single stock futures business.

The commissions compromised on a margin requirement for all accounts, securities and futures, of 20 percent. That is the same margin requirement as for stock options, an investment vehicle that competes with single stock futures as a risk management tool. (Both hedge risk in trading and single stock futures can be created synthetically through a combination of buying and selling options.)

The CFTC and the SEC blended industry standards in the final margin rules, which were approved on August 2, 2002. They have summarized the margin rules as follows:

- Minimum initial and maintenance margin levels for outright positions in security futures are 20 percent of "current market value," or the daily published or quoted daily settlement price of the security future.
- Self-regulatory authorities can set margin levels lower than 20 percent of current market value for customers with certain strategy-based offset positions involving security futures and one or more related securities or futures.
- The types of collateral that are acceptable as margin deposits are identified and standards for the valuation of such collateral are established.
- Uniform standards for the withdrawal of margin by customers and security futures intermediaries are established.
- Procedures for undermargined accounts are set forth.

For both veteran stock traders and veteran futures traders, the margin treatment of single stock futures will be different from what they are used to. Futures traders will need to adjust to slightly higher margins, while stock traders will need to adjust to the fact that their accounts will be "marked to market" on a daily basis, after the close. If market movement causes an account balance to fall below the required margin levels, the trader will be required to deposit additional funds, in the form of a margin call.

For example, if a trader's single stock future opened at $110 (the value of the single stock futures contract on 100 shares would be $11,000), margin requirements would total $2200 (20% × $11,000). If the closing price fell to $105 one week later, the trader's equity would have decreased by $500 ($5 × 100), to $1700. However, the minimum margin required for $10,500 worth of stock would be $2100. This would result in a margin call for $400 ($2100 - $1700). On the flip side, however, if the stock price rose by $5, the trader would have earned $500 for the account.

Tax Treatment

Everyone knows the U.S. tax code is a complicated mess of rules too dense for a non-CPA to grasp. That being said, this section will be relatively brief. It is best to direct specific questions to a qualified accountant.

As with margin, the main concern in developing rules for taxes was parity between the treatment of stock options and that of single stock futures. Prior to the CFMA, all regulated futures contracts and listed non-equity options were characterized as section 1256 contracts. Section 1256 contract status was important because it allowed 60 percent of capital gains and losses to be long-term and 40 percent short-term regardless of the actual holding period and because it allowed positions to be marked to market at year-end. In contrast, equity options, unless traded by a dealer, did not fall under section 1256. (To be considered a dealer in equity options, one must be registered with a national securities exchange as a market maker or specialist in listed options.)

To maintain parity between equity options and security futures, regulators made the following resolutions under the CFMA:

- Security futures contracts are not section 1256 contracts unless they are held by a dealer in security futures contracts.
- Security futures contracts held by nondealers are generally taxed in the same manner as listed equity options held by nondealers (new Code §1234B).

At this writing, the definition of a security futures dealer has not been determined and will have to be determined by the Treasury after receiving input from exchanges. Dealer status need not be based on affirmative obligations, such as market making, but instead may simply be based on the amount of trading an investor does.

Security futures contracts raise a number of additional tax considerations, such as straddle rules, wash sale rules, constructive sale rules, and much more. For more specific information, contact an accountant.

The following tax charts simplify the tax code for security futures products.

TABLE 2-1

Tax Chart for Security Futures Contracts

	Timing	Character	Holding Period	Making/Taking delivery of stock
Dealers*	Mark-to-Market	Capital gain/loss	60% long-term; 40% short-term	Same as cash settlement
Non-dealers (long)	On termination	Capital gain/loss	Short-term unless held for more than one year	Treated as purchase of stock Holding period tacks
Non-dealers (short)	On termination	Capital gain/loss	Apply short sale rules	Treated as sale of stock
Non-dealers (hedging long stock)	May give rise to "constructive sale"	Capital gain/loss	Short sale or straddle rules apply	Treated as sale of stock

*Revenue Procedure 2002-11 provides procedures for determining who is a "dealer".
© 2002 Erika W. Nijenhuis

TABLE 2-2

Security Futures Contracts—Information Reporting

Information Reporting	Security Futures Contracts	Other Stock Index Contracts ("Regulated Futures Contracts")	Equity Options
Entering into contract	No	No	No
Closing by delivery of stock	Yes if stock is sold (report as sale of stock)		
No if stock is purchased	Yes (report as purchase or sale of contract)	Yes if stock is sold (report as sale of stock)	
No if stock is purchased			
Other closing transactions (cash settlement; offset)	Not clear*	Yes (report as purchase or sale of contract) Market generally does not report	

*IRS regulations do not specifically address these transactions. The market can be expected to interpret existing rules consistent with the treatment of equity options, unless the IRS issues guidance requiring information reporting.

© 2002 Erika W. Nijenhuis

Shorting on an Uptick Rule

A key advantage of trading single stock futures is that you will be able to short the contract without waiting for an uptick. This differs from when you are selling a stock. In order to sell an outright stock position short, an investor must wait for the stock to rise in price again. This rule dates back to the Securities Exchange Act of 1934, in which the SEC prohibited selling a stock after a price drop. Ideally, the rule was adopted to prevent forms of market manipulation such as bear raids, in which investors sell short in an effort to drive the price of a security down.

There is no such rule in the futures industry, and the rule for securities is sometimes considered to be outdated, as the volume was much lower and trading strategies were much simpler in the early 1930s.

Insider Trading Restrictions

According to the SEC web site, "Insider trading is illegal when a person trades a security while in possession of material nonpublic information in violation of a duty to withhold the information or refrain from trading." Securities laws prohibit any deceptive actions in the offer, purchase, or sale of securities. These extensive laws provide the foundation for disciplinary actions against fraudulent insider trading.

In the futures industry, trading on nonpublic information is generally not prohibited by CFTC or NFA rules. However, for the purposes of trading single stock futures, insider trading and other forms of trading based on nonpublic information will be violations of SEC Rule 10b-5, which generally prohibits insider trading, and NFA Compliance Rule 2-37(a), which states, "No Member or Associate shall violate Sections 9(a), 9(b), or 10(b) of the Commodity Exchange Act or any applicable regulation thereunder in connection with any security futures product." (Those sections of the Commodity Exchange Act detail what is considered to be insider trading and how those actions are penalized.)

Restricted-Stock Rules

A restricted stock is an unregistered acquired stock from the issuer or the affiliate of an issuer in a private nonpublic offering. For example, stock issued to employees of a company could be restricted stock.

Rule 144 of the SEC explains what must be done with restricted stock. It requires that "persons who hold restricted securities may sell them only in limited quantities and that all sales for restricted stock by control persons must be reported to the SEC."

In order to comply, futures commission merchants (FCMs) will now ask whether a potential customer is a control associate in any of the companies whose stock underlies futures contracts on a single stock futures exchange. If the customer is a control associate, he or she is likely to be monitored more closely by the FCM to ensure that he or she does not engage in market manipulation.

The NASD has not included any rule regarding restricted stock and has "not included provisions concerning position limits and the reporting of security futures positions, which will instead be addressed by each exchange or market trading security futures as appropriate."

Fees

The SEC is funded via a fee on every security trade that is conducted—another difference, as the CFTC does not collect fees on trades. Section 31 fees will apply to single stock futures, and the exchanges will incur these fees. They may or may not pass them on to the customer. The fee is $0.009 per round turn transaction. The U.S. Treasury will receive the money from these fees. (Fee rates are subject to change depending on the SEC's annual budget.)

The Roles of the NFA and the NASD

The NFA and NASD are self-regulatory organizations (SROs) that work under the CFTC and the SEC, respectively. They handle some of the finer points of regulation and audit brokerage firms to ensure that each firm is adhering to industry standards. The bottom line is that they have worked together to protect you, the trader. These two organizations together developed the new standards for single stock futures. In general, because the securities industry is more heavily regulated than the futures industry, the NFA has adopted many rules or reinterpreted existing rules so that they mirror similar NASD rules.

To the average investor, this information is probably about as exciting as reading through tax laws. But the bottom line is, it's your money, and it never hurts to learn about your broker's legal obligations. The following is a synopsis of key rules designed to govern security futures products.

NFA

The CFMA mandated that in order for members of the NFA to trade security futures products, the NFA become a "limited purpose national securities association." Basically, this means that the NFA has had to adopt customer protection rules similar to the NASD rules that were already in place. These rules among other things, outline supervision of security futures product brokers, customer suitability, fair commissions, best execution, and discretionary account practices.

In terms of supervision, each firm offering security futures products activities is required to designate a security futures products principal, who must have passed the Futures Branch Manager Examination (Series 30). This principal will be responsible for supervising discretionary trades and the opening of customer accounts and approving promotional materials, for which the NFA has added rules specific to security futures products.

The NFA has also developed a customer suitability rule for single stock futures. Before a customer can trade futures, FCMs or introducing brokers (IBs) must obtain information on the customer's previous investment experience, estimated annual income, and net worth. Before the customer can trade single stock futures, FCMs or IBs must now also inquire whether the account is for speculative or hedging purposes and determine the customer's employment status, marital status, and number of dependents. Based on this information, the security futures principal will determine if the prospective customer is suited to trade security futures products. Once the account is approved, brokers cannot make recommendations that are ill suited to a particular account.

The NFA also implemented a new fair commissions rule, which is designed to ensure that your broker does not overcharge you. It is an interpretive notice that states that charging commissions based on costs, plus a reasonable profit, is allowed. Also, the member is allowed to take into account volume and services provided when setting commission levels.

Another new NFA rule is the equivalent of the NASD's best execution rule. Basically, this means that NFA members must put their customer's interests before their own. Your broker cannot trade ahead of an order that you place and must place orders in your best interest. Also, if you request that a trade be placed in a specific market, your broker must follow those instructions. If you do not give specific market instructions, your broker must take the following into consideration before placing your order: "price volatility, liquidity, depth, speed of execution and pressure on available communications; the size and type of transaction; and the location, reliability and accessibility to the customer's intermediary of primary markets and quotation sources," as well as the fees and costs associated with trading in each market.

In line with this best execution rule, your broker must not channel an order through a third party unless you instruct him or her to do so. If your broker does so without your permission, he or she must show that it was in your best interest pricewise and timewise.

NASD

If you choose to trade security futures products in a securities account, you will want to be aware of the rules that will pertain to your account and your broker. As you'll see, many of these rules mirror the NFA rules.

The NASD has proposed to the SEC several amendments to current rules and one new rule, Rule 2865, for the regulation of security futures products. As specified by the CFMA, the amendments closely parallel current rules for stock options. These rules will pertain only to security futures held in securities accounts. The proposed rule amendments and rules cover three areas: education requirements for industry professionals, communication with the public, and opening and maintaining customer accounts.

In order to engage in security futures product activities, various firm representatives must complete an additional education requirement, addressing security futures directly.

This requirement is available through the NFA's and the NASD's web sites, but a firm may alternatively develop its own internal requirements consistent with those outlined by the associations. The NASD is also working to revise the standard tests for these firm representatives to include security futures products. Once this is done, a person who passes a revised NASD exam will not have to complete a separate continuing education requirement.

The NASD also has certain rules about communicating with the public, covering advertisements, sales literature, and record keeping regarding security futures products. All of these forms of communication must have a risk disclosure statement, and three disclosures about security futures products must be included: (1) In a communication, discussion of the advantages of security futures must be balanced by disclosure of the risks associated with these products, (2) the communication must warn that security futures products are not suitable for all investors, and (3) "exaggerated, unwarranted, or misleading" statements about security futures are prohibited. A registered options and security futures principal must approve all ads and submit them for NASD approval. In addition, records of security futures product ads and correspondence must be kept, along with information on past recommendations, actual transactions, and completed worksheets.

Rule 2865 is a new rule that has been specifically developed for security futures products like single stock futures. It deals mainly with how customer accounts will be opened and maintained. Under this rule, the NASD may impose restrictions that it deems necessary to maintain an orderly market and to protect investors. NASD members must comply with this rule when trading security futures products.

The first part of the rule outlines what information a broker/dealer (B/D) must provide before opening an account and what records it must keep in maintaining that account. First, a B/D must provide a risk disclosure statement prior to conducting any security futures product transactions. Once the account has been approved and opened, the B/D must send a confirmation of each transaction and a monthly account statement if there has been account activity in the preceding month, detailing money positions, entries, interest charges, and any special charges, if there is no activity, the B/D must send a statement quarterly.

The second part of the rule deals with the information that customers must disclose before opening an account. A customer must provide information on his or her investment objectives, such as safety of principal, income, growth, trading profits, or speculation; employment status, estimated annual income from all sources; estimated net worth exclusive of family residence; estimated liquid net worth, such as cash, securities, or other liquid assets; marital status and number of dependents; age; and investment experience, such as the number of years the customer has been investing and the size and frequency of various types of transactions, such as transactions involving commodity futures, options, stocks, bonds, and other financial instruments. Provided that the customer meets a minimum net equity established by the B/D and the information is verified, the security futures principal can approve the account.

If applicable, an account form may include sources of background and financial information and the dates and various signatures required for account approval. Fifteen days after approval, a customer shall receive a written agreement of his or her account and a risk disclosure statement. The B/D will then maintain a record of the customer's background, financial information, and complaints.

If a customer opens a discretionary account, giving someone else the authority to trade in his or her place, the B/D must comply with a few additional rules. First, no one can exercise discretionary power to trade security futures in a customer's account or accept orders from a person other than the customer unless this power has been given in an agreement. On the day it is entered, each discretionary order shall be approved and initialed by the branch office manager or by the principal qualified to supervise security futures activities. Again, records of discretionary transactions must be kept.

The suitability clause of Rule 2865 refers to the customer's suitability to make certain trades and suitability to deal with the risks of those trades. Basically, it comes down to the trader's ability to incur loss and to fully understand each trade. According to this clause, each broker is required to know each of her or his customers' investment objectives, financial situation and needs, and any other information necessary to determine how that customer should trade. With all of this information in mind, the broker must have a "reasonable basis" for recommending a trade. A broker must recommend only trades that are appropriate given the customer's investment experience and financial background. Every NASD member shall also try to avoid trading ahead of customers' orders.

Each member shall investigate the background of any person "prior to making such a certification in the application of such person for registration" with the NASD.

"A person associated with a [NASD] member who opens a securities account or places an order for the purchase or sale of securities with a [registered B/D]" must notify her or his employer of her or his intention of opening an account and, if the employer requests, provide duplicate copies of confirmations, statements, or other information pertaining to that account, unless the account was established prior to employment.

The final rule amendment deals with short sales. Normally, under NASD regulation, you cannot sell short unless you can deliver the security. This amendment clarifies that this restriction will not apply to security futures products.

The bottom line is that many regulators from both industries spent a lot of time developing rules to protect traders who choose to use single stock futures. A great deal of compromise was seen on the part of regulators from both the securities and the futures sides, and this has resulted in a valuable new tool for hedging risk or speculating on future price movement in the underlying stock price.

CHAPTER 3

Single Stock Futures Trading Outside the United States

Regulatory wrangling put the United States well behind other countries around the world in terms of the introduction of single stock futures trading. Currently, there are more than a dozen exchanges outside of the United States that offer single stock futures contracts. But, better late than never, and, actually, the additional time has allowed for education of investors and preparations at U.S. exchanges and may have put the United States in a stronger position as it begins to offer this new trading vehicle. Among the many countries that offer trading in single stock futures are Australia, Canada, Finland, Hong Kong, Hungary, the Netherlands, Singapore, South Africa, Spain, Sweden, and the United Kingdom. The OM Stockholmbörsen in Sweden and the Helsinki Exchange in Finland have traded single stock futures for more than a decade.

TAKING A LOOK AT VOLUME

In 2001, Spain's MEFF earned top ranking in terms of single stock futures trading volume, with nearly 8.8 million contracts changing hands. However, overall volume at some of the other exchanges has been limited. In 2001, five of these eleven exchanges—Montreal, Sydney, Euronext Amsterdam, Hong Kong, and Singapore—did not trade even close to 100,000 contracts in the entire year (see Table 3.1).

While the lack of volume in single stock futures at some of these exchanges contributed to skepticism about the viability of these products here in the United States, our exchanges have stepped onto a very different playing field. Many of those countries do not have an active base of futures traders, whereas the United States does. Familiarity and experience with

TABLE 3.1

Volume of Single Stock Futures in Foreign Markets

	2000	2001
MEFF R.V. (Spain)		8,766,165
LIFFE (now Euronext.liffe; U.K.)		2,325,744
OM Stockholmbörsen (Sweden)	2,144,767	1,468,018
Budapest Stock Exchange	456,510	879,049
SAFEX (South Africa)	29,991	811,156
Montreal Exchanges		17,206
Sydney Futures Exchange	8,817	12,545
Euronext Amsterdam	773	8,367
Hong Kong Exchanges	3,322	7,756
Singapore Exchange Ltd.		6,575
Helsinki Exchange	N/A	N/A
Total	2,187,670	13,423,532

(Source: *Futures Industry* magazine, January/February 2002)

the futures markets seems to be a key to success. Two of the exchanges with the lowest volumes are actually quite young exchanges. For example, the Hong Kong Futures Exchange Limited was established in 1976. A quarter of a century is not much, considering that U.S. futures exchanges were established in the nineteenth century. Also, at the end of 2001, some of these markets, such as Singapore, had not even been open for trading in single stock futures for an entire year.

Further adding to the skepticism is the fact that options are generally traded more heavily than single stock futures in foreign markets. Many traders understand how to trade options, while futures remain unfamiliar to them; thus, they still trade options more frequently than futures. However, the difference between the volumes of options and futures is much slimmer in successful single stock futures markets, such as Euronext.liffe.

COMPARING TWO SUCCESSFUL FOREIGN MARKETS: MEFF AND EURONEXT.LIFFE

Single stock futures have seen success and are somewhat actively traded on two foreign exchanges: MEFF (the Spanish futures and options exchange) and Euronext.liffe (formerly the London International Financial Futures and Options Exchange). The United States can look at these exchanges, to a degree, as models for success and for clues to how single stock futures can augment our existing markets. These exchanges will also offer competition to the U.S. exchanges, as U.S. investors may eventually be able to trade in these highly liquid markets.

MEFF

While MEFF offers only nine single stock futures contracts (versus Euronext.liffe's 140 single stock futures), it is the leading exchange in terms of single stock futures trading volume. In the first nine months of 2003, more than 8.5 million single stock futures contracts were traded, compared to 5.1 million contracts in the same period for Euronext.liffe, its nearest competitor.

Why has MEFF seen so much success? The exchange modeled its single stock futures product on its successful options contracts. The similarity attracts traders who are already familiar with options and are interested in a new hedging tool.

At MEFF, both stock options and stock futures contracts are based on 100 shares of the underlying stock, and they both have quarterly expirations and physical settlement. The futures can also be settled in cash. When you settle a contract in cash, you receive or pay the cash value of the stock, which is generally based on the opening price of the stock on the expiration day; you do not receive any stock. After payment, neither the buyer nor the seller has any further obligations under the contract. When you settle the contract through delivery, you receive or deliver the stock. If you must deliver the stock but do not own it, you must purchase it or have your brokerage firm purchase it for you.

Offering both types of settlement avoids disputes regarding the integrity of the settlement price. Cash settlement occurs only for an equal number of buyers and sellers. The contracts to be settled by delivery are assigned through a lottery system. For example, if there are 100 long contracts and 90 short contracts that have opted for cash settlement, 90 of these contracts are going to be settled in cash. The remaining 10, which are randomly chosen, will be settled by delivery of the underlying stock by the clearinghouse. MEFF offers both types of settlement to ensure interest in single stock futures, thus also increasing liquidity.

MEFF also applied its successful options market-making system to its single stock futures, which increases the liquidity of these contracts. As payment for providing liquidity, market makers receive a percentage of the members' trading fees based on the amount of liquidity they provide. Market makers agree to take the opposite end of customers' trades in exchange for a fee. This is an incentive system that helps to ensure a liquid market for single stock futures.

In addition to liquid markets, a key ingredient of the success that MEFF has seen in its single stock futures trading is its proprietary trading system. MEFF, a leading electronic exchange, developed the S/MART trading system, which offers a typical response time of $\frac{3}{10}$ of a second.

Euronext.liffe

Few exchanges seem to understand the importance of reliable electronic trading systems and their ability to make products accessible to millions of traders around the globe better than Euronext.liffe. This understanding and the ability to incorporate it into the workings of the exchange has catapulted Euronext.liffe to the position of the second-largest single stock futures exchange in terms of volume, even though the exchange began trading single stock futures only on January 29, 2001. Since then, Euronext.liffe has traded more than 11 million universal stock futures contracts (the name used by the exchange is different from that in the United States, but the concept is the same). While MEFF's success is attributable to the fact that the exchange has made its single stock futures comparable to its options, Euronext.liffe's success can be attributed to its global accessibility.

Euronext.liffe trades in five currencies: sterling, euro, dollars, Swiss francs, and Swedish krona. The underlying stocks of universal stock futures come from the U.K., the United States, and continental Europe. This global accessibility has pumped up the exchange's total activity. In 2001, an average of €612 billion was entrusted daily to its trading platform, making it one of the largest electronic exchanges by value.

Much of the reason that Euronext.liffe, a wholly electronic exchange, is so accessible is that its LIFFE CONNECT trading platform extends to 26 countries and is used by a variety of financial institutions—banks, brokerage firms, and other institutions. Therefore, much of Europe's financial community is already familiar with its workings. Much of the United States is also linked to LIFFE CONNECT.

In order to ensure reliability for its thousands of customers, LIFFE CONNECT requires the independent software vendors connected to its system to conform to all the technical requirements set by Euronext.liffe, and the vendors must also be accredited by the exchange.

The LIFFE CONNECT system offers several other features that are attractive to new customers and maintain the reliability of the system. One of these is to allow traders to request quotes from other market participants. Another useful feature for traders is LIFFEstyle Online, which provides historical market information on all Euronext.liffe markets to customers at any time. This information is constantly updated by the Euronext.liffe market and enables nonprofessionals to obtain quick access to data.

In addition to Euronext.liffe's customer-friendly technology, another factor in the exchange's success is how it promotes liquidity, which it has done in several ways. First, many universal stock futures are covered by at least one designated market maker. Doing this guarantees a continuous two-way market with a maximum spread in a minimum size.

The exchange also encourages liquidity through its low margin requirements, which can be as low as 6 percent. This offers customers an incredible amount of leverage, as they could potentially control £100,000 worth of stock for about £6000.

Finally, Euronext.liffe offers only cash settlement on 134 of its contracts to avoid delivery issues that may arise. For example, a short squeeze could occur if not enough stock were available to buy. Also, customers can accept cash payment no matter what type of account they hold. For example, if they do not have a stock account, they would not be able to accept a delivery of stock. Avoiding these potential problems also enables smoother trading with other European Union countries. Thus, the simplicity of this type of settlement may have some appeal to traders across Europe.

However, Euronext.liffe also offers physical delivery on six of its contracts to suit the settlement systems in Finland, Norway, and Denmark, where universal stock futures are not settled through an auction system.

CLOSER TO HOME—WHERE TO TRADE SINGLE STOCK FUTURES IN THE UNITED STATES

Currently, there are four exchanges that offer or have announced an intention to offer single stock futures: NQLX, OneChicago, Island Futures Exchange, and Amex. Each offers its own unique benefits to traders, depending on where their trading interests and preference lie. NQLX and OneChicago opened trading in a portion of their listed single stock futures on November 8, 2002, with a plan to roll out other contracts on a frequent basis.

NQLX, a wholly electronic exchange, was a joint venture of the NASDAQ Stock Market, Inc., and Euronext.liffe until June 2003, when NASDAQ pulled out of the joint venture, giving its stake to Euronext.liffe. NQLX is independent and uses LIFFE CONNECT as its trading platform. In August 2001, it became the first exchange to be recognized by the CFTC as a single stock futures exchange. As of October 7, 2003, the exchange offered futures on 88 individual stocks, including General Motors Corp., Johnson & Johnson, and Microsoft, as well as futures on six exchange-traded funds (ETFs) and futures on three broad-based indexes.

NQLX's now sole parent company, Euronext.liffe, is already experienced in trading single stock futures, and its platform, LIFFE CONNECT, is located at more than 500 sites in 26 countries. Its experience and global connectivity offer tremendous advantages to prospective single stock futures traders.

OneChicago is a joint venture of the Chicago Board Options Exchange (CBOE), the Chicago Mercantile Exchange (CME), and the Chicago Board of Trade (CBOT). The CFTC approved it for trading in June 2002. OneChicago will also operate exclusively as an electronic exchange, and orders may be entered either through CBOEdirect or through the CME's GLOBEX 2. As of October 7, 2003, OneChicago had competitively listed 94 single stock futures, including futures on General Motors Corp. and Microsoft, as well as one ETF contract and 15 narrow-based indexes.

The CBOE, the world's largest stock options exchange, began listing stock options in 1973 and index options in 1982. The CME is the largest equity futures market in the United States, and the CBOT is one of the busiest futures exchanges in the world.

Island Futures Exchange was approved by the CFTC to trade single stock futures in February 2002. Island Futures Exchange is an affiliate of Island ECN, which has become one of the leading exchanges for NAS-DAQ securities, executing approximately one out of every six trades in NASDAQ securities. As of this writing, it has not set up a market-maker program to ensure liquidity, as OneChicago and NQLX have done. Instead, Island intends to succeed by offering traders the lowest possible price. Island has yet to list stocks for futures trading, but it has developed contract specifications.

Amex, in contrast to all other single stock futures exchanges, will offer single stock futures in an open-outcry pit, placing the new product alongside its options. Amex is the second-largest options exchange in the United States and is assuming that it can translate its success in open-outcry options into success in open-outcry single stock futures. As of this writing, Amex has not yet listed any single stock futures or developed contract specifications. However, exchange spokespersons have said that although Amex single stock futures have been perceived as strictly pit-bound, that's somewhat of a misconception. Virtually all of the smaller order types—retail-type options orders—are now handled electronically via automatic execution on the exchange's Auto-Ex system. Amex hasn't yet decided at what size it will allow automatic execution for single stock futures, but if an order isn't executed through Auto-Ex, it will be routed to the electronic book. More complicated or large orders will be electronically routed directly to the specialist.

WHAT CAN U.S. EXCHANGES LEARN FROM MEFF AND EURONEXT.LIFFE?

The U.S. markets' ability to succeed will depend largely on the ease with which they enable customers to use single stock futures and on their ability to compete with foreign exchanges, particularly when foreign exchanges offer futures on U.S. stocks. U.S. exchanges need to focus on three factors to ensure volume for single stock futures and to make their products competitive with foreign single stock futures.

The first factor is technology. U.S. exchanges must start leaning toward online trading and moving away from open outcry as much as possible. It's very difficult to run two different types of trading platforms, electronic and open outcry, and have the process be cost-effective. The costs of running the exchange are generally passed on to the customer in fees, so it will be cheaper for customers to trade with wholly electronic exchanges.

Three of the four exchanges that offer or intend to offer single stock futures in the United States have already done this. Island, NQLX, and OneChicago are all-electronic markets. Amex, on the other hand, still clings to a degree to an open-outcry method for single stock futures trading and anticipates that it will be successful based on the success of its options market, the second largest in the United States.

Another essential tool for developing the single stock futures markets is the market maker. Just as the two top foreign exchanges use market makers to ensure liquidity, the U.S. exchanges have quickly solicited market makers for their single stock futures in the hopes of securing liquidity, an essential quality in any successful market. Thus far, both NQLX and OneChicago have contracted with market makers, but they work in different manners.

Under OneChicago's plan, there are lead market makers (LMMs), each of whom is responsible for making two-sided markets in listed single stock futures and narrow-based indexes, not unlike the situation in the equities markets. The OneChicago system provides "participation rights" for the LMMs. If an LMM's price is the best bid or offer, and if an order comes in and the market maker "hits" it, the LMM will have the right to 30 percent of the trade. However, if a market maker or a customer comes along and enters an order that betters the LMM's best bid or offer, then the LMM cannot participate in the trade unless it comes in with an even better bid or offer—a "market improver."

NQLX, on the other hand, is not using a lead market maker (specialist-type) system like OneChicago's. Market makers receive reduced fees, good systems capacity to put quotes on the screen, and also the ability to interact with a portion of the order flow that they bring to the market, but only under strict rules. For example, after executing one-half of a customer's order against the best prevailing price in the order book, the market maker is allowed to immediately execute the other half of the customer's order against its own trading interest at the same price. This is known as internalization, and it is common in the equities markets. NQLX believes that under this system, the market participants that have set the best price in the order book are rewarded, while the market maker's customers are sure to get their orders executed at the best price on the exchange's market.

Third, the ability to trade seamlessly across borders will become a factor in determining the success of the U.S. exchanges. Euronext.liffe and Eurex, the two leading European derivatives exchanges, have boosted their own volume by creating "borderless" trading between exchanges. Thus, European customers already trade between countries' exchanges, provided that each country is a member of the European Union.

Foreign exchanges, such as Euronext.liffe, do offer single stock futures on U.S. companies. However, American individual and institutional investors are not yet allowed to trade these vehicles, as the Commodity Futures Modernization Act (CFMA) requires any foreign exchange that wants to offer single stock futures to American investors to be registered as a futures or securities exchange under either the Commodity Exchange Act or the Securities Exchange Act. Thus far, no foreign exchange has applied for listing by either the CFTC or the SEC, but nothing in U.S. law prohibits foreign exchanges from listing U.S. stocks.

However, American investors should be able to trade on foreign exchanges soon. The CFMA requires that the commissions develop rules regarding foreign exchanges. Furthermore, section 12 of the Securities Exchange Act requires that the commissions promote fair competition.

So far, U.S. exchanges cannot list foreign-security futures products for trading unless the underlying securities are registered with the SEC, according to the CFMA. However, the commissions may determine, in developing rules to permit U.S. exchanges to list foreign products, that in order to promote fair competition, securities do not necessarily have to be registered with the SEC.

The last factor to consider is margin. As mentioned before, the margin on universal stock futures is as low as 6 percent. Unfortunately, U.S. exchanges probably won't be able to permit such low margin levels for retail investors, but large institutional investors may receive the benefits of low margins. Although 20 percent margin is still low in comparison to the 50 percent margin required for trading stocks, the lower margins on foreign exchanges may attract some U.S. investors.

WHAT DOES IT ALL MEAN FOR YOU, THE INVESTOR?

Finally, U.S. investors and traders have access to a trading vehicle, single stock futures, that has already been successfully utilized by foreign investors in nearly a dozen countries around the world. The success of MEFF and Euronext.liffe offers U.S. exchanges valuable lessons about what traders want and need in order to utilize this product efficiently. Several of the U.S. exchanges have already incorporated key factors for success, a market-maker system and all-electronic trading systems, into their single stock futures trading program.

Now that you have learned some of the history behind single stock futures trading outside the United States, let's get down to business, with some information that can help you, as a trader, to utilize this vehicle here in our country. Let's turn to the next chapter, which will help you to understand pricing differences between single stock futures and the underlying cash security.

4

Understanding the Difference Between the Pricing of a Stock and the Pricing of a Futures Contract on the Stock

In trading, it all comes down to price. Buy low, sell high. Sell high, buy back low. The difference between the price of entry and the price of exit equals profit. Those of you who have traded futures will be familiar with the concept of basis, or the difference between the underlying cash price of the commodity and the price of the futures contract. This chapter will outline some key considerations to be aware of when looking at the price of a single stock future and the different approaches to pricing the underlying cash security. After all, if you don't know if you're getting the right price, you won't know how to trade effectively.

PRICING OF A STOCK

If you are reading this book, you probably already have a basic understanding of how stock pricing works. You probably also know that there is no sure-fire method of determining a stock's fair value. However, pricing models can provide a basis for comparing the qualities of two different stocks. Armed with that information, you can enter your trades more confidently than the uninformed investor who follows "hot" tips.

Traders can choose from a plethora of models for assigning dollar value to stocks. These models range from relatively simplistic models to complex models for serious number crunchers. Simple methods include the PEG value and forward P/E value methods. According to the PEG value pricing method, the P/E ratio of a fairly valued stock should be equal to the growth rate of the stock, where PEG = (P/E)/(% earnings growth) and PEG value = current price/PEG. (Percent earnings growth can be expressed in terms of a single year's or multiple years' growth. This pricing method cannot be applied to stocks with negative growth rates.)

The forward P/E is based on the idea that stocks typically trade at a constant P/E, and therefore that the future value of a stock can be calculated by comparing the current P/E with the future P/E. (Analysts' predicted earnings are used for this pricing method.) The forward P/E = price (P/E, current)/(P/E, future). (This pricing method cannot be applied to stocks with negative current or future earnings.)

If you are interested in tackling more complex models, they generally include more variables, such as the following:

- Book value
- Future earnings
- Dividend rates
- Risk-free rate of return
- Risk of the stock
- Time

Although it appears that including these six variables would make for an impossible equation, only two of them truly vary. Time and risk are calculated differently depending on which pricing model you use. The current book value, the future predicted earnings, and the risk-free rate of return are fixed. Dividends are fixed for at least 3 months and may or may not change after that period of time. Some companies do not offer dividends at all.

PRICING A FUTURES CONTRACT BY DETERMINING FAIR MARKET VALUE[1]

In futures trading, it is no different. To be a successful trader, you must educate yourself. Of course, the methods by which futures traders and stock traders determine price differ greatly.

In pricing a futures contract, you are trying to determine the contract's fair market value. Fair market value is the theoretical value of the futures contract. In theory, the price of a single stock futures contract should equal the value of the underlying stock plus the interest rate less dividends, calculated over the life of the futures contract. The result of this calculation would be the fair market value. (See Table 4.1.)

Most investors and exchanges, such as the Chicago Mercantile Exchange, have used this equation for years to calculate the fair market value of futures on stock indexes such as the S&P 500, but it can also be used for single stock futures. Many traders have made the assumption that single stock futures will trade at a premium to the underlying common stock, similar to the premium at which S&P 500 futures have traded (relative to the cash S&P 500) for most of their 20-year history. However, while many single stock futures will trade at a premium to their underlying stock, traders need to know that many others will trade at parity or perhaps even a discount to the underlying stock.

To better understand how single stock futures might be priced in relation to their underlying security, let's take a look at three stocks with different dividend yield attributes: one with no dividend yield, one with a small dividend yield, and one with a relatively large dividend yield.

No Dividend Makes a Difference

Traders need to be aware of the difference that a dividend will make. First, we will look at an already actively traded single stock future, that for Microsoft Corporation, which at this writing was the world's largest software maker and the second-largest stock in the S&P 500 index. Microsoft pays no dividend, making the input into the fair value equation a little simpler. Table 4.2 lays out the data for Microsoft that can be fed into the fair-value equation.

Usually, a stock that has little or no dividend yield relative to interest rates will trade at a premium to the cash. Each successive futures contract will have a little greater premium as one goes forward in time. This has

TABLE 4-1

Fair-Market Value Equation

$$\text{Fair market value} = \text{cash}[1 + (r - d)(x/365)]$$

where cash = price of underlying common stock

r = interest rate or financing costs (usually 3-month LIBOR)

x = number of days until expiration

d = dividend yield of underlying common stock

TABLE 4-2

Microsoft Corporation (MSFT)

MSFT common stock price:	$52.10
Interest rate (3-month LIBOR):	1.80%
Dividend yield on common:	0.00%
Days to Sep 02 expiration: 26	
Days to Dec 02 expiration: 118	
Days to Mar 03 expiration: 208	

Fair value of Sep 02 futures:

$$\text{MSFT futures} = 52.10[1 + (0.018 - 0.00)(26/365)] = \$52.17$$

Fair value of Dec 02 futures:

$$\text{MSFT futures} = 52.10[1 + (0.018 - 0.00)(118/365)] = \$52.40$$

Fair value of Mar 03 futures:

$$\text{MSFT futures} = 52.10[1 + (0.018 - 0.00)(208/365)] = \$52.63$$

Data as of August 27, 2002.

been the case with S&P 500 futures for most of the last 20 years. Interest rates were almost always higher than the S&P 500 dividend yield, and thus the futures were priced at a premium to the cash. In this example, though, rates are lower than dividend yields for only the second time in the last 20 years, and the futures over cash premium has disappeared completely.

When Dividend Yield Is the Same as Interest Rates

The second example (Table 4.3) is Boeing Corporation (BA), whose dividend yield is about the same as interest rates.

Interestingly, when dividend yields and interest rates are at the same level, there is no advantage to holding either the futures or the underlying stock, as the entire middle portion of the fair value equation collapses to 1.00. Hence, the futures and the cash at expiration are priced identically!

Big Dividend Effect

The last example (Table 4.4) is Philip Morris, now Altria Group, Inc., (MO), an important member of the S&P 500 that pays a rather large dividend.

TABLE 4-3

Boeing Corporation (BA)

Boeing Corporation common price: $ 37.14

Interest rate (3-month LIBOR)   1.80 %

Dividend yield: 1.80 %

Days to Sep 02 expiration: 26

Days to Dec 02 expiration: 118

Days to Mar 03 expiration: 208

Fair value of Sep 02 futures:

$$BA \text{ futures} = 37.14[1 + (0.018 - 0.018)(26/365)] = \$37.14$$

Fair value of Dec 02 futures:

$$BA \text{ futures} = 37.14[1 + (0.018 - 0.018)(118/365)] = \$37.14$$

Fair value of Mar 03 futures:

$$BA \text{ futures} = 37.14[1 + (0.018 - 0.018)(208/365)] = \$37.14$$

Data as of August 27, 2002.

This is an important point for traders to consider. Large dividend yields clearly affect the pricing of single stock futures relative to the underlying stock. In fact, Philip Morris futures should trade at a significant discount to the underlying stock. When dividend yields far outstrip interest rates, the futures have to be priced at hefty discounts to compete with the large payout of a high-dividend-paying stock, as the interest earned (1.8 percent short rates) can't compete with the yield (in this case 4.8 percent).

Why You Need to Price Single Stock Futures

So, why go to the trouble of pricing single stock futures, with their multiple expirations and dividend inputs? The answer is easy enough: for the same reason that professionals price stock index futures—or any futures contract, for that matter. Any professional trader always has a firm handle on pricing, as her or his profits or losses depend on accurate pricing of futures relative to the cash instrument.

TABLE 4-4

Philip Morris (MO)

Philip Morris common price:	$47.58
Interest rate (3-month LIBOR)	1.80%

Dividend yield: 4.88%

Days to Sep 02 expiration: 26

Days to Dec 02 expiration: 118

Days to Mar 03 expiration: 208

Fair value of Sep 02 futures:

$$\text{MO futures} = 47.58[1 + (0.018 - 0.048)(26/365)] = \$47.48$$

Fair value of Dec 02 futures:

$$\text{MO futures} = 47.58[1 + (0.018 - 0.048)(118/365)] = \$47.12$$

Fair value of Mar 03 futures:

$$\text{MO futures} = 47.58[1 + (0.018 - 0.048)(208/365)] = \$46.77$$

Data as of August 27, 2002.

Even "plain vanilla" speculators have a good handle on pricing. Ask any pro what happens when you constantly purchase financial instruments, whether futures, options, or anything else, above their fair value. Take it the next step. If the Sep 02 futures on Philip Morris were theoretically priced at $47.48, then it would make good sense to try to execute your order at or around that price (or even below it). Purchasing single stock futures well above $47.48 or selling them way below that figure is a prescription for less than optimum results.

If those reasons can't convince you to do this extra bit of homework, maybe this real-life experience will motivate you. David Lerman, an author and the associate director of equity products at the Chicago Mercantile Exchange, offers this example as a reason for all traders to know fair market value of the futures product they are trading.

A few years back, a trader called Lerman, screaming about how "bad" his fill in S&P 500 futures had been. He called at 1:30 in the afternoon.

Lerman: "Did you place your order about 30 minutes
ago?"

Trader: "Yes . . . how did you know?"

Lerman: "Did you know what fair value was when you placed
the trade?"

Trader: "No."

Lerman: "Did you place an order to buy an S&P 500 futures
contract at the market?"

The trader admitted that he had placed a market order to buy one
June S&P 500 contract. Not in the mood for these types of questions, the
trader again asked Lerman how he knew the time of the trader's order.

THE POINT

At 1:00 P.M., the following prices were flashing on Lerman's screen:

S&P 500 cash: 1400.00

Cash/futures theoretical basis: 10.00

Cash/futures actual basis: 10.10

The theoretical basis, or the fair basis, is the cash value of the
S&P 500 subtracted from the theoretical fair value. The actual basis is
the cash value of the S&P 500 subtracted from the actual futures price.
A rather large order to buy then entered the pit and drove the futures
up over their fair value. This is usually a temporary occurrence, and the
futures will sooner or later return to equilibrium or near equilibrium.
(This usually occurs in a matter of minutes.) The result was as follows:

S&P June futures: 1412.00

S&P June futures fair market value:1410.00

S&P 500 cash: 1400.00

Cash/futures theoretical basis: 10.00

Cash/futures actual basis: 12.00

The trader's market order to buy S&Ps hit right when the market was trading at 1412.00 He got filled at 1411.80, 1.80 points above fair value. Within minutes, the market did what it always does and returned to equilibrium. His trade hit right in the middle of this market activity. This produced an immediate loss of 1.80 points in the position ($450.00).

If the trader had known a little bit about fair value, he would have known that futures were a bit above the market price, and he could have waited until the price got back in line with the theoretical fair value.

Fair market value mathematically ties together dividends, financing costs, and time to expiration and produces a fairly accurate (no pun intended) picture of where a futures contract should be trading. In reality, the prices of single stock futures will fluctuate above and below fair market value throughout the trading day. Rarely does anything trade exactly at fair market value.

Fair market value also reflects differences between single stock futures and their underlying stocks. First, stocks can pay dividends, whereas futures do not. According to our fair-market-value equation, then, when dividends increase, single stock futures prices should decrease relative to the price of the underlying stock. If the dividend yield equals the interest rate, then the futures price will be equivalent to the cash price. This rarely occurs, but it has happened in index futures. In November of 1993, interest rates and dividend yields on the S&P 500 were identical; thus the theoretical fair-value equation would give you equal values for the futures and the cash markets.

The second difference highlighted by these equations is the interest rate applied to futures contracts. For example, in the foreign exchange market, the futures price is the same as the cash price plus the interest rate. Upon expiration of the futures contract, the interest rate has zero value because there is no longer an interest-rate differential. There is no cost of storage, and the price difference between the cash currency and the futures contract on the currency theoretically diminishes. Interest rates should have the same effect on single stock futures. When interest rates increase, the price of single stock futures prices should increase, and once a contract reaches expiration, the price of the single stock futures contract and the price of the stock should be nearly the same.

Other Variables That Affect Pricing

Other factors also come into play in the pricing of a single stock future. One of these is whether the stock is hard to borrow (i.e., borrowing to effect a short sale is difficult). Stocks that are extremely hard to borrow usually either have a small float (number of shares outstanding) or have a very high risk profile, causing firms to restrict short sales. This was the case with some Internet stocks during their parabolic rise in the late 1990s. Hard-to-borrow stocks are usually more costly to borrow, and the pricing of futures on such stocks will reflect this cost. However, the vast majority of single stock futures will be on large-cap stocks that have a huge number of shares outstanding, rendering the hard-to-borrow issue moot.

Short-term supply and demand also influence price. Extreme bearish sentiment can drive single stock futures to a steep discount to cash as well as a discount to fair value. Conversely, bullish sentiment can have the opposite effect. For the knowledgeable trader, these swings can provide some extraordinary opportunities.

Other variables that may complicate the calculation of fair market value include the choice of interest rates, the time and uncertainty of dividends, and the selection of a compounding method. Some additional costs that are not in the equation, such as the potential costs for physical delivery, regulatory fees, and possibly costs for the transfer of certificates, are likely to affect the actual value of the futures contract. Despite these floating variables, the basic idea is straightforward: Single stock futures prices should mirror current stock prices, relevant interest rates, and expected dividends over the life of the futures contract.

To briefly review how the pricing of a single stock futures contract will work, take a look at the following:

- If stock prices increase, the prices of single stock futures should increase.
- If interest rates increase, the prices of single stock futures should increase relative to the price of the underlying stock.
- If dividends increase, the prices of single stock futures should decrease relative to the price of the underlying stock.
- The greater the number of days until expiration, the greater the premium to the underlying stock at which the single stock futures contract will trade.

FUTURES MARKETS ANTICIPATE FUTURE EVENTS

While you calculate fair market value to determine whether you're getting the best price on a futures contract, market activity will reveal the price of the underlying stock. One of the key economic functions of the futures markets is price discovery. The futures markets offer traders and the public the opportunity to "discover" the current value of 5,000 bushels of corn or the S&P 500 index. The same is true in the single stock futures market: Traders and the public have the opportunity to discover the perceived market value of an underlying stock. In fact, the single stock futures market will have some advantages over the stock market in its ability to predict price movement.

More transparent markets will be a big advantage that traders of single stock futures will have over players in the cash market. The bottom line is that futures traders will have additional clues that will help them to gauge the potential direction of prices, including the ability to observe "smart money" trading activity in the single stock futures markets. For example, a member of a board of directors at a company may choose to trade single stock futures in his or her account, and you may choose to utilize this information in making your trading decision.

Another key advantage in single stock futures trading is that you do not have to wait for an uptick to short a stock future, which could lead to an interesting situation. It could be that in the short term, the single stock futures market will be more price-sensitive on the downside than the cash market. In other words, the single stock futures market could more quickly find "fair market value" on the downside in reaction to some sort of company news, as traders won't have to check with their broker to see if the stock is available for borrowing and then wait for an uptick in order to sell short. They will be able to act on their bearish outlook immediately in the single stock futures market.

Even if single stock futures do not provide a more cost-efficient way to short stocks, the result could be that the futures market will anticipate sell-side price movement more quickly, while the cash market will anticipate buy-side price movement more quickly.

CONSIDERATIONS OF VOLATILITY AND LIQUIDITY

As a trader, you are probably looking for volatile and liquid markets, as these two factors offer the opportunity to make profits. Both volatility and liquidity can affect price. Volatility does have a downside when it is sparked by a lack of liquidity (a small number of buyers and sellers). For example, in thinly traded markets, prices can fly up and down in a volatile fashion, as there are not many bids and offers at each price to slow the movement down. In a highly liquid market, volatility can decrease (as it will take more buyers and sellers at each price to move the price higher or lower). Traders who are interested in getting involved in the single stock futures market may want to check the various exchanges' web sites; OneChicago and NQLX post daily volume and open interest figures on their sites. This can be a useful tool to determine which single stock futures trade actively. Generally, higher volume and open interest figures translate into more liquid markets, with better fills.

Volatility

Volatility is the measure of an underlying stock's tendency to move up and down in price over a period of time. Ever since futures began trading in the U.S. in the nineteenth century, one of their main functions has been to protect investors from the aggressive price swings of a volatile market. Single stock futures are likely to provide that function as well by tempering the volatility of their underlying stocks.

You, as an investor, must look at the prices of individual stocks compared with the price of the overall market. If a stock is highly volatile, its price level will swing up or down over a wider range than the overall market.

The CME introduced S&P index futures in 1982, which coincided with the start of one of the greatest bull markets in this century. Some observers note that S&P futures allowed fund managers and investors to hedge in appropriate ways, which could have decreased overall market volatility.

Investors and portfolio managers could combine trading the stock market with the use of stock indexes. Let's say they expected the overall stock market to go up, but they were not sure what to expect from a specific stock or group of stocks that they were holding. (Remember, a specific stock does not necessarily move in the same direction as the overall market or with the same volatility.) Therefore, they could hold on to the stock and purchase a stock index futures contract to take advantage of the expected upward move. If they were bearish over the short term, they could short the futures market in order to temporarily hedge a particular stock or an overall portfolio.

The fact that players in the futures market were allowed to go short, rather than to liquidate, at times of concern reduced the volatility of the market, as investors could hedge their portfolios. They could select the futures contract that most closely resembled their stock portfolios, using the S&P 500 or Composite for broad-based portfolios, the Russell 2000 or Value Line for small stocks, and the MMI for portfolios similar to the Dow Jones Industrial Average.

Single stock futures allow you to do the same, but also enable you to perfectly tailor the hedge to your specific stock holdings. For example, if you owned shares of XYZ Corporation and expected poor earnings in the near future, but wanted to hold on to the stock, you could short the single stock future on XYZ and hedge your position, without giving up your shares. Single stock futures give you the opportunity for a flawless hedge in your individual stock portfolio, as opposed to estimating which index may resemble your portfolio.

Initially, futures on stock indexes, such as the S&P 500, encountered skepticism, just as single stock futures have, but once investors realized their potential as a strategy, their volume soared, creating liquid markets for these futures.

Liquidity

Liquidity exists when a market is broadly traded, so that buying and selling can be accomplished with small price changes and bid/ask spreads are narrow. Liquidity is essential for any futures market if it is to reflect fair market value, and an even flow of liquidity prevents volatile price swings. The single stock futures market has several factors in its favor that have contributed to liquidity from day one, and thus should prevent high volatility.

The first benefit of single stock futures contracts is that they are standardized (like all exchange-traded futures contracts). Standardization simplifies the communication between a customer and a broker because the broker needs to know only the number of contracts and the price that a trader wants. When a customer phones a broker and places an order to buy two contracts of GM for December delivery, the broker needn't worry about how many shares are involved or where they will be delivered.

Standardized delivery also allows almost any hedger or speculator with sufficient capital to enter the market easily because there's no confusion about what's on the block. Increased participation by hedgers and speculators increases liquidity, and increased liquidity means lower transactions costs for both institutional and individual investors.

Another factor that is likely to boost liquidity in the single stock futures markets is the existence of market makers. Market makers agree to take the opposite side of customer orders and to maintain a certain bid/ask spread for their single stock futures. When the customer buys the ask and sells the bid, the market maker has the opportunity to sell the ask and buy the bid and thus is able to profit on the bid/ask spread. Appointing market makers to single stock futures will guarantee market liquidity. NQLX has created "primary market maker" status, and OneChicago has created "lead market makers" to trade single stock futures. NQLX primary market makers will compete against other market-making firms by making the best prices on single stock futures as well as exchange-traded funds and futures on broad-based indexes listed by the exchange. OneChicago has assigned lead market makers to a specific group of products.

COSTS FOR THE TRADER

A final consideration: What is the cost, or price, of trading single stock futures? Lower transaction costs and lower margin requirements mean that single stock futures are a cost-effective way of managing risk for both individual and institutional investors.

Single stock futures will have lower capital requirements than the stock market. As we have already discussed, to buy stocks, you must put down at least 50 percent of the value, or the margin, of the stocks you wish to buy. To trade single stock futures, you will have to put down only 20 percent of the value of the contract, also known as the performance bond, which is the same amount you put down to trade stock options.

For example, if you were to trade Bank of America (BAC) single stock futures, the margin or performance bond would be $1600 for a $8000 position: $80 (cost of BAC) $\times$ 100 (shares) $\times$ 20% = $1600. In the cash market you would have to pay $4000: $80 (cost of BAC) $\times$ 100 (shares) $\times$ 50% = $4000. With the remaining $2400, the investor could sell three Bank One (ONE) futures contracts at $40 per contract to hedge market risk and thus trade the relative strength and weakness of Bank of America and Bank One.

For institutional investors, margin could be the factor that influences upside movement. Also, it could ultimately prove to be cheaper for an institution to conduct trades through the futures markets, as it could utilize a short-term interest rate, generally about 2 percent, rather than a broker-dealer interest rate of around 6 percent. If it is cheaper to conduct trades in the futures market because of the interest-rate differential, an institution might want to buy in the futures market.

Finally, a firm will likely charge anywhere from $8 to $18 per round turn to trade single stock futures, narrow-based indexes, or exchange-traded funds. This charge generally includes exchange fees, regulatory fees, operating costs, and commissions.

There's a lot to consider when determining the pricing of individual stocks and single stock futures. But most investors and traders find success when they zero in on a methodology that works for them. By just doing your homework, you will be one step ahead of other investors in the arena. Just think back to that S&P trader who didn't take the time to calculate the fair value of his trade. Taking the time to do so can help you become a more successful trader.

---

[1] The majority of the information in this section was taken from articles by David Lerman in the July 2002 and October 2002 issues of *SFO* magazine.

5

Basics of Fundamental and Technical Analysis

Once you've decided that you are interested in trading single stock futures, or any other type of financial instrument, you'll need to do your homework and develop a trading methodology that works for you. There are two main types of market analysis, fundamental and technical. Some traders use just one or the other. Others use a combination of both. Every trader and investor needs to find a method that works for him or her. When trading single stock futures, as when trading any other market, you'll need to have an opinion about whether the market is going up or down and when, and in order to develop an opinion, you'll need to do some analysis.

Fundamental analysis is the study of economic data, including factors that affect supply and demand, such as production, consumption, export numbers, and a myriad of other information. This differs from technical analysis, which is the study of price charts. Traders who are pure technicians believe that "it is all in the charts." This means that pure technicians believe that the current price of single stock futures, or whatever market is being traded, captures all known fundamental information that is currently out there and all the current opinions of traders who are willing to put their money down on a trade. When traders use charts, they look for repetitive, historical patterns in order to derive clues regarding overall direction of prices, also known as the trend. An old market saying is "the trend is your friend." Determining the direction of the trend may be the first important step in studying a market. And there are several ways to go about doing that. First, let's take a look at some of the basics of fundamental analysis.

FUNDAMENTAL ANALYSIS

Fundamental analysis is the study of the underlying factors that affect supply and demand, and, hence, the price of a futures contract. In the simplest terms, when supply becomes scarce, the price will go up. When supply is plentiful, the price will go down. The trick is figuring out how or why supply may become scarce or plentiful. To help make this determination, fundamental analysis uses the following supply/demand equation: Existing stocks + production − usage = supply.

When you are doing fundamental research on single stock futures, you may want to research a company and its stock by reading Securities and Exchange Commission (SEC) reports and annual reports. These reports provide abundant amounts of information right at your fingertips, assuming that the company you are researching is large enough. (Most single stock futures contracts are on larger companies' stocks, so it shouldn't be too difficult to find the information.)

SEC Reports

Most publicly held companies must file financial reports with the SEC. If a company has $10 million or more in assets and at least 500 shareholders, it is required to file statements, periodic reports, and other forms. This information is available on the SEC's web site.

If a company is subject to reporting requirements, it must file information with the SEC about

- Its operations
- Its officers, directors, and certain shareholders, including salary, fringe benefits, and transactions between the company and management
- The financial condition of the business, including financial statements audited by an independent public accountant
- Its competitive position and material terms of contracts or lease agreements

Annual Reports

Many companies also provide copies of their annual reports to the public, either electronically or on paper. These reports include much of the same information that is required to be filed with the SEC. Information in an annual report may include, but is not limited to

- Financial highlights, such as net revenues, net earnings, assets, book value per share, and so on
- The nature of the business
- The company's business principles
- Financial information (more than just highlights)
- The names of board members, officers, and directors
- Shareholder information

Other Factors

Other stock market analysts use fundamentals such as corporate profits, interest rates, economic conditions, and public expectations, all of which contribute to the overall direction of the market. Each one of these fundamental factors affects individual stocks differently. For example, higher corporate profits usually equate to higher stock prices, while higher interest rates usually mean lower corporate profits. Finally, investor psychology also affects the direction of stocks. If the public is optimistic, prices usually go up. Pessimism drives prices down.

Besides educating yourself through reports, you should also track stock market news. Corporate actions that affect stocks will also affect the price of single stock futures and narrow-based indexes. For example, if Microsoft declared a 2-for-1 stock split, there would be no change in the futures contract; the contract itself would still represent 100 shares. However, the number of futures contracts outstanding would double, and the original price of the contract on all open contracts would be cut in half.

Markets Move on Unexpected News

When looking at fundamental factors (such as corporate profit reports) or at bigger-picture economic news (such as U.S. government data on the economy), which does affect overall movement of stock prices, it is important to remember that markets move on expectations. For example, let's say that Dell is scheduled to release its first-quarter earnings report on a specific day. As a matter of course, a variety of analysts' projections will be issued ahead of the data release. The price of Dell single stock futures will include the expectations, an average of all the known estimates that have been made public. Markets react or trade up or down in the wake of unexpected news or data. So, if first-quarter earnings are expected to be $1.05 per share, but a figure of $1.35 per share is released, Dell single stock futures will most likely see at least an initial knee-jerk reaction to the upside, based on the unexpected surprise in the earnings data.

Some fundamental traders also like to monitor U.S. government reports on the overall economy, including data on the labor market, overall gross domestic product growth, inflation, and consumer activity. These data have the potential to affect both individual stocks and the overall major stock indexes. Again, traders should remember that these reports tend to have the most impact when the news is unexpected, either sharply better than expected or sharply worse than expected. Heading into data releases, markets and stocks tend to reflect overall expectations in their prices. Thus, the markets tend to show the biggest reactions when the reported figures are out of line with these expectations.

The U.S. government releases a bevy of major economic indicators throughout the month. Some of the major ones with which traders may want to become familiar include the following:

The employment situation. This report is usually released by the Department of Labor on the first Friday of every month. The data detail the number of nonfarm jobs created in the United States during the previous month. The overall unemployment rate represents the number of unemployed people who are currently looking for work. While this is considered a lagging economic indicator, it is closely watched by financial-market participants and often sparks reactions in the stock market.

Gross domestic product. The Department of Commerce tracks these data, which are issued in advance, preliminary, and final forms for each quarter. The report reveals overall output from the United States, including all goods and services, and is a broad indicator of the overall economic pace.

Personal income and outlays. This report, also released by the Department of Commerce, details overall personal income levels and can be used as a gauge of consumer health.

Consumer price index. This report, released by the Department of Labor, monitors shifts in price inflation at the consumer level.

Consumer confidence index. This monthly release is considered a leading economic indicator, as the public's perceptions of the general outlook for the economy and the security of their own employment have a direct impact on their spending and savings habits, which, in turn, affect the overall economy.

Much of the fundamental data can be longer-term in nature and can help traders and analysts develop opinions on the longer-term trend. Sometimes traders choose to utilize fundamental data to determine the overall longer-term trend and then use technical methods to identify shorter-term entry and exit points. Now let's turn to technical analysis to see how this can be helpful in trading.

TECHNICAL ANALYSIS

While stocks and commodities differ, the same basic rules of technical analysis apply. In technical analysts' view, every fundamental factor that can influence a market is reflected in the current price. This method of analysis involves looking at the movement of prices over time and tries to discern chart patterns and other clues about the future direction of prices. Technical analysts base their prognostication of future price trends solely on the analysis of price activity. They contend that the price of a futures contract reflects every single bit of fundamental information that is known by anyone who can even remotely affect the price of the commodity. Every fact that is known about supply, demand, and, perhaps most important, the psychology of the public ends up in the price charts. So, in a nutshell, price action is the composite opinion of everyone involved in the markets. That is why learning to analyze price action is so important to anyone who is trading stocks, futures, or options.

Some people say that technical analysis is an art, not a science. The bottom line is that charts are pictures of price activity. Through the study of historical price patterns and the use of a variety of additional technical tools, the seasoned technician can identify trends and, perhaps even more important, signals that those trends are going to change. These could be a warning flag to either take profits on a position or initiate a new position in the opposite direction.

The Trend Is Your Friend

Technical analysis provides a visual picture of supply and demand. A daily bar chart, for example, is composed of a series of lines, each one representing one day. The open, high, low, and closing prices for a given day will form the bar for that session. In general, a group of bars that are moving higher represent an uptrend, while a group of bars that are moving lower signal a downtrend in price. A bull trend on a chart can be defined as a series of higher highs and higher lows. Conversely, a bear trend can be seen as a series of lower lows and lower highs. As mentioned earlier, there is an old saying in the market that "the trend is your friend." The basis for this saying is that many traders like to trade with the trend, as it can be safer to have the trend on your side.

The function of technical analysis is to monitor price changes in order to gauge the probable strength of demand compared with the pressure of supply on a futures contract at various price levels and then to predict the direction, length, and velocity of the next move. Although some price patterns may be clearly visible to a majority of traders, others may exist only in the eye of the beholder. Technical analysis can be a subjective form of study. What one analyst sees, may not be what another analyst sees. Before one can dive into the world of head-and-shoulders patterns, Fibonacci retracements, gaps, and moving averages, it is important to understand the basics of how a price chart is formed.

The Different Types of Price Charts

An isolated price does not mean a lot. Is it high or low? Is it moving up or down? Technical analysts use various types of charts to depict the relationship of one price to another. Values are reflected on the vertical scale, and time on the horizontal scale. On some charts, only the close is important; on others, the open is significant. On some charts, time is a critical element; on others, it is not a factor at all.

There are several types of formations that traders study in looking for clues to which way the market will go. While we mentioned the bar chart earlier, there are other types of chart formations, which include the line chart, the candlestick chart, and the point-and-figure chart.

Line Chart

One of the simplest charts is the line chart or close-only chart, which uses only one price for a time period, generally the close (see Figure 5.1). A series of dots on the chart represents the prices for consecutive time periods, and you just connect the dots to see the market's movement over time more clearly. This is the type of chart used for many moving-average studies.

Bar Chart

As mentioned earlier, perhaps the most popular type of chart is the bar chart, which clearly shows the high price and the low price for a period (see Figure 5.2). The period may be a week, a day, 60 minutes, 1 minute, or some other interval. Analysts look at prices in different time frames, depending on what time frame they are looking to trade. However, the basic bar-chart analysis is the same for all time frames.

FIGURE 5.1

Line Chart

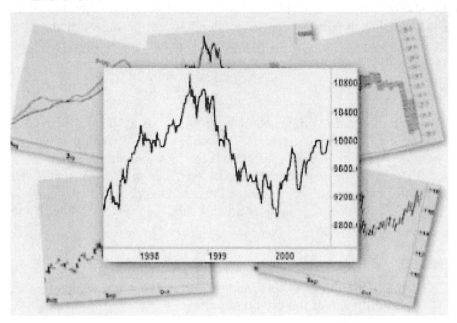

FIGURE 5.2

Bar Chart

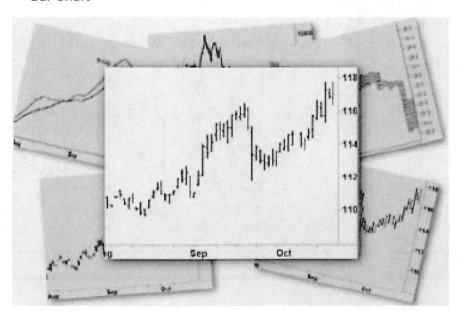

A horizontal line on the right side of the high-low price bar indicates the closing price for a period on a bar chart. The opening price is marked by a horizontal line on the left side of the bar. However, the features of the bar chart that usually get the most attention are the high and the low, because they represent the extent of traders' opinions about prices for the period shown (see Figure 5.3).

Candlestick Chart

This type of charting originated in Japan hundreds of years ago and has become very popular since the 1980s (see Figure 5.4). With this type of chart, the open in relation to the close is the most important feature.

The focus of attention in the candlestick chart is the *body*, that is, the difference between the open and the close for the period. If the close is higher than the open, the body is usually shown as clear or white; if the

FIGURE 5.3

The high and the low represent the extent of traders' opinions about prices for the period shown.

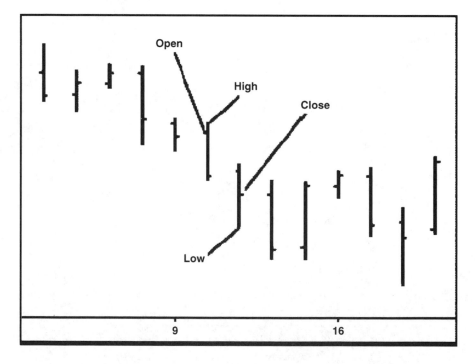

FIGURE 5.4

Candlestick Chart

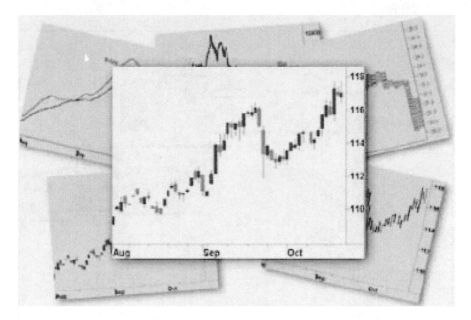

close is lower than the open, the body is usually shown as black or a solid color (see Figure 5.5). As a result, you get a quick visual picture of the day's price action by just glancing at a candlestick chart.

The price action during the period that occurs outside of the body shows up as tails or shadows that sometimes look like the wick of a candle (see Figure 5.6). As in the bar chart, they indicate the high and low boundaries of traders' thinking about prices for the period, but they are not considered to be as important as the body.

While all of the same information—the daily price high, low, open, and close—appears in both the candlestick chart and the bar chart, proponents of candlestick-chart analysis point to earlier reversal signals, which may not be evident on a bar chart. Candlestick-chart analysis includes a number of colorful names for chart patterns—engulfing patterns, shooting stars, hanging men, haramis, and many others that are unique to this type of analysis. Each candle pattern provides a visual picture of the supply/demand balance.

Next to price, time is the most important component of most charts, whether they are close-only, bar charts, or candlesticks. Price action usually

FIGURE 5.5

The body is the difference between the open and the close for the period.

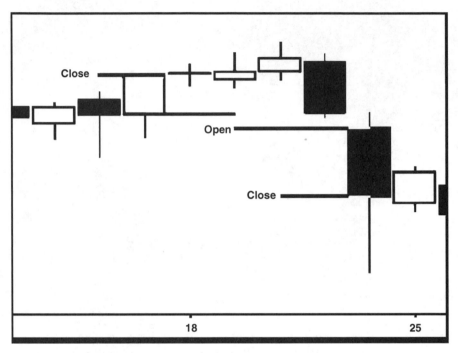

reflects what happens during a specified period, whether that period is a month, a week, a day, or a minute.

Point-and-Figure Chart

One type of chart that pays virtually no attention whatsoever to time is the point-and-figure chart (see Figure 5.7). Not only is time irrelevant on this chart, but the open and close also mean nothing. Only the high and the low are significant, because the complete focus of this chart is on reaching specific price points.

Perhaps the most crucial step in point-and-figure analysis is the very first step: determining what the value of a box should be (see Figure 5.8). The value can be a tick or it can be some larger unit of value, depending upon the time frame in which you are trading. Assume a value of 1 for each box. Now the building of the point-and-figure chart can begin. Assume that prices are moving upward and have reached the values of 8, 9, 10, 11, and 12. An X would go in each of those boxes in the same column to represent rising prices.

FIGURE 5.6

Tails or shadows indicate the high and low boundaries of traders' thinking about prices for the period.

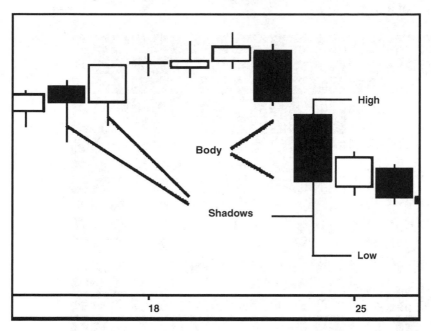

FIGURE 5.7

Point-and-Figure Chart

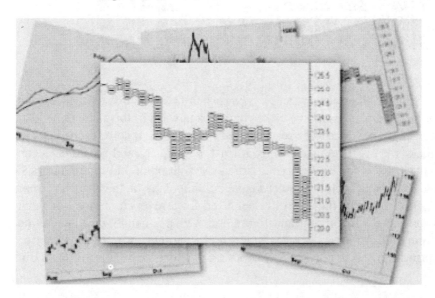

FIGURE 5.8

The first and most crucial step is determining the value
of a box.

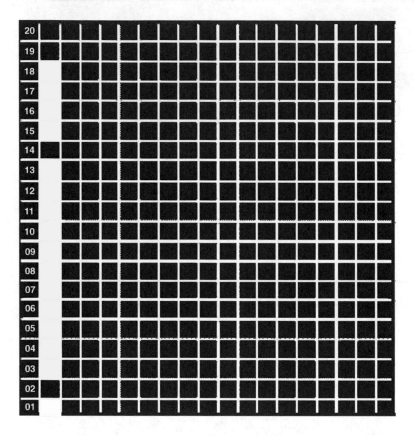

If the market hits 13, an X goes in that box; when it reaches 14, the same thing happens, and the chart continues upward in this manner as long as new highs continue to be reached (see Figure 5.9). At some point, however, the market will stop advancing, at least temporarily, and no more Xs can be added. Now comes the second crucial step in point-and-figure analysis: How many boxes will it take before the column of Xs on the chart reverses?

Typically, the number of boxes used for a reversal is three, or what is known as a 1-by-3 point-and-figure chart. If an X cannot be added to the column of Xs to indicate a new high, the low comes into play. If the price is sitting at 13, as in our example, nothing happens—perhaps for days. But

FIGURE 5.9

If the market hits 13, an X goes in that box; this continues as long as new highs are reached.

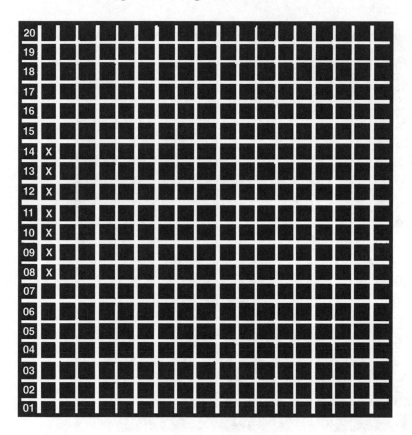

if the price has dropped by the value of three boxes (in this case, to 11), a
column of Os begins one column to the right of the Xs and one box below
the high X (see Figure 5.10).

Once the column of Os starts, the low price is the key (see Figure
5.11). If it forms a new low, an O is added to the bottom of the column of
Os, as we have done in boxes 10 and 9 in Figure 5.11.

When an O for a new low cannot be added to the column of Os,
the focus is once again on the high. If the high price represents a three-
box reversal, a new column of Xs starts. One signal to buy comes when
a column of Xs exceeds a previous column of Xs or, better yet, two or
three previous columns of Xs (see Figure 5.12).

FIGURE 5.10

If the price has dropped by a specific value, a column of
Os begins one column to the right of the Xs and one
box below the high X.

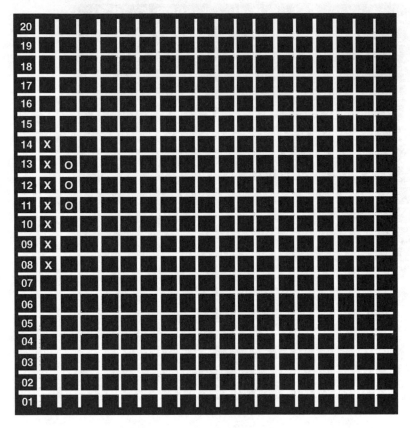

All of this may sound very complicated, but fortunately, many of
today's technical analysis software packages include point-and-figure
charting as one of the analytical alternatives. All you have to do is
enter the parameters for the box size and reversal values you want and
you have an instant Xs and Os point-and-figure chart. Point-and-figure
charts have not been as popular recently as other types of charts and
are considered an "old-fashioned" method of charting. However, proponents of this methodology say that because only price matters, this
type of chart can filter out a lot of "noise," which may be seen in sideways markets.

FIGURE 5.11

Once the column of Os starts, the low price is the key.

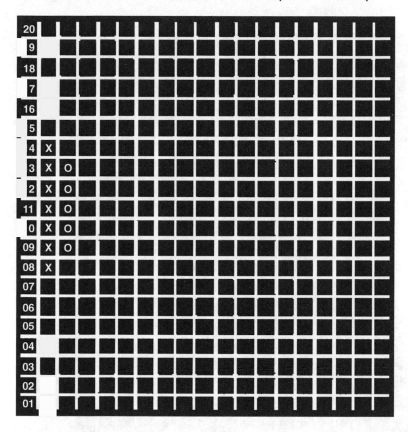

Most charts require some type of mark for each time period, even when there is little or no price movement. A point-and-figure chart based only on prices and not on some arbitrary time period requires little work when nothing is happening. It saves its entries for those times when prices move enough to warrant it.

Now that you understand the different types of charts that are available to the technician, the next chapter will outline some basic chart patterns and their meaning. The field of technical analysis is large, and there are many different methodologies. In this book, we will touch on some of the more basic forms, including trend and pattern recognition, retracements, and moving averages. But for those who are interested in delving deeper into this field, numerous books specializing in technical analysis are available.

FIGURE 5.12

One signal to buy comes when a column of Xs exceeds
a previous column of Xs.

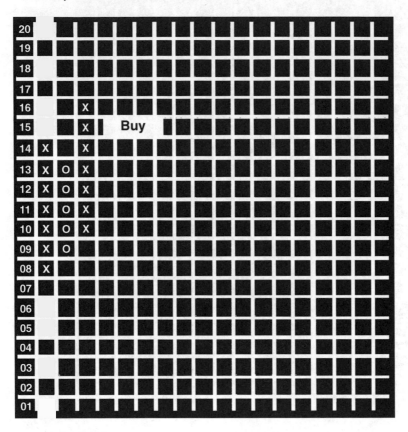

CHAPTER 6

Significant Chart Patterns and Other Technical Tools

To trade single stock futures successfully, you will probably need at least one of a variety of technical methods to assist you. The previous chapter explained fundamental analysis and the various types of charts used by technical analysts. It is now important for you to learn how to read the data within those charts and to determine how chart patterns can influence trading decisions. Determining these chart patterns, or trends, is a necessity when you are employing technical analysis in a trading strategy. Trend lines, support and resistance, market-reversal indicators, and trading cycles can help to predict future market movements. Any serious technical trader who studies the long-range charts will tell you that when it comes to technical analysis, history indeed does repeat itself.

Technical analysis can require extensive study, particularly when you are delving into the many indicators that analysts use, such as the relative strength index and stochastics. For more detailed information on any of the chart types or technical studies, ask a broker to recommend some of the numerous books, classes, and seminars available on these subjects. This chapter is only a starting point for further study.

THE TREND LINE

The trend line is a basic technical analysis tool. Some of the best-known market adages are "trade with the trend" and, as mentioned earlier, "the trend is your friend." These old sayings are so well known because, for the most part, they're true. Prices tend to stick to these straight trend lines, and even when they bounce off a trend line, they are often drawn back to it because most traders want to trade the trend. For example, if prices increase abruptly, buyers will hold back because they don't want to pay more than anyone else is willing to pay (unless there is a very good reason to do so). This action causes prices to return to the trend line.

There are three types of trend lines: an uptrend line, a downtrend line, and a sideways trend line. An uptrend line is a series of higher highs and lower lows. This type of trend line gives you a signal to buy in a given market. When you spot what you believe to be a trend, draw a straight line along the bottom of the lows to show the uptrend and extend it to show where the momentum of the upward advance should take prices if the uptrend continues at its present pace. Uptrend lines should be drawn so that they connect lows and thus are drawn below prices (see Figure 6.1).

A downtrend is a series of lower highs and lower lows; it signals that you should sell in a given market. Draw a straight line across the top of the highs to show the downtrend and where the momentum of the downward advance should take prices if the decline continues at this pace. Downtrend lines connect highs and thus are drawn above prices (see Figure 6.2). Sideways trend lines are drawn below prices and connect lows.

But spotting and following the trend is not always as easy as it may appear. Almost anyone looking at Figures 6.1 and 6.2, for example, would agree that they show an uptrend and a downtrend, respectively. These trends are easy to spot after they have occurred, but they are not easy to detect before a significant number of highs and lows have been established.

So how do you know if you've really spotted a trend? One confirming indicator that technicians look at is volume: The greater the volume, the greater the significance of a price trend.

Volume will also tell you when traders think that prices are moving too far or too fast. For example, in a normal uptrend, when prices move too far above the trend line, volume will decrease until prices return to the trend line. Conversely, in a downtrend, the volume is usually greater when prices are falling than when they are rallying.

A substantial change in volume can be a warning flag that a trend reversal is imminent. In a downtrending market, volume usually increases before the trend reverses. If a market is in an uptrend, volume usually decreases before a reversal. The reason is that prices can fall from their own weight, but they need constantly increasing buying activity to trend higher.

Trend lines can be used as a buy or sell signal. They can reveal how much confidence traders have in their positions and alert you when that confidence begins to wane. The trend can be your friend if you learn how to analyze it, using volume and other technical indicators as well.

FIGURE 6.1

Uptrend Formation

Eurodollar Daily Bar Chart

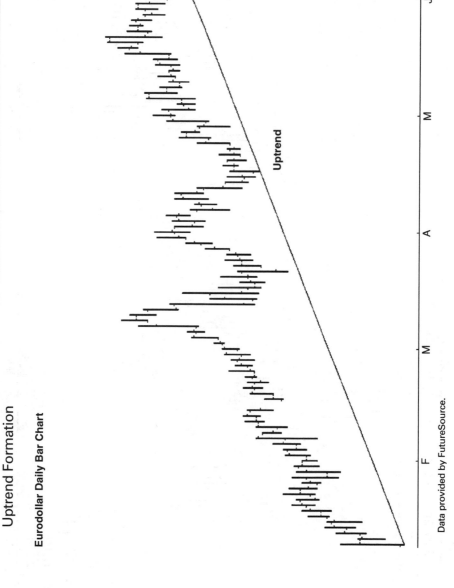

Uptrend

Data provided by FutureSource.

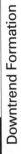

FIGURE 6.2

Downtrend Formation

Sugar Daily Bar Chart

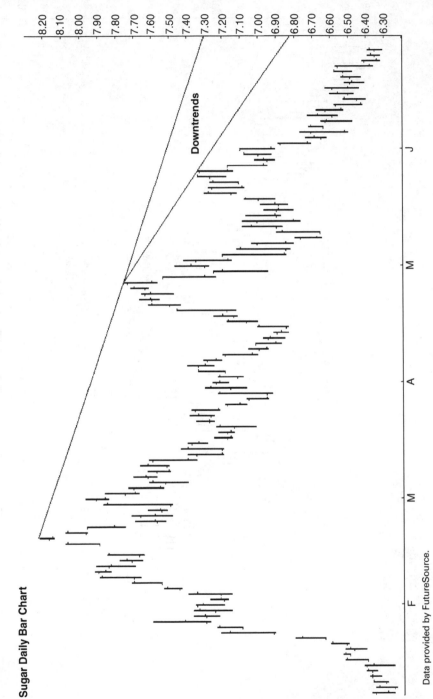

Data provided by FutureSource.

SUPPORT AND RESISTANCE

Have you ever watched a stock or commodity move up 5 points, level off for a few days, and then move up again, forming a pattern that looks like a staircase? Or maybe you've seen a stock retrace downward after a bullish rise and rest at one price level, only to fall again.

A basic tenet in reading the charts is the concept of *support* and *resistance*. Basically, support and resistance are previous highs and lows—old price points on the chart, often at old significant turning points—which come into play as the price nears those points at a later time. Fundamentally, a support price level is one at which you can expect increased demand to emerge, keeping prices "supported" (see Figure 6.3). Conversely, resistance on the price chart occurs when selling or supply pressures the market and prevents prices from rising above a certain point (see Figure 6.4).

Typically, when demand increases, so does volume. Then volume will typically decrease when the price decreases. Lack of activity and demand initiate a price slump. The price will rebound from the slump when it reaches a level that attracts buyers, and volume will rise again as buyers take advantage of the low price. A support level then forms as prices trade sideways or move up.

When the price of a single stock future, or any other price, hits a resistance level, there is the potential for selling pressure to emerge. Prices level off or sink lower. As with support levels, changes in volume tip you off to resistance levels. If volume is down, you know that traders are offsetting their long positions because the price has become "too high."

If you can determine where prices may stall during a bull move or find support during a decline, you can find out when to enter or exit markets, where to place protective stop orders, and how to anticipate the size and length of anticipated moves.

As you study charts, you'll also notice that previous resistance levels often become support levels, and vice versa. For example, a single stock future could rally through a resistance level shortly after bullish news is released. As the stock future's bullish move loses steam, it retraces down to that old price point, which had previously acted as resistance on the move higher and is now a support.

CHART PATTERNS

There are many types of patterns that form on the charts, and the "look" of these formations often actually explains their names. For example, a double bottom or top really looks like a double bottom or top. If you are interested in potentially trading off of technical patterns, you will find that

FIGURE 6.3

Support Level

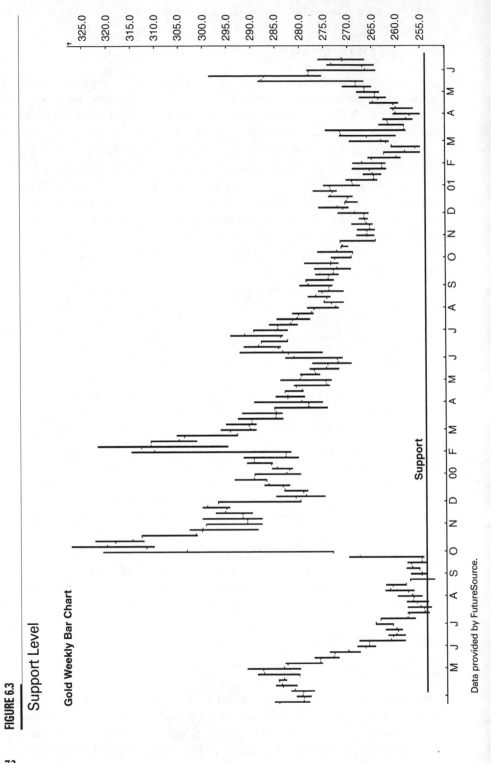

Gold Weekly Bar Chart

Data provided by FutureSource.

FIGURE 6.4

Resistance Level

Japanese Yen Weekly Bar Chart

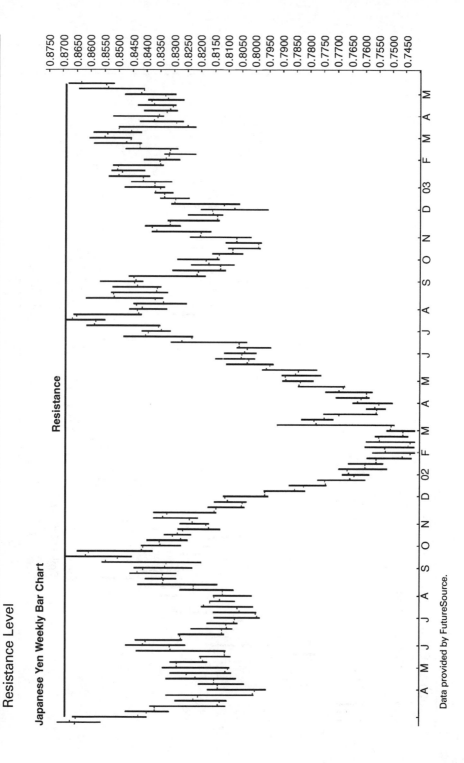

Data provided by FutureSource.

FIGURE 6.5

Spiked-Bottom Formation

Eurodollar Daily Bar Chart

Data provided by FutureSource.

FIGURE 6.6

Spiked-Top Formation

▶ Daily Gold Bar Chart

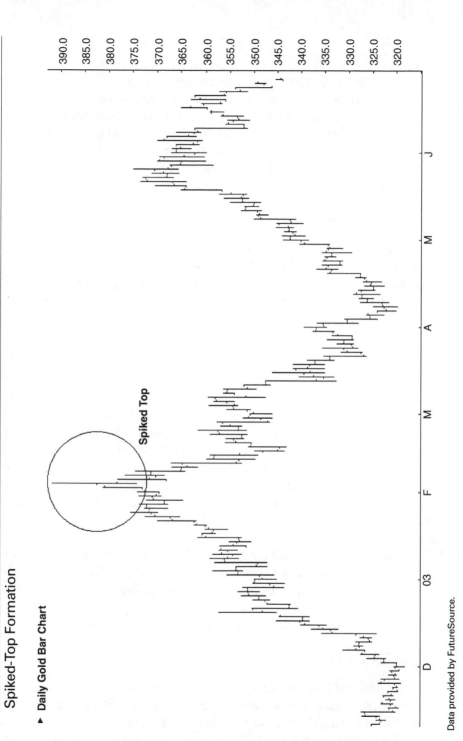

Data provided by FutureSource.

these formations tend to recur on all types of charts and for all time frames. So, how does this work? One answer may be that while a particular chart may be depicting the price action of a single stock future or a corn contract, the basic elements that drive prices up and down, including fear and greed and supply and demand, are the same, no matter what particular market you're studying. Basically, different stages of fear and greed and supply and demand unfold in a pictorial fashion, and these various patterns have been named and catalogued by market technicians.

Reversal Formations

Technicians have found that reversal formations suggest that a market has completed its run and is in the process of changing direction. Reversal formations include, among others, the spiked or "V" top or bottom, where prices spike to a high or a low and then make a sharp turn in the other direction, or—which is more common—an "M" top or a "W" bottom.

Spiked Tops and Bottoms

Spiked, or V, bottoms (see Figure 6.5) form in shaky markets, when traders aren't sure what is going to happen next, as the market has just experienced some unexpected bleak news. No one trusts his or her own market forecasts or anyone else's at this point. Then more unexpected news hits, and traders rush to exit their longs. The panic selling causes the price to plummet steeply and hit a point substantially lower than where the fall began. Then, if traders realize that the news was not nearly as bad as they thought, the price stops falling and, almost as suddenly as it fell, begins racing up sharply. Spiked tops (Figure 6.6) follow a similar scenario in reverse.

It is important to watch market data closely because these formations move fast and can be hard to predict. Take care not to change your position from long to short or from short to long before you know that the trend has changed. You may think the market has stopped plunging downward, but it may just be pausing, only to plunge even deeper.

Multiple Tops and Bottoms

Multiple tops and bottoms are a series of spiked tops and bottoms, a series of market peaks and valleys. The double top (Figure 6.7) looks like an M. Prices rally to a steep high, settle back about half as far, rally again to a high that is lower than the previous high, and finally decline past the interim low.

FIGURE 6.7

Double-Top Formation

Euro Currency Daily Bar Chart

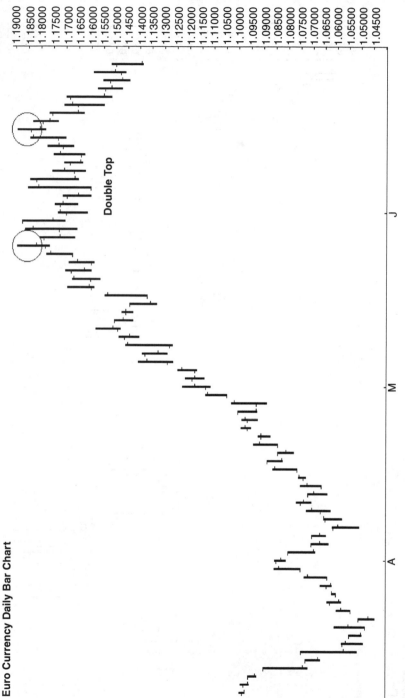

Double Top

FIGURE 6.8

Double-Bottom Formation

Swiss Franc Weekly Bar Chart

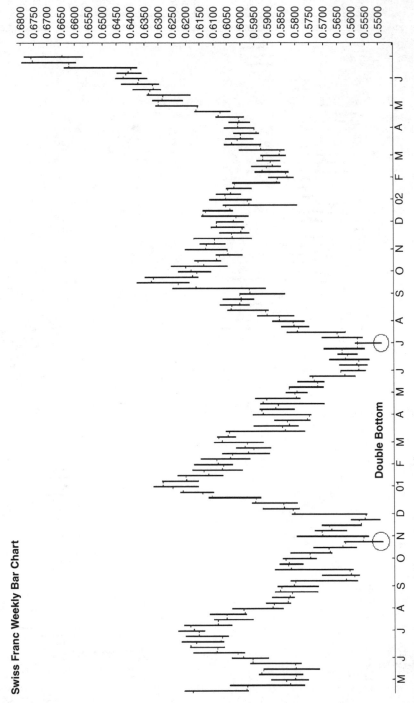

Double Bottom

Data provided by FutureSource.

The break below the interim low signals that a top is in place and that the market is about to head lower. The double bottom (Figure 6.8) resembles a W and forms in the opposite way from an M formation.

Double and triple tops and bottoms are common formations on price charts, yet they are also the most misleading. We characterize these formations as misleading for several reasons. First, stocks and commodities trend up and down all the time, so if you are not an experienced technical analyst, you may begin to see M and W formations on every chart. Be careful; many of these "formations" can be false signals.

Second, it is almost impossible to accurately identify a double top or bottom until the reversal in the trend is apparent and prices have moved above or below the vertex, or the interim high or low that is between the two halves of the double top or bottom. By the time this happens, the formation is complete, and many trading opportunities have passed.

Finally, the formation could become a triple top or bottom. If you act when it is only a double, the market could get the best of you. Volume generally increases around the peaks, but even this is not reliable, as studies have shown a lot of variation in volume.

Gaps, Island Reversals, and Continent Reversals

Another type of pattern analysis involves monitoring gaps, or areas on a chart where no trading takes place at all (see Figure 6.9). A *simple gap* on a daily chart can occur from one day to the next when a market opens at a higher level than the previous day's high. In general, gaps to the upside are considered to be signs of market strength, while gaps to the downside reveal price weakness. There are several different types of gaps, and some of these gaps are part of well-known reversal formations, including the island reversal and the continent reversal.

One kind of gap, known as an *exhaustion gap,* often occurs at the end of a price trend. For example, an exhaustion gap can reveal that buying energy (in an uptrend) is losing momentum. Sometimes, in a rising market, there will be one last burst of energy by the bulls before prices reverse and move lower. The same can be true in a weak market: In a last burst of energy on the downside, sellers push prices to a sharply lower open below the previous day's low. However, the sellers are unable to defend the new price lows, and the trend soon reverses to the upside.

Another type of gap, called a *breakaway gap,* can signal a new trend or a shift from a sideways mode. Sometimes an exhaustion gap will be closely followed by a breakaway gap in the opposite direction; this can form a powerful reversal pattern known as an island top or

FIGURE 6.9

Gaps

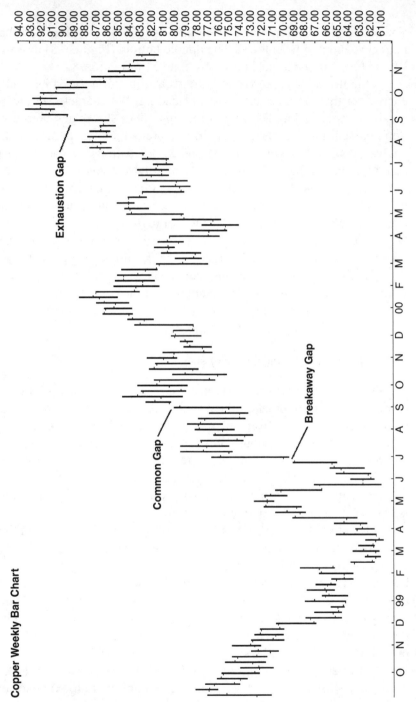

Copper Weekly Bar Chart

Data provided by FutureSource.

bottom (see Figures 6.10 and 6.11). This pattern is called an island because the price bar or several bars that make up the pattern actually look like an island, surrounded by gaps on the price chart.

An island reversal can occur at either a market top or a market bottom and reliably indicates that the current market trend is likely to reverse. Less commonly, if an island reversal forms over several weeks or months, it is referred to as a continent reversal (see Figure 6.12).

A gap that can help you project a move's continuing potential is known as a *measuring gap*. These gaps generally occur roughly midway through a market move. After making a move higher, for example, a market may jump into new higher territory, leaving a gap where no trading has taken place. If the market maintains its strength, this may be viewed as a measuring gap that indicates the halfway point of an extended move. Technicians can actually use such a gap as a measuring tool in order to calculate an objective, or how much farther the move has to go on the upside or downside, depending on which direction the gap occurred.

Key Reversals

A key reversal pattern is a one-day formation that can signal an important trend change. Like an exhaustion gap, a key reversal pattern represents a last gasp by the buyers or sellers in an established trend. In an uptrend, a key reversal pattern can occur when the price pushes to an extreme new high for the move on an intraday basis, but then closes lower, generally below the previous day's close (see Figure 6.13). Conversely, in a downtrend, a key reversal day can evolve when sellers push prices to a new low for the move, but then buying emerges, pushing the single stock future to a settlement above the previous day's close.

On the day following a key reversal, confirmation will occur if prices move higher than the previous day's high or lower than the previous day's low. This reversal pattern tends to be more meaningful if it is accompanied by high volume.

Key reversals, like island and continent reversals, alert you to the possibility of a trend change; they are not definitive indicators of trend change. You should use them in conjunction with other technical tools and analyze them with the entire market situation in mind.

The Head-and-Shoulders Formation

Along with the trend line, the head-and-shoulders chart formation is probably one of the best-known chart patterns. Everyone, from novice

FIGURE 6.10

Island Reversal at Bottom

Dow Jones Futures Daily Bar Chart

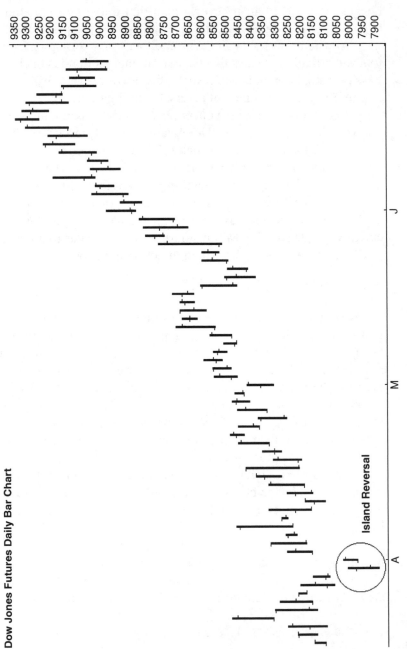

Island Reversal

Data provided by FutureSource.

FIGURE 6.11

Island Reversal at Top

Eurodollar Daily Bar Chart

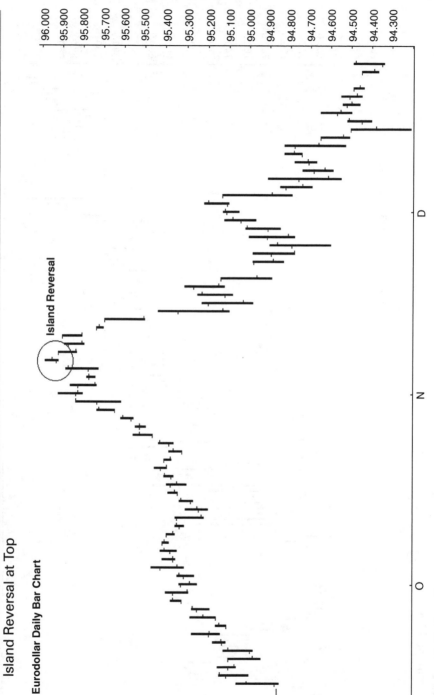

Data provided by FutureSource.

FIGURE 6.12

Continent Reversal

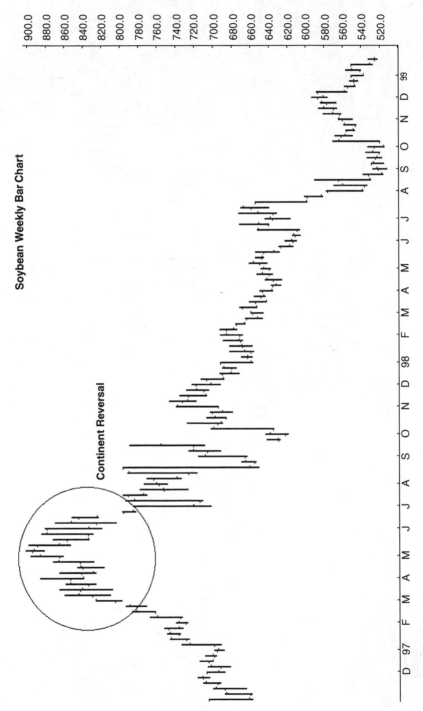

Soybean Weekly Bar Chart

Continent Reversal

Data provided by FutureSource.

FIGURE 6.13

Key Reversal

U.S. Treasury Bond Daily Bar Chart

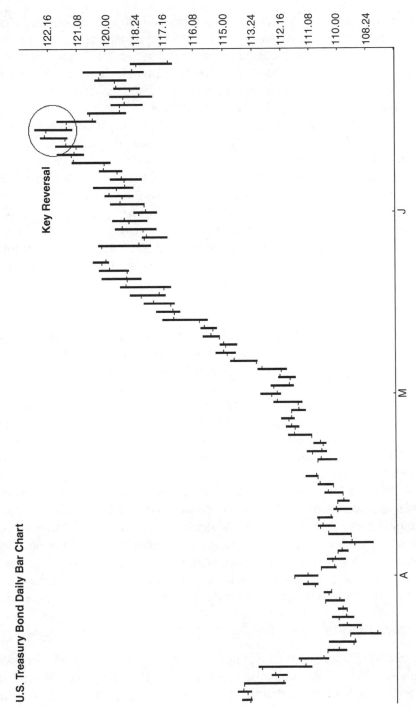

Key Reversal

Data provided by FutureSource.

traders to floor traders, sees these patterns and tries to trade them. And, since technical analysis can be a self-fulfilling discipline, the greater the number of traders who recognize a particular pattern, the more likely it is that its projection will become market reality. Because the head-and-shoulders formation is so well known among technical traders, it has also become one of the most reliable of formations.

A head-and-shoulders formation, whether upright or inverted, indicates a major trend reversal in the chart of a single stock future, or any other commodity or stock. It represents three successive rallies and reactions, with the second rally, or head, reaching a higher point than the other two rallies (see Figure 6.14). The first rally forms the left shoulder, and the third rally forms the right shoulder. Granted, this formation is seldom perfectly and simply formed. It may be angular instead of rounded, and there may be multiple heads and/or shoulders. The head-and-shoulders formation alerts you to the end of an uptrend. The inverted head-and-shoulders formation signals the end of a downtrend.

Volume is the key. Again, as with other chart formations, always watch volume closely, because it is a confirming indicator for various technical patterns. It clues you in to what the market is really thinking, as it represents the actual buying and selling power behind the price move. The greater buying power behind a rally will be demonstrated in above-average volume figures. For example, with the head-and-shoulders pattern, as the left shoulder forms, volume tends to expand on the rally and contract on the sell-off. When the head forms, volume is high during the rally, but the overall volume may be lower than the overall volume that formed the left shoulder. The overall volume of the third rally and reaction is even lower. It fails to reach the high established by the head (the second rally).

With this pattern, the actual confirmation of a top or bottom occurs when the so-called neckline, a trend line drawn off the bottom of the shoulder points, is broken. After the neckline is broken, sometimes a market will retest the neckline (now called either neckline support or neckline resistance.) This is a type of retracement, and as long as the neckline holds on this test, the pattern will be valid. A retracement move to test the neckline can be an opportunity to enter the market or to add to your position.

Calculating Price Objectives

Head-and-shoulders formations not only reliably indicate trend reversals, but also forecast price objectives. You can calculate the price objective of a head-and-shoulders formation by measuring the distance between the

FIGURE 6.14

Head and Shoulders

Ten-Year U.S. Treasury Note Weekly Bar Chart

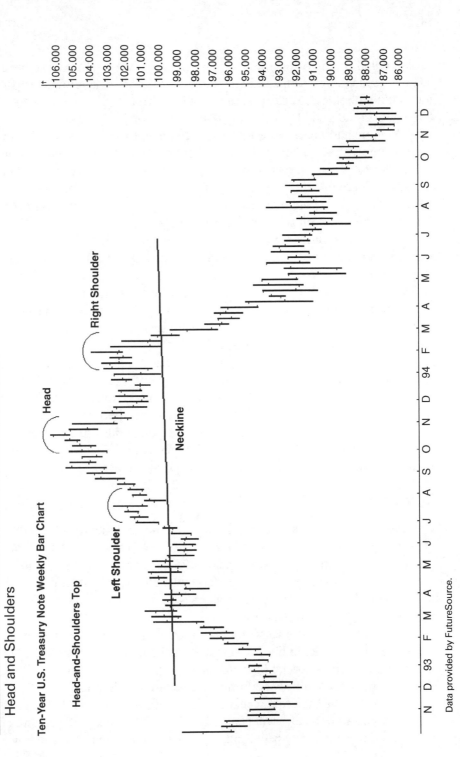

Data provided by FutureSource.

neckline and the high (or low) made by the top (or bottom) of the head. Then you add that price measurement to the neckline to determine the pattern's ultimate price target. Be sure to double-check your price objectives, and confirm the trend by reviewing other indicators.

Volume and open interest also supply clues to the trend. While volume is simply the number of contracts that are traded during each session, open interest is the number of outstanding or open contracts in each single stock future or other commodity. These figures reflect the total number of long or short contracts. The two are always equal, because for every long position, there must be an opposing short position.

When the trend reversal begins, volume should increase, and open interest should build in the direction in which the market is trending. Review what the traders with reportable positions and commercial hedgers are doing. Their activity is reported to the public by the Commodity Futures Trading Commission every Friday afternoon in the Commitment of Traders report. To see these data for yourself, go to www.cftc.gov/cftc/cftccotreports.htm.

Highlight on your charts the areas where the move may encounter resistance and study the price action as these points are reached. Does the volume pick up or slow down? Does the price movement bust right through the resistance, or does it stop at a resistance barrier? The answers to these questions will let you know whether you should stay in the market and look for a second, third, or fourth objective or whether you should take your profits and look for a new trading opportunity.

Retracements

One technique for measuring the potential of a reversal move is to look for what analysts call *retracements* (see Figure 6.15)—that is, how much of a previous move will the market retrace before it finds a top or bottom? If the market skyrockets, how many traders will sell and take their profits? If the market plummets, how many traders will short the market? Exactly how great a retracement will occur?

Fortunately, retracements commonly occur in calculable mathematical proportions. To determine how great a retracement will occur, calculate the distance from important highs to important lows and analyze how the particular market previously performed under similar circumstances. You'll find that most markets often repeat retracement patterns, and that when a market begins to retrace, it will generally retrace 33 percent, 50 percent, or 66 percent of the distance between the previous significant high and low.

As with support and resistance levels, you can use this information to time the market, that is, to select a point where you will take your profits or reenter the market.

Some key points about retracements:

- A retracement of 50 percent is a popular goal.
- A market that makes a shallower retracement—say, only 33 percent of the previous move—is a stronger market than one that has a deeper setback of, say, 66 percent of the previous move.
- A retracement target that coincides with a support or resistance point, such as a prior low or high, is a much more significant zone to watch.

There are a number of other techniques that you can use to measure price potential, including Fibonacci ratios and methods developed by W. D. Gann that have both price and time elements. If you study Fibonacci ratios, for example, you might see a 0.618 retracement of the previous move as a target. These techniques require their own course of study.

The Rounded Bottom

A rounded bottom formation is a technician's dream because it is recognizable, is reliable, and alerts you to an upcoming long-term trend. Unlike many reversal formations, it gives you time to make trading decisions.

A rounded bottom forms as the price of a commodity slowly falls, reaches bottom, and then slowly rises again. (See Figure 6.16). It develops out of an increasing oversupply situation. As supplies of a commodity become plentiful, buyers purchase only what is necessary, believing that the commodity will become less expensive tomorrow.

As buyers wait to see if the price movement develops into a major bear market or if it is just a reaction to the main trend in the form of a retracement, volume for the commodity drops off. The supply-demand equation becomes balanced, and a long, flat bottom develops.

As the price remains at a low, buyers begin to take advantage and increase their buying. Demand once again builds. Traders anticipate increased activity and bid up prices. Volume reflects the price activity, and a bull market may erupt.

Variations of the rounded bottom are horizontal channels or flat formations. They appear long and sideways on price charts. These develop when a commodity or index has created a base for a major move. Prices begin trading in a narrow range, and traders feel that the market has little

FIGURE 6.15

Retracements

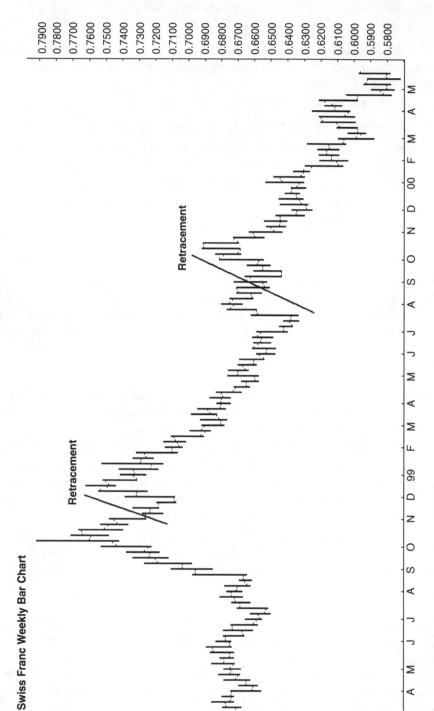

Swiss Franc Weekly Bar Chart

Data provided by FutureSource.

FIGURE 6.16

Rounded Bottom

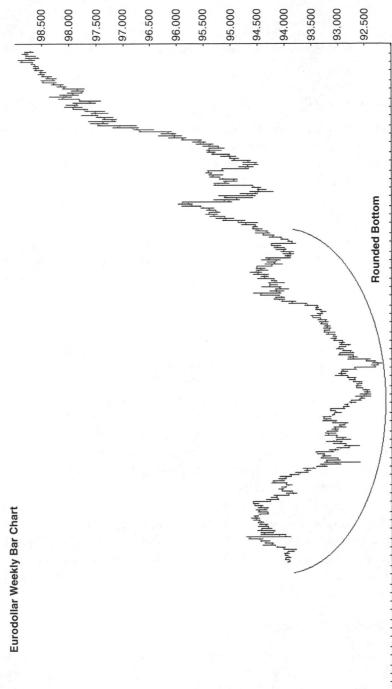

Eurodollar Weekly Bar Chart

Rounded Bottom

MJ J A S OND98FMAM J J A SOND99 FMAM J J A SOND00FMAM J J A SOND01FMAM J J A SOND02FMAM J J A SOND03FM

Data provided by FutureSource.

potential, so volume is low. The market is flat on these trading plateaus. It can move up or down away from the plateau, depending on what news heats it up.

Continuation Patterns

Another set of chart formations is called continuation patterns. As their name suggests, these formations indicate that while prices may have moved into a temporary sideways, consolidative type of mode, an eventual resumption of the previous trend is likely.

Triangle Formations

The triangle formation develops when the momentum behind a trend loses steam. For example, if a commodity or single stock future is rallying in a bullish trend, sometimes a market will pause in a consolidative mode, and a triangle can form. Basically, a triangle forms when zigzag price action occurs (see Figure 6.17). This is identifiable to the market technician, as one is able to draw trend lines connecting the points across the top and those across the bottom of this zigzag action. Generally, prices will "break out" of this zigzag action and continue in the direction of the previous trend.

When the uptrend line and the downtrend line meet, a symmetrical triangle is formed. Prices move into the apex of the triangle. More than half the time, prices continue in the direction in which they were going when they entered the triangle, thus continuing the trend.

There are three main types of triangles that tend to appear on charts: symmetrical, ascending, and descending triangles.

In a symmetrical triangle, prices tend to coil evenly, while in an ascending triangle, the bottom line angles up to meet the level top line. This triangle suggests that the commodity is available at the price level of the top line, but that there are no sellers below that price level. Prices rise and finally break out to the upside. The descending triangle is just the opposite and indicates lower prices.

Flags, Pennants, and Diamonds

Flags, pennants, and diamonds are other continuation formations that operate much like triangles, but offer their own individual twists on chart analysis (see Figure 6.18). Typically, these types of continuation formations also indicate a period of consolidation. The same type of analysis

FIGURE 6.17

Triangle Formation

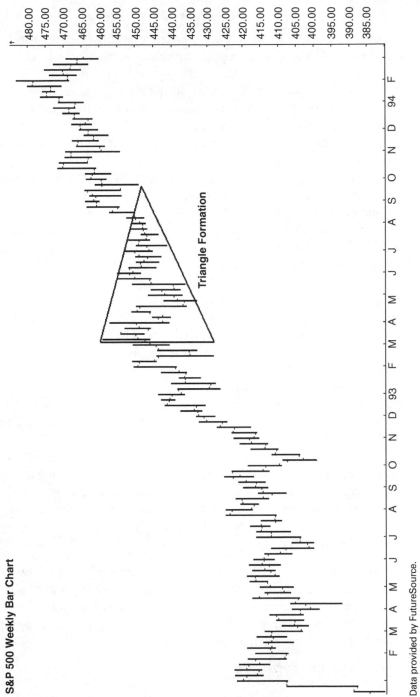

S&P 500 Weekly Bar Chart

Triangle Formation

Data provided by FutureSource.

applies in downtrends, where flags and triangles provide congestion areas that may look like a stair-step arrangement as each new level of lower prices develops.

The flag formation is slanted on a 45-degree angle. The flag is a small countertrend move against the direction of the main trend, a resting period during which bulls and bears sort out who will lead the market. Typically, a breakout of the flag signals a new leg in the direction of the main trend that is in place.

Some analysts use the flag to project how far the trend might go. They measure the length of the "flagpole" and add that to the point where the market breaks out of the flag. This becomes a potential price target. Keep in mind that this is not an exact science. The target can become a self-fulfilling prophecy. If the flag angles down, it is actually an up flag because prices will head up when they break out of the formation. A down flag, then, angles up, and prices will be going down.

According to some analysts, the tighter and neater the flag formation, the more reliable it will be. Quickly formed flags tend to be more reliable than slowly, sloppily formed ones. The length of the pole supporting the flag may also indicate how far the price trend will continue after it breaks out.

Like flags, pennants fly from "poles," but they look like symmetrical triangles. The up pennant forms out of buying activity and signals a continuation of the uptrend. Again, pennants that are more quickly formed tend to be more reliable.

The diamond formation develops when prices fluctuate wildly. Then the excitement fades and the prices dwindle to a point, forming a diamond. Predicting these formations is quite difficult because they can signal a trend reversal just as easily as they can signal a trend continuation.

Volume Tells the Story

As always, keep an eye on volume when you are analyzing the formations just described. It usually sinks as the formation develops and then escalates as the breakout occurs. Also, do not use these formations as your sole trend indicators. Volume can be a useful confirming indicator, along with other technical tools, such as moving averages.

SIMPLE MOVING AVERAGES

Analysts have developed numerous technical indicators, such as the aforementioned charts, over the years to give them a more comprehensive reading

FIGURE 6.18

Continuation Formations

Eurodollar Daily Bar Chart

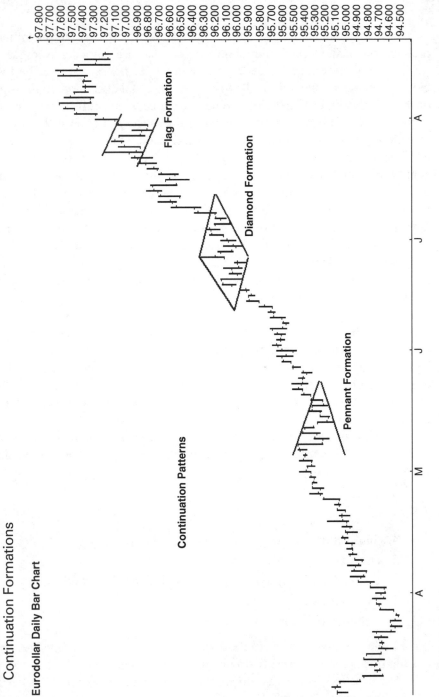

Continuation Patterns

Flag Formation

Diamond Formation

Pennant Formation

Data provided by FutureSource.

of price action. Not all of these indicators can be covered here, but one of the predominant techniques used through the years has been moving averages.

A moving average is based on one price per period—it may be the close or the open, the high or the low. The price can even be a composite of the open, high, low, and close. Whatever price you use, be sure to keep it consistent so that the data are meaningful. Once you choose the price, the concept of the moving average is simple: Add up all the prices for the number of periods that you want to include in your study, then divide the sum by the number of prices used to get a simple moving average. At the end of each period, add the new price and subtract the oldest price. Before the advent of computers, market technicians did this work manually every day, but now traders can have access to this type of information with the mere click of a button. Moving averages are a common technical tool that is widely available in software charting packages.

Analysts use a number of variations on the moving average to place more weight on more recent prices, such as exponential moving averages, weighted moving averages, and displaced moving averages. However, the basic signal from moving averages is that if a shorter-term moving average crosses above a longer-term moving average, this is a buy signal because it indicates that prices are moving up; if a shorter-term moving average crosses below a longer-term moving average, this is a sell signal because it indicates that prices are moving down. The moving average crossover, as simple as it is, is the basis for some successful trading systems.

Moving averages smooth out the price activity of a commodity over a period of time. For example, to calculate a 4-day moving average, you would

1. Select the first 4 days' prices.
2. Total them.
3. Divide by 4.
4. Subtract the first day's price and add the fifth day's.
5. Divide the new total by 4.
6. Subtract the second day's price and add the sixth day's.
7. Divide the new total by 4.
8. Continue doing this with each day's price.

Table 6.1 gives an example of a 4-day moving average using the closing prices for a Microsoft single stock futures contract.

For a better perspective on market movement, chart the calculated moving average on a graph. You can even chart moving averages right on single stock futures price charts in order to compare the moving average

TABLE 6.1

4-Day Moving Average

Day	Price	Total	4-Day Moving Average
1	57.08		
2	56.93		
3	56.47		
4	54.81	225.29	56.32
5	56.72	224.93	56.23
6	57.85	225.85	56.46
7	57.9	227.28	56.82
8	58.13	230.6	57.65
9	56.99	230.87	57.72
10	58.43	231.45	57.86
11	57.8	231.35	57.84
12	57.69	230.91	57.73

Note: This data was collected prior to Microsoft's 2-for-1 stock split effective February 2003.

with the actual price activity. In a downtrending market, the moving average usually remains above the current market price. In an uptrend, it tends to stay below the market price. The point at which the moving average crosses the actual price is a critical point.

Of course, you don't necessarily have to chart the moving average on top of the actual price chart. Perhaps your goals are more general. In this case, you can still use moving averages to indicate a trend. For example, the 4-day moving average just described would provide the short-term trend. If you wanted to view the bigger picture, you could calculate a 200-day moving average to represent the long-term trend.

Another use of moving averages is to generate specific buy and sell signals. The averages become a mini-trading system. To do this, you need to chart two different moving averages. Common ones are the 4-day moving average, for a fairly short-term trend, and the 9-day moving average, for a longer-term trend.

If both averages are moving higher, buy the market. Buy in the price range between the averages, and place stops below the slower moving average. Before you buy, wait for prices to sink into the zone below the slower moving average.

If both averages are moving lower, sell the market. Again, place sell orders in the price range between the averages. Place stops above the slower moving average. Wait for the market price to rally into this zone of the slower moving average. Sell short only when this occurs.

When you're placing a long-term trade, make sure both moving averages are headed in the same direction, and use a long-term moving average, such as a 50- or 100-day moving average.

A Weighted Moving Average

Perhaps you believe that the most recent price is a stronger indicator of the market trend, enabling you to anticipate trend changes sooner. If so, you may prefer to use a weighted moving average (see Table 6.2). To calculate a weighted moving average, simply do the following:

1. Arrange the numbers to be averaged in chronological order, with the most recent number last.
2. Multiply the oldest number by 1, the next by 2, the next by 3, and so on, until you reach the most recent number.
3. Multiply the most recent number by a factor equal to the total number of entries. (If you are averaging five numbers, the most recent number will be multiplied by 5.)
4. Now add all the results and divide by the sum of the multipliers. This will give you the weighted moving average.

Notice that this weighted moving average is less than a simple moving average because greater emphasis is placed on the most recent values in this declining market. In a rising market, on the other hand, the weighted moving average would be higher than a simple moving average.

Weighted moving average:
        843.19/15 = $56.21

Simple moving average:
        282.01/5= $56.40

Whether you prefer a weighted moving average to a simple moving average or vice versa, moving averages are an excellent tool for confirm-

TABLE 6.2

Weighted Moving Average

Day	Price	Weighing Result Factor
1	57.08 − 1 =	57.08
2	56.93 − 2 =	113.86
3	56.47 − 3 =	169.41
4	54.81 − 4 =	219.24
5	56.72 − 5 =	283.6
Totals	282.01, 15	843.19

ing trends. But as with all trading techniques, you should always moderate their use with experience and good common sense.

Chart analysis can be a useful tool in trading single stock futures. Traders may want to study the charts of the underlying cash stock to get the "best" reading of historical price information for the single stock future. In addition to remembering that the "trend is your friend," the following rules of technical analysis can be useful to remember:

Ten Technical Analysis Trading Rules[1] :

1. When a trend line is established, it is likely to continue.
2. The longer term the chart (15-minute, hourly, daily, weekly, monthly), the more reliable the trend line.
3. The greater the volume of trading when a trend is established, the greater the trend's significance.
4. In uptrending markets, when prices move too far too fast, trading volume decreases and prices decline.
5. In downtrending markets, volume is higher when prices are declining than when they rally.
6. Markets tend to give warnings before major trend changes occur. Be alert for these signals.
7. If a market is in an uptrend, volume usually drops just prior to the market's reversing its direction.

From All about Futures (New York: McGraw-Hill, 2001).

8. Volume usually increases in downtrending markets just before a reversal of trend.

9. Markets tend to test their trend line, by making shallow penetrations, before they plunge through it. These dips are warnings of impending trend reversals.

10. The steeper the trend, the more unstable it is and the more likely that a reversal of trend is imminent.

CHAPTER 7

Advanced Trading Considerations

We've gone over the basics, and now it's time to delve into some of the more advanced trading strategies that you may want to consider. There are a number of ways to trade successfully, but you will need to find a methodology that you are comfortable with and that works for you. After you've mastered the basics, this chapter can offer some ideas on more sophisticated strategies.

Single stock futures offer opportunities to profit, with a chance of loss, from increases and decreases in price. The most common form of speculation is straight buying and selling, which you will be able to do with single stock futures. If you are bullish on a stock, you will buy the futures contract on that stock, anticipating that its price will rise. If you are bearish, you will sell the futures contract on the stock. But single stock futures offer more advanced trading strategies than just straight speculation. Securities futures products can be used in a variety of ways, from opportunistic to risk-averse investment scenarios, and there are multiple ways to apply each strategy.

OPPORTUNISTIC SPECULATION

Spreading Opportunities

A more advanced way to speculate is through spreading. *Spreading* simply means that you expect to profit from a change in price relationships. One way to profit is to purchase a contract expiring in one contract month and sell another contract expiring in a different month. For example, you could buy one September General Motors (GM) single stock futures contract and sell one December GM single stock futures contract. This is called a *calendar spread.*

Commodity traders often employ calendar spreads for grains, coffee, crude oil, and other physical commodities, as supply and demand conditions may vary substantially from contract to contract because of growing conditions, delivery issues, and seasonal factors. These types of conditions don't affect certain financial futures, such as S&P futures and single stock futures, but traders must consider variables such as interest rates and dividends. However, spreading opportunities resulting from these differences can sometimes be small and may take a while to develop.

In contrast to the prices of many physical commodities, which are affected by often unpredictable factors, the prices of different contract months for single stock futures will have a reasonably consistent relationship to the price of the underlying stock, dependent on the yield curve, the expected dividends, and the borrowing demand for that particular stock. Absent a dividend, the back month will trade at a premium to the front month, or a higher price. For example, in December, June contracts will trade at a premium to March contracts. But when that spread narrows or widens beyond the norm, traders can capture those spreads to make a profit.

Another spreading strategy is what is known as *pairs trading.* In this strategy, you would purchase and sell two different stocks within the same industry, but in the same contract month. In other words, you would buy the strong stock and sell the weak stock and profit from the difference.

For example, if you wanted to speculate in the pharmaceuticals industry and you believed that Pfizer (PFE) would have stronger growth than Bristol-Myers Squibb (BMY) between now and June, you might decide to buy June Pfizer futures and sell June Bristol-Myers Squibb futures.

If the volatility of each single stock futures contract is the same, you may want to be dollar-neutral in your trade. To do this, you need to ensure that your trades involve an equal dollar value. For example, you could buy two Pfizer futures contracts at $30 per share for every three Bristol-Myers futures sold at $20 per share. Tables 7.1 and 7.2 illustrate how this example might play out if each contract is 100 shares.

Let's look at another example. If you believed that personal computers were going to take off to the upside, a possible trade idea would be to buy Dell Inc. (DELL) and sell International Business Machines (IBM).

TABLE 7.1

Opening Position	Price at Liquidation	Gain or Loss	Price at Liquidation	Gain or Loss
Buy 2 PFE at 30	$33	$600	$27	–$600
Sell 3 BMY at 20	$23	–$900	$17	$900
Net gain or loss		–$300		$300

Note that this example does not include fees and commissions.

TABLE 7.2

Opening Position	Price at Liquidation	Gain or Loss	Price at Liquidation	Gain or Loss
Buy 2 PFE at 30	$33	$600	$27	–$600
Sell 3 BMY at 20	$17	$900	$23	–$900
Net Gain or Loss		$1500		–$1500

Note that this example does not include fees and commissions.

Because the volatility of each contract differs, you would want to execute this trade based on the volatility of each contract, not on the dollar value, as in the previous example.

If Dell single stock futures contracts were trading at $30 and you figured that they generally had an intraday price change of about $1, and if IBM was trading at $90 and generally had an intraday price change of about $3, in order to execute a pairs trade, you would need to make sure that the average daily price change for each contract would be equal. And the higher the volatility, the fewer contracts on that stock you would trade, and vice versa. To accomplish that for this example, you would buy three times as many Dell contracts as you would sell IBM contracts in order to act on your bullish view of Dell.

If you are interested in exploring pairs trading, Msn.com offers a charting comparison tool for market sectors versus individual stocks that can be a valuable analysis tool. For example, an overlay could be done with DELL, IBM, and the industry sector line. If Dell is above the industry line and IBM is below it, one pairs strategy could be to sell Dell single stock futures and buy IBM single stock futures, on the assumption that both will return to the sector line.

Examples of potential spreading opportunities:

One single stock future against a competitor's single stock future: ExxonMobil (XOM) versus ChevronTexaco Corp. (CVX)

A single stock future against a future on a broad-based index: Microsoft (MSFT) versus the NASDAQ 100

A single stock future against a future on a narrow-based index: Johnson & Johnson (JNJ) versus the pharmaceuticals index

A narrow-based index against another future on a narrow-based index: software stocks versus hardware stocks

A narrow-based index against a future on a broad-based index: retail stocks versus the S&P 500

Single Stock Futures as Arbitrage Tools

Arbitrage is similar to spreading, but slightly more complicated. While both strategies take advantage of price discrepancies, arbitrage enables investors to capitalize on price discrepancies between equivalent products caused by market inefficiencies. These inefficiencies can include anything from lack of price transparency to lack of liquidity. The trick in arbitrage is finding a buyer or seller when the market is illiquid and finding information when the market is not transparent. As arbitrageurs simultaneously buy and sell equivalent products in different markets, price discrepancies are smoothed out, so their actions benefit all market participants. This differs from the basic idea behind spreading, which is that the prices of similar products should have a relationship to each other. For example, the prices of S&P futures and Dow futures should theoretically move in the same direction.

Currently, one area in which arbitrage commonly occurs is the cash foreign exchange market. As there is no designated exchange for cash currencies, banks set their own rates. Ideally, the price of a currency should be the same at every bank. However, as those prices are not always the same, arbitrageurs can take advantage of the different rates offered by different banks. An arbitrageur could call five banks to discover the different rates these banks offered and capitalize on the discrepancies between those rates.

Single stock futures will shake up the trading landscape for both futures and stocks as traders learn how best to "play" this new instrument. Whenever a new product enters the scene, the most skilled traders develop techniques to eliminate the market's inefficiencies and temper its volatility. Arbitrage opportunities for single stock futures may arise from the following: spreads between the bid and ask, futures trading far above or below fair value, volatility in the underlying stock market, and nonfungible contracts. Interestingly, however, in the early days of trading, the bid/ask spreads on these instruments are quite tight.

If there is high volatility in the underlying stock market, the futures market may not accurately reflect stock prices on a continuous real-time basis, and so arbitrageurs will buy the cash market and sell the futures market or vice versa, depending on which price is overvalued or undervalued. Program trading firms have done this for years with stocks and stock index futures and options. Now, more investors may capitalize on market inefficiencies, as single stock futures can be easier to use than stock index futures or options.

Without fungibility, which is the ability to trade the same instrument across exchanges, there may be market inefficiencies. Currently, single stock futures on OneChicago and NQLX are not fungible, so, theoretically, the two exchanges' prices for the same product could vary, and a skilled arbitrageur could buy one and sell the other. For example, both exchanges offer a futures contract on shares of Microsoft, so those contracts should theoretically trade at the same price. If the prices are not the same, an arbitrage opportunity would exist.

Let's say you are long Microsoft at NQLX at 54.50 and you see that NQLX has a bid at 54.65. If you placed a market order to sell, you would get filled at 54.65, but you also see that OneChicago has a bid at 54.75. However, if you decide to sell Microsoft futures at OneChicago to pick up the extra 10 cents, the margin required for holding both positions on two exchanges, though relatively low, could eat up the 10-cent gain. In other words, once you unwind your positions, the cost of arbitrage could cause you to lose the edge you gained in the first place, when you could have used the extra margin money to invest elsewhere.

It has been suggested that by the end of 2004, there may be options on single stock futures. This will unleash another opportunity for arbitrage: arbitrage between single stock futures and their options. Right now, if you wanted to arbitrage an option with a single stock future, you would have to do an indirect arbitrage between the stock, the stock option, and the single stock future. Although few people will engage in this three-legged arbitrage, for those of you with the interest and resources to take advantage of a direct arbitrage, rest assured that options on single stock futures will come.

RISK-AVERSE HEDGE STRATEGIES

If you are an individual trader with a stock portfolio, single stock futures offer a superior vehicle for hedging your cash stocks in a variety of ways. Used properly, they can help you lock in profits and protect against losses.

Just as option traders can use calls and puts to hedge the risk of their stock positions and create trades that are adaptable to their needs, stock traders can buy and sell single stock futures for the same purpose. Hedging single stock futures may also be used to employ modern portfolio theory, a theory that holds that diversification reduces company-specific risks. According to the National Futures Association, "Generally, hedging is the purchase or sale of a security future to reduce or offset the risk of a position in the underlying security or group of securities (or a close economic equivalent)." Hedging helps to protect, to an extent, your securities position from an unfavorable price swing, but in return for this insurance, you give up the potential to profit from a favorable price move. So if you want to lock in a price for the sale or purchase of an underlying security at a future date, you can hedge with single stock futures. Let's take a look at a sell example and a buy example.

Security futures products can be used to hedge price volatility and to fine-tune market exposure:

- Hedge a long cash equities position with a short single stock futures position.
- Hedge a 401(k) position in company stock until the next open selling period.
- Delete a stock from a broad-based index.
- Overweight or underweight a sector within a diversified portfolio using narrow-based indexes.

Using the Sale of Single Stock Futures to Protect Your Cash Position

If you are long a particular stock, you can sell futures on that stock to reduce your risk. You can adjust your short position to meet your financial needs by increasing or decreasing the number of futures contracts.

Assume that you own 1000 shares of Home Depot (HD) that have appreciated since you bought them. You would like to sell them at the current price of $35 per share, but there are taxation or other reasons for holding them until the next calendar year. You could sell ten 100-share Home Depot futures contracts for next-year delivery, then buy back those contracts in the next calendar year when you sell the stock. If the stock price and the futures price change by the same amount, the gain or loss in the stock will be offset by the loss or gain in the futures contracts (see Table 7.3). This is known as a *perfect hedge*. In reality, many hedges will be imperfect. Nonetheless, they provide the ability to protect against risky market positions.

Again, by varying the number of single stock futures you trade against your stock position, you can modify your risk. To hedge 50 percent of the position in this example, you would sell 5 single stock futures on Home Depot instead of 10.

Buying Narrow-Based Indexes to Hedge a Sector

Let's look at a buy example. Assume that in August, a mutual fund in which you have invested expects to buy stocks in the oil and gas industry with the earnings of bonds that will mature in November. If regulations allow, the mutual fund can hedge the risk that the stocks it intends to invest in will increase in value between August and November by purchasing futures on a narrow-based index of stocks from that industry. When the mutual fund buys the stocks in November, it will also close the security futures position in the index. Assuming the relationship between the single stock futures and the stocks in the index remains steady, the profit or loss from the futures contract will offset the price change in the stocks, and the mutual fund will have locked in the price at which the stocks were selling in August.

Subtracting a Stock from the Index (Target Hedging)

Target hedging is a technique in which you sell single stock futures on those stocks in your portfolio that you think may underperform. It allows you to tailor a strategy for your particular index fund in a more specific

TABLE 7-3

Price in December	Gain or Loss on Futures	Gain or Loss on Cash Position	Effective Selling Price
$25	$10,000	–$10,000	$35,000
$35	$0	$0	$35,000
$45	–$10,000	$10,000	$35,000

Note that this example does not include fees and commissions.

fashion than just selling index futures. For example, if a particular stock or handful of stocks is causing your portfolio to sag, or if you think they may do so in the near future, you can sell futures on those stocks to offset the losses in the underlying position and thus take advantage of the rally in the rest of your portfolio.

Microsoft alone has about a ten percent weight in the NASDAQ 100 index, although this is down from close to 25 percent several years ago. While key rulings in antitrust lawsuits triggered a tough period for the software giant's stock, many investors still believed that technology was a buy. In retrospect, that belief was unfounded. However, this was a period during which traders might have used single stock futures effectively. Traders could have sold Microsoft futures and bought NASDAQ futures to play on their belief that the NASDAQ overall was still going higher. However, these traders would have wanted to ensure that asset values were the same before entering into that kind of trade. Had the NASDAQ index moved higher and Microsoft lower, the result might have been more positive. Remember, however, that the index as a whole could have moved lower as well. As we view today's market, subtracting a dominant stock in the index might not have been enough. But if we look at the example conceptually and apply it to other situations, subtraction is a viable strategy.

Hedging Forward Commitments of Stock

Other uses of single stock futures that might arise could include hedging forward commitments of stock, such as 401(k) contributions, tender offers, and bonuses. For example, to protect a position in a limited-access account, such as a 401(k), you can sell single stock futures to assure you that your funds will be intact when you go to withdraw them.

Taking Advantage of Tax Laws in Hedging

If you trade futures regularly, you probably know that single stock futures do not receive the 60/40 tax treatment that other futures receive. Although interpreting tax laws can be complicated, familiarizing yourself with a few of them may be to your advantage. For example, under Section 1223(16) of the Internal Revenue Code, if you receive stock in delivery against a long single stock future, the holding period for the security begins at the purchase date of the single stock future, which is a definite benefit over options. The single stock futures trader has a better opportunity to extend the holding period in order to be taxed at the long-term capital gains rate, since the holding period includes the time the contract is held.

Keep in mind that you must always factor other fees and commissions into your trading plan, in addition to taxes on your trading activities. For further explanation of and education on other tax advantages, consult a qualified CPA.

The bottom line is that single stock futures can be an effective tool that offers you unprecedented flexibility in speculation and hedging. They can be used as a speculative instrument, to take advantage of directional moves, or, perhaps even more importantly, they can allow you a means of protecting your 401(k) holdings or other cash stock investments from short-term market losses.

CHAPTER 8

The Options Market and Single Stock Futures

As an investor in 2003 and beyond, you may have experienced the bottom-line benefits of one of the greatest bull markets of all time during the 1980s and 1990s. But, you also may have experienced the financial pain that bears brought down in the first couple of years of the new century. The recent economic uncertainty and financial market volatility have added a great degree of risk to investments. Investors on every level have been forced to search for lower-risk investment vehicles in order to achieve greater investment success. The buy-and-hold philosophy of investing, at least for the short-run, may have run its course. As we have discussed throughout this book, single stock futures are a new investment tool that offers investors another way to hedge price risk as well as to take advantage of the market from a more opportunistic vantage point. But this chapter will tackle another angle. In some ways, single stock futures are similar to the options market. If you've traded options before, you may see the similarity in concept. However, after a brief overview of the basics of options, we'll also highlight how and why single stock futures could be a better alternative under various scenarios.

Some may believe that the ideal investment vehicle is one that offers a profit potential at a predetermined risk of loss. If the maximum loss can be precisely calculated prior to committing funds and the profit potential is far greater than the risk, this unique investment may be ideally suited to today's market. If this investment also reduces the need to place stops to protect against minor reversals, it has come even closer to perfection.

SIMILARITIES BETWEEN OPTIONS AND SINGLE STOCK FUTURES

Although options seem to fit the definition of the ideal investment vehicle, single stock futures contracts also have similarities to the "ideal" investment vehicle. For example, both of these tools are based on the value of another financial instrument, stocks (or, in options, futures contracts). Furthermore, to trade either of these instruments, a trader needs to deposit only 20 percent of the value of the contract, giving her or him greater leverage on her or his investments. Finally, both of these instruments can be used as hedging tools to protect the value of stock holdings. As you can see, options and single stock futures can potentially compete for traders' dollars as risk management and market speculation tools. This chapter can help you determine which would be the best tool for you.

Single stock futures offer certain advantages over options. An important advantage is that the value of single stock futures is not affected by time decay, an effect we'll explain later in the chapter. Their value is based on the value of the underlying stock plus interest rates minus dividends, which is a much simpler pricing model than that of options. In addition, when trading options, you have to wait until the stock hits the agreed-upon price before you can take advantage of the option. If the stock never hits that price, you are out the cost of the option. If you trade futures, you can take advantage of the contract, no matter what the price of the underlying stock is. Thus, you can still take delivery of the stock and hold it indefinitely.

However, for the more risk-averse trader, one of the main advantages of options is that the risk is predetermined. To help you plan risk management or speculation strategies that suit your financial needs, we'll review some of the strategies and benefits of options and compare them to those of the newest derivative, single stock futures. Your interest in these strategies may grow even more once options on single stock futures come into being; according to the Commodity Futures Modernization Act, they may legally begin trading in December 2004. (No specific plans for these options have been released by exchanges, at press time.) This chapter is not meant to explore all uses of options; it is merely a brief guide. After all, entire books have been written on this subject, so clearly it cannot be covered fully in just a few pages.

OPTIONS BASICS

Puts and Calls

An option is the right, but not the obligation, to buy or sell a stock or underlying futures contract at a specified price during a specified period of time. The two basic types of options are the *put* and the *call*. A call option is the right to buy at the specified price on or before the option's expiration date.

You would purchase a call option if you expected a stock or a futures contract to rise. A put option is the right to sell; therefore, you would buy a put option if you expected prices to decline. You could also sell a put if you expected prices to rise, or sell a call if you expected prices to fall.

Options on futures and stocks provide the buyer with rights, not obligations. The term *right* indicates one of the primary differences between futures and options. With futures, an obligation is created for both the buyer and the seller. The buyer must take, and the seller must make, delivery unless the position is offset prior to delivery. In the case of options, a unilateral obligation is placed on the writer (seller) of the option; that is, only the option writer is obligated to perform. The buyer of the option may exercise the option, but may also decide to abandon it and let the option expire. In the event that the option is exercised, the option writer must deliver or accept delivery of the underlying stock or futures position. Once the writer has received notice from the buyer that the option will be exercised, the writer cannot offset his or her option position.

Options Premium

A premium is the value of an option, or the amount that you would pay an option writer to guarantee you a price on your stock or futures contract. The premium on an option can be calculated as follows: Premium = intrinsic value + time value. Intrinsic value is the amount an option would be worth if it were to expire immediately. For example, if S&P futures were trading at 1060 and your call option gave you the right to buy S&P futures at 1050, you would have an immediate 10-point profit and should be willing to pay the value of 10 points, or $2500 (10 points × $250), for that option.

The second part of an option premium is time value, which is less definite than the intrinsic value. By definition, time value is the amount of the premium that exceeds intrinsic value. However, if time value is not concrete, how do you know whether it exceeds intrinsic value? In order to fully grasp the concept of time value, it is necessary to understand some of the factors that contribute to the creation of this value. The first factor is the time until expiration. You can reasonably assume that the right to buy something is worth more if you have 12 months to decide than if you have only 3 months. The option buyer is asking the writer to pre-price the underlying product, regardless of future market performance. The writer must be paid for this risk, so, reasonably, 12 months' worth of risk costs more than 3 months' worth.

Options premiums are also influenced by short-term interest rates. Higher interest rates may cause premiums to drop in order for the options to attract more investors. However, if the rate of return for other investment vehicles is lower, options do not have to be competitively priced and premiums will be higher.

Options Volatility

Volatility probably influences option prices more than other variables and is one of the most complex influences on options pricing. So, although there may be many mind-bending mathematical reasons for volatility, let's zero in on some basic reasons. If S&P futures are at 1050 and will remain at that price for a year, there is little risk in selling a 1050 call option. But if S&P futures trade between 1010 and 1070 during the same week, there is significantly greater risk associated with the 1050 call option. Once again, the writer of the option must be paid for assuming that risk. The greater the likelihood that the option will trade through the strike price, thus increasing the chance that the buyer will exercise the option, the higher the premium must be to accommodate the risk taken by the writer. The common thread running through each of these components of time value is risk. Anything that increases the writer's risk will increase option premiums, regardless of the source of that risk. Any time that the amount of risk decreases, option premiums will fall.

Strike Price

The strike price is the price at which you may buy or sell the underlying futures contract or underlying stock. An at-the-money option has a strike price that is close to the price of the underlying security. An in-the-money call (put) option has a strike price that is below (above) the current price of the underlying security. An out-of-the-money call (put) option has a strike price that is above (below) the current price of the underlying security.

THE OPTIONS ADVANTAGE

Options provide investors with price insurance, whether the investors are trading futures or stocks. The buyer, or holder, of an option has the right, but not the obligation, to receive a position in the underlying futures contract or stock at a predetermined price (strike price) on or before a specific date (expiration date). As we reviewed in Chapter 1, a futures contract requires the purchase or sale of the underlying security if the contract is held to expiration. Likewise, if you hold a stock position, you are subject to any market movement. An option buyer, on the other hand, may elect to let the option expire without exercising her or his rights or can exercise the option to her or his advantage. For this reason, an option resembles insurance, with a premium being paid to insure against the possibility of a change in price. If the price change does not occur, the individual purchasing the option loses only the premium paid.

For example, if you want to hold onto your stock because you believe its value will rise in the long run, but you are concerned about the possibility of plummeting prices in the short term, you can hedge your position by buying a put option. If you bought a stock at $30 and bought a put option with a $30 strike price, you would have the opportunity to sell the stock at $30, even if the price dropped well below $30.

Another way to protect your stock position from falling prices would be to sell a call option. Again, you can secure a minimum price for your stock. Not only would this offer some price protection, but you would also receive the premium for assuming the risk of selling an option. Should the market rise, you would be able to keep the premium and perhaps even the stock if the option buyer chooses not to exercise his or her rights. (Chances are, however, that you would sell your stock to option buyer.)

A more speculative way to take advantage of the benefits of options is to buy options instead of stocks or futures. For example, if you are bullish on a particular stock, but you are unsure about buying the actual stock, you can buy call options, which will give you the right to purchase the stock at a prestated price, the strike price. If the market moves upward as you predicted, you can then buy the stock at a price that is lower than the current market price. If the market doesn't move upward, you will be out only the premium, which would be less costly than buying the actual stock.

Another way to secure the purchase price of a stock is to sell a put option. You could sell someone an option to sell his or her stock at a specified price. However, you must be aware that selling or writing options tends to be riskier than buying them. The risk involved in writing options is completely opposite to the risk and reward potential of buying options. The writer of an option is exposed to unlimited risk with the prospect of only limited rewards, whereas the buyer of options assumes limited risk with the prospect of potentially unlimited rewards. The primary incentive for writing either put or call options is the premium income, while the major risk for an option writer is the risk of exercise. An option writer should keep in mind that the buyer of the option can exercise at any time.

Whether and when to exercise a profitable option is entirely up to the option buyer. To compensate for this obligation, the call writer receives money from the call buyer in the form of a premium. It is this premium money that motivates all writers to participate in the market. However, for the novice options trader, it may be best to stick with buying options.

As we've noted briefly here, investors can speculate and manage risk with options, and in the next few sections we'll present more advanced strategies. Options offer investors a plethora of trading strategies from which to choose in order to meet their individual trading needs.

OPTION SPREADING

Spreading, as discussed in Chapter 6, involves taking advantage of price discrepancies through a combination of buying and selling. Again, because spreading involves a combination of trades, it's a slightly more advanced strategy than only buying or only selling. Spreading opportunities are far more numerous in options than in futures because spreading is available between a much wider variety of strike prices and expiration dates than there are commodity delivery/expiration dates. An option spread is similar to a futures spread, consisting of a long and a short position (a call and a put) in one option, with the call and the put having either different strike prices or different expiration dates. Investors can also spread to reduce the risk inherent in writing either a put or a call option.

Time Spreads

Time spreads, or calendar spreads, involve options with the same strike price but different expiration dates. In executing a time spread, the main goal is to take advantage of the tendency of the time value of an option to decay quickly prior to expiration. Generally, a put or call with a closer expiration date is sold (written), and a put or call with a farther expiration date is purchased.

The put or call with the farther expiration loses its time value more slowly, which limits the risk of such a position by eliminating the potential for unlimited loss on sharp upside (downside) moves. For example, a spreader in S&P options on futures might write (sell) a March 1030 S&P call for a $1500 premium and purchase a June 1030 S&P call for a $2000 premium. The spread would be established for a net debit of $500 premium. The original debit represents the maximum possible loss as long as the spread remains in effect. In order to make a profit, the spread would have to widen to more than 2 points. Both the passage of time and the price movement of the underlying futures contract have the potential to affect this spread.

The difference between the two options is likely to increase as time passes because the nearby option will lose its time value at a faster rate than will the distant option. The price of the underlying contract is the prime determinant of how much profit will be derived from a spread. If the spread position is established by selling the nearby option and buying the more distant when both options are at the money, the spread will be profitable if the futures prices remain relatively constant, and will tend to produce losses if the prices change. The spread will be at its widest when the price of the futures contract is closest to the exercise price of the option. The spread will narrow as the price moves away from the exercise price in either direction. In the previous example, an S&P futures price of 1030 at the March option expiration date would cause the March 1030 call to expire without value, while the June 1030 contract might have time value left. The spread could be closed out at double its original cost. If prices were considerably higher or lower than 1030, the spread would narrow, as both options would lose their time values.

Even if the S&P price should increase slightly, this strategy will still yield a profit, provided that at the time the March call expires, the premium difference between the March and June options is greater than the initial net cost of the spread. Moreover, the maximum net loss will occur only if at the time the March call expires, the June call no longer has any time value. This will happen only if it is so far out of the money that no market exists for it or so far in the money that its premium is totally a reflection of its intrinsic value.

Bull Spreads

Option spreads that involve options with the same expiration date but different exercise prices are called *price spreads*. If an investor thinks that the stock market is going to rise, she or he might purchase a call. With the March S&P futures at 1010, a call with a 1000 strike price might be purchased for a 20-point premium (20 points $\times$ \$250 = \$5000). If you do not want to risk the entire \$5000, an alternative would be to write a call with a higher exercise price. In this case, the March 1010 S&P call could be sold for, perhaps, a 15-point premium, or \$3750. The spread could be put on a 5-point debit. Such a spread is called a *bull spread,* and the risk in the position is limited to the amount of the original debit. Risk limitation does not come without a price, however, as the profit potential of the spread is also limited.

The maximum profit from a price spread is computed by subtracting the original debit from the difference between the exercise prices of the two options. In this example, the debit is 5 points and the difference between exercise prices is 10 points, for the possibility of making 5 points. A price above 1010 at the March expiration would see both options trading at their intrinsic value. The difference between them would be the maximum: 10 points. If the price was lower than 1000, both calls would expire without value, and the maximum loss would occur.

Bull Call Spreads

One of the strategies an investor may employ is a bull call spread, meaning that the investor is bullish on market prices. The bull call spread involves buying one option and writing (selling) another option. This is done by buying the call option with the low strike price and selling the call option with the high strike price.

The guidelines for the bull call spread are well defined. The maximum net loss involved is the net premium cost. The maximum net profit that can come from this spread is the difference between the strike prices of the two options less the net premium cost. As an example of a bull call spread, suppose that an investor who is expecting higher stock prices notes in July that the September S&P futures price is 1050. To profit from the anticipated price increase, he buys a September 1050 call at a premium of $5000 and sells a September 1100 call at a premium of $1000. His maximum potential profit is $8500 (the strike price difference of $12,500 less the net premium cost of $4000). His maximum potential loss is the $4000 net premium cost.

In order for the investor to realize the maximum profit, the futures price at expiration must be equal to or above the strike price of the option written. If it isn't, the investor's profit or loss will depend on whether the value of the purchased call at expiration is more or less than the net premium cost. If the futures price in the previous example increased only to 1060, the $2500 gain would be less than the net premium cost of $4000, and the investor would have lost $1500. As the futures price increased, say, to 1070, the investor would have a $1000 profit—that is, a $5000 gain minus the $4000 net premium cost.

The investor can modify the risk/reward potential on a bull call spread through the selection of the strike prices, and the associated premiums, at which the calls are bought and written. For example, with the September S&P futures price at 1050, the investor could buy a September 1070 call at a premium of $2500 and write a September 1100 call at a premium of $1000. The investor's maximum risk is the $1500 net premium cost, and the maximum profit is $6000 (the $7500 strike price difference less the $1500 net premium). Although the potential loss is relatively small, a substantial increase in the futures price (from 1050 to 1100) is required in order to real-ize the maximum profit. The investor's expectations during the life of the option and his or her tolerance for risk determine what spreading opportu-nities to take. The choice involves which strike price to buy and which strike price to write. But as these examples illustrate, once the math of the spread has been calculated, the risk/reward potential will be clear to the investor.

Bull Put Spreads

An alternative to the bull call spread is the bull put spread. This strategy also involves profiting on an increase in the market. A bull put spread con-sists of purchasing a put option with a low strike price and selling a put option with a high strike price. The maximum profit potential for the investor is the premium difference. The maximum loss the investor could incur is the difference in strike price less the net premium received. For example, suppose that in December, the March S&P futures price is 1040. To profit from an expected increase in the futures price, an investor pays a premium of $2500 to buy a March 1040 put and collects a premium of $9000 by writing a March 1070 put. The net premium received is $6500. If the futures price at expiration is 1070 or higher, neither put will be exer-cised, and the investor's net profit will be $6500 (the net premium received). The maximum loss of $1000 ($7500 - $6500) will occur if the futures price at expiration is 1040 or below.

Points to remember about option bull spreads:

- A bull spread produces profits only when the spread narrows.
- The maximum profit is the difference between the strike price and the debit (the amount by which the cost of the long side exceeds the proceeds from the short side).
- The maximum loss is the debit.

Bear Spreads

The strategies to benefit from a declining market are simply the opposite of those used in a rising market. A bear call spread during a period of declining stock market prices offers clearly defined risk and reward guidelines. The investor who is risk-averse knows in advance the maximum net profit and the net loss possible.

If you thought stock market prices were headed lower, you might have reversed the process described earlier and sold (wrote) the 1000 call for a premium of 20, while buying the 1010 call options for a 15-point premium. The spread would be established for a 5-point credit. Such a spread is called a *bear spread*. Any price below 1000 on the underlying futures instrument at the time of the options' expiration would cause both calls to expire worthless, allowing you to retain the entire 5-point premium. The maximum loss would occur at any price above 1010 at expiration, because the options would be selling 10 points apart at their intrinsic value.

Points to remember about option bear spreads:

- A bear spread leads to profits when the spread decreases.
- The maximum profit is the credit (the amount by which the proceeds from the short side exceed the cost of the long side).
- The maximum loss is the difference between the strike price and the credit.

STRADDLE STRATEGIES

So now you know what to do if you have a bullish or bearish market outlook, but what if your outlook is a little fuzzy? What if the market is moving sideways? How can you profit in a consolidating market? The answer is the straddle. Using this strategy, you can position yourself for a big market move even though you don't know which way the market will swing. As with most strategies, there are two variations: the long and the short.

The Long Straddle

To execute a long straddle, you would buy both a long call and a long put position with the same strike price and the same expiration date. If you are to profit from this strategy, a major market move must occur before the options expire. In fact, the profitability of this move is theoretically unlimited until the bull or bear market ends. If the market doesn't move at all, you're out your paid premium and any associated transaction costs.

For example, suppose a stock is at 78, and so you buy a call and a put for that stock at 78. If the price of the stock rises, you'll exercise your call option. If it goes down, you'll exercise your put option. If it's stagnant, you will be out only your premium.

The Short Straddle

There is an opposite trading strategy, the short straddle. Instead of buying a put and a call, you sell a put and a call. This strategy is best if you expect the market to be flat for the life of the options sold.

The short straddle is particularly appealing because it allows you to benefit from the normal decay in an option's time value as it approaches expiration. In a profitable scenario, neither option is exercised, so you keep the full premium on both the put and the call. A major price move, on the other hand, could be very expensive.

CREATING SYNTHETIC FUTURES WITH OPTIONS

Anyone who initially opposed single stock futures trading in the United States may have used the argument that equivalent positions can already be created using a combination of options. However, this strategy, particularly for a novice options trader, may be a bit cumbersome and more complex than necessary, as you'll see in the following examples. This combination strategy is called the *synthetic long* or *synthetic short.*

Synthetic Long

To create a synthetic long position, you would purchase a call option and then sell a put option, where the two legs of this position share a common strike price and expiration date. Of course, if you intend to execute a long strategy, you must be bullish on the direction in which you expect the market to head.

For example, let's say that after analyzing the stock market, you think that the Dow will head higher. Instead of buying a futures contract on an index like the S&P 500, you choose to trade a synthetic long, so you buy a call and sell a put. Assume for simplicity's sake that the S&P 500 is trading at 350 and that both the call and the put are in the money. The call costs you 2 index points to buy, and you receive 2 index points for selling the put. Let's look at three possible scenarios for this strategy.

If your bullish prediction proves true, your call gains in value and the put will expire worthless. You win on both legs. You can close out or exercise your call, and you retain the premium you received for selling the put. However, if prices drop, you will lose on both legs. You lose the premium paid for your call, as the call expires worthless. The trader to whom you sold the put exercises it, obliging you to deliver a short futures position that is in the money.

The third possibility is that the market does not move either up or down. In this case, you break even, less the transaction costs. The 2-point premium you received for selling the put balances the 2-point premium you paid for the call. (Remember that the transaction costs are doubled in this strategy compared to those for taking a straight futures position.)

This example is a very simple one. The two options do not necessarily have to have the same strike price. If the put is in the money and the call is not, you'll have a credit, whereas if the call is in the money and the put is not, you'll have a deficit because the premium you receive for the put will not cover the cost of the call. The problem with this strategy, however, is that the underlying futures contract or security will have to move farther in order for you to begin profiting on the trade.

Advantages of This Strategy

Why would you want to pay double the transaction costs when you could hold a straight futures position? This is the reason: The synthetic long strategy can be used to convert a long call or short put option position to a futures position with the same advantages and risk. For example, suppose you have already bought a call option. Should you decide that the market is definitely moving upward, you could make the most of your position by gaining the short put premium. Doing this would create a synthetic long position.

The Synthetic Short

If your market outlook is bearish, you can create a synthetic short, just as you can create a synthetic long, in order to mimic a short position in the futures. To create a synthetic short, you would buy the put and sell the call with the same expiration and, preferably, the same strike price. The risks of holding a synthetic short position are equal, but opposite to those of holding a synthetic long position: If prices rise, your call will be exercised and your put will expire worthless.

COMPARING THE BENEFITS OF SINGLE STOCK FUTURES TO OPTIONS

As you can tell from the previous examples, both options and single stock futures can be used for hedging and opportunistic moves. Because these trading tools are so similar, you should know the differences between them, as you'll want to use the tool that is most suitable to your trading strategy.

While it is possible to create synthetic single stock futures using a combination of options, it is far easier to just trade a single stock futures contract. Single stock futures can be cheaper because there is no premium, as there is with options, and there is only one round-turn transaction cost for a single stock futures contract, as opposed to two for a synthetic single stock future created with options.

So how do security futures and options compare dollar-wise? Let's say that you and a friend each anticipate an increase in ABC, which is currently trading at $25 a share. You purchase one ABC 25 call covering 100 shares of ABC at a premium of $5 per share. The option premium is $500 ($5 per share × 100 shares). Your friend purchases an ABC single stock futures contract covering 100 shares of ABC. The total value of the contract is $2500 ($25 share value × 100 shares). The required margin is $500 or 20 percent of the contract value.

The most that you can lose is $500, the option premium. You break even at $30 per share, and make money at higher prices. Your friend, on the other hand, can begin profiting at any price above $25, though she may lose more than her initial margin deposit should the price fall. Note that if the price of ABC rises to $40 per share, you make $1000, whereas your friend makes $1500. (Note, however, that if the price plummets to $10 a share, you would lose $500, whereas your friend would lose $1500 if she did not offset her position in time.)

TABLE 8.1

Price of ABC at Expiration	Your Profit or Loss	Your Friend's Profit or Loss
40	1000	1500
35	500	1000
30	0	500
25	–500	0
20	–500	–500
15	–500	–1000
10	–500	–1500

Note that the expiration month and transaction costs have been left out of the example for simplification.

As you can see from Table 8.1, single stock futures may be a better investment alternative in some cases. With single stock futures, you do not have to wait for the price of the stock to rise past the cost of the premium in order to make money.

If this were a hedging situation, single stock futures might again be a better alternative. Say you and your friend both own ABC stock and expect its price to decline, but would like to hold on to the stock. To limit your losses, you hedge with a 20 put, for a premium of $500. Your friend chooses to sell single stock futures on ABC instead; the value of the contract will be 100 (shares) × 25 (current share price) + interest – dividends (or fair value, which we reviewed in Chapter 4). In this situation, if the stock drops to 23 by the option's expiration date, you lose money on your stock and also lose the premium, since the stock never reached the strike price. Your friend's losses, on the other hand, are offset by an increase in the value of her short single stock futures position, since she buys back her single stock futures position at a lower price than that at which she sold it.

ASSESS YOUR OWN STRATEGIES AND GOALS

With any trading strategy, you will need to compare the risks and rewards, and also assess your own risk tolerance. Should you determine that you prefer predetermined risk in trading, options may suit your trading style for speculation and hedging. If you decide that the potential for greater profit overshadows the potential for greater risk, single stock futures may offer the advantages of a simpler and less expensive vehicle to express your trading opinions.

CHAPTER 9

The Electronic Connection: Trading Single Stock Futures Online

The advent of electronic trading over the last several years has clearly opened "doors of efficiency" to individual traders, with pluses that simply didn't exist in years past. Now, with an Internet connection and a level of hardware and software consistent with your trading needs, you can trade from the comfort of your own home or office. Electronic trading has leveled the playing field, so to speak—individual investors can now have access to markets, on a real-time basis, in a way that was never before possible.

Currently single stock futures trade on all-electronic exchanges, so this chapter introduces you to the world of online trading systems. NQLX and OneChicago are wholly electronic exchanges. If and when Island ECN introduces securities futures products, it, too, will be wholly electronic. These days, new exchanges find that creating an electronic platform rather than a floor-based model is both dramatically more cost-effective and more what the public is seeking for most types of trading. Products can be launched and delisted easily. Trading pits never have to be built. Trade execution is simpler and, in most cases, as reliable or more reliable. And the electronic connection can actually add liquidity to the markets, as it allows more players access to these contracts. Electronic trading has already had the effect of adding liquidity to securities, futures, and options markets, and it should help to increase participation in single stock futures as well.

If you're not already familiar with online systems, you should be. They are changing the way trading is done—quickly. A point: Just because single stock futures contracts are traded through an electronic platform like

NQLX's or OneChicago's does not mean that you *have* to trade without the assistance of a broker or that you *must* personally trade online. You may choose to work with a broker and have him or her transmit your orders electronically to NQLX or OneChicago. Or, your brokerage firm may have its own electronic trading system, to which the firm's customers have access. This would indeed, then, allow you to make your own trades via computer. The only point here is that exchanges have electronic platforms rather than trading floors for single stock futures, and thus you have choices as to how you *personally* transact your business.

If you do decide to trade single stock futures (SSFs) online, you may have the opportunity to see current markets in action, just as the floor traders in the pit would see current bids and offers. The markets can move rapidly, and you can see this when you are watching an online system. The bid/ask prices may sometimes change faster than you can blink. Don't let that speed thwart your desire to trade. Electronic platforms level the playing field for individual traders—you will probably see the same bid/ask information as the market makers, who are on the other side of trading single stock futures. You no longer have to wait for your broker to contact you or try to get through to your broker—you yourself can place your buy and sell orders with the click of a mouse once you learn how to navigate the system.

INFORMATION PROVIDED BY ONLINE SYSTEMS

A brokerage firm's online system normally provides two things: order information and market data services. On your trading system, you will usually see these two types of screens. Order information includes your buy/sell information, stop information, market quantity, commodity, time, duration (good-till-canceled or day order), and market status (filled, unable, rejected, canceled).

Market data services include quote information in bid/ask terms, quantity in terms of size, and depth of market (all the bids/asks below and above the market). Depth of market includes all bid/ask prices—bid prices are below market price, and ask prices are above market price.

Other common screens that may be found within a trading system are position reference, parked orders, and viewing reports. A *position reference* screen offers users information on order management, including what orders were filled and which orders were canceled. There is an order portion for inputting buys and sells and order specifications, which detail the type of order—for example, a limit order or a market order. The position reference screen also allows the trader to see the quote window and to monitor real-time profits and losses. Clearly, it is extremely helpful for traders to be able to monitor all of this information on one screen at a glance.

A *parked orders* screen allows a commodity trading advisor (CTA) to put trades into a basket and then send all the trades in at the same time. But parked orders do not benefit only professional traders. They give a customer the ability to have a trade or set of trades waiting to be sent to one or more exchanges. This way, these orders aren't actually at the exchange(s) and potentially getting filled before you might want them to be filled. For example, let's say you want to place the following orders:

Buy 2 SSF @ Market

Sell 3 SSF @ Market

Buy 2 SSF @ 7750 Limit

Sell 10 SSF @ 7800 Limit

If you had all of these orders "parked," you could place them all simultaneously when the market conditions seemed appropriate to you, rather than having to enter each of them individually and risk getting "slipped" because you couldn't place them quickly enough.

A *viewing reports* screen allows traders to access previous activity reports. Customers are able to click on a certain month and day to see what trading activity they initiated during those sessions.

TYPES OF ONLINE SYSTEMS

There are two types of online systems from which to choose: *browser-based systems* and *stand-alone systems*. Each has its own benefits and drawbacks.

Browser-Based Systems

Browser-based systems are web-based systems (Microsoft Internet Explorer and Netscape Navigator are examples of web-browsing systems) that are made up of a series of web pages that allow you to enter orders, view working orders, and get quotes. E*Trade and Ameritrade are examples of firms offering this kind of system. The main advantage is that traders can log into these systems from anywhere.

There are many other benefits to these systems. First, nearly everyone who uses the Internet can use a browser-based system and will be comfortable with its format. Second, a browser-based system is easily upgraded. When your brokerage firm's webmaster changes one or more of the web pages, you and everyone else who goes to that page will see the changes. You do not have to do anything in particular to see updated material on the web page. Finally, since most web browsers are standardized, there is very little need to customize programming or worry about how certain functions may operate.

However, like any system, a browser-based system has drawbacks as well. First, web pages are static, so they do not have the ability to stream real-time information unless they incorporate Java, a type of programming language. A browser-based system that uses Java can be much slower than a stand-alone system and more restrictive in how it can be programmed. End users still have to download a considerable amount in order to allow Java programs to work in conjunction with their browsers and must keep in step with newer versions of the Java program. Another drawback is that a web-based system has trading information spread out across many pages. Moving through these pages can be time-consuming and could cause the investor to miss or to be late for an opportunity.

Stand-Alone Systems

A stand-alone system is a program that you download directly onto your computer. Like a browser-based system, it allows you to enter orders, view working orders, get quotes, and do everything else that you can do through the browser-based system.

As with a browser-based system, there are pros and cons. First, unlike a browser-based system, a stand-alone system can stream various types of information. This means that you can enter an order and see exactly when it gets filled without having to refresh any information. This feature also can allow for streaming quotes, real-time profit/loss calculation, and faster order execution. It enables you to be as up-to-date as possible on all of your trades. Second, a stand-alone system can take advantage of a web browser for various purposes, such as generating various reports and charting, but a web-based system cannot take advantage of a stand-alone system, since a web page cannot launch a program.

However, if a company develops a stand-alone system, it has to be more conscious of the various operating systems that its customers have. For example, because no two operating systems function in exactly the same way, there is the potential for some users to have more difficulty in using the program. In addition, you will have to actually install the program on your own computer, which may require more time and effort than using a web-based system, since a web-based system usually requires nothing more than a web browser.

WHAT TO LOOK FOR IN AN ONLINE SYSTEM

When comparing what is available, you'll need to examine two aspects of online trading systems: the trading system itself and its features, and the type of customer service available to system users.

What the System Offers

First off, check to see whether the system in which you are most interested is a browser-based or stand-alone type. From there you can determine which is more suitable to your needs. In addition to the type of system, you should also research the ability to view depth of market information, which is considered one of *the* most important tools in an online trading system. It shows the most recent bid/ask price, the quantity of contracts, and the next bid/ask prices.

Depth of market is an important tool in deciding whether to buy, sell, or stay out of the market because it gives you the ability to see the relative strength of the buy side and the sell side. For example, let's say you know the bid and ask of a particular single stock future to be 83.00 and 83.25, respectively. But to make money in the market, you would like to know where the market is going—up or down—and where there might be support or resistance. Let's say that you now have the ability to view depth of market as shown in Table 9.1.

You can see by the depth on the asks that at 83.75 there are 155 contracts offered to sell, at 84.00 there are 231, and at 84.25 there are 285. This may indicate that there is a resistance, or strength, on the sell side, while for the bids there is some variable resistance on the buy side.

What the System Providers Offer

To ensure that you will receive the best service, you should also look into the support system that a company provides for online trading. We all know that technical problems can occur, so you should at least know that you will receive the best customer service, even when the system is not functioning properly.

First, ask if the system offers backups for a variety of key information. For example, look for email backup to receive statements or

TABLE 9-1

Bid Quantity / Bid Price	Ask Quantity / Ask Price
34 / 83.00	66 / 83.25
122 / 82.75	98 / 83.50
112 / 82.50	155 / 83.75
58 / 82.25	231 / 84.00
136 / 82.00	285 / 84.25

As displayed in this table, depth of market for futures contracts is often shown as the aggregate number of contracts at a particular price, five prices deep.

order status in case you are unable to check your account online. Also, your futures commission merchant (FCM) or broker/dealer (B/D) should provide system status on its web site and email notification of trading/exchange system status in the event that you are not able to log on to the system. This will help to clarify whether the problem is due to a malfunction of your computer or is a trading system malfunction.

Look for a trading system that offers an offsite disaster recovery program—the ability to run all of the company's essential operations from a different location. The goal is to make the recovery as seamless and transparent as possible to you, even though all of the company's operations have been moved to another physical location. As its name implies, an offsite disaster recovery program sets up fallback procedures in case of a disaster, such as a fire, loss of electricity, or, in a worst-case scenario, something similar to the events of September 11, 2001.

For example, an offsite disaster program should ensure the following:

- All current important information and data are backed up to another location at regular intervals.
- All exchanges and the FCM or B/D that are currently connected for trading through the main office are also connected at the remote location.
- All clearing operations can be run from the offsite location.
- There is enough computer equipment and appropriate data lines for Internet access and other various functions.
- All pertinent employees can do their necessary jobs.

SIMULATED TRADING

Another key element about which traders should think long and hard when choosing an online system is the opportunity to trade in a simulated environment. This can offer a number of advantages. First, you can test the system to see if it works the way it is intended to work. Why buy the actual product without knowing if it works for you? Second, the cost of education in trading can be lessened if a trader can trade a real-time account in a simulated environment. Losing a simulated $50,000 is much cheaper than losing your real, hard-earned $50,000. A simulated environment offers you an opportunity to learn many important market lessons; in fact, making mistakes in a simulated setting can possibly help you avoid them later. Finally, simulated trading offers market participants the chance to get a feel for new products, such as single stock futures or narrow-based index futures.

There are many different choices when it comes to online trading systems, and when you are shopping for something this important, it is worth taking your time and asking questions. An efficient and reliable online trading system, teamed with excellent customer service, is an important and necessary ingredient in the toolbox of any successful online trader.

10

Selecting a Broker and a Brokerage Firm

When you make the decision to trade single stock futures, you'll also need to find a broker that is equipped to offer these products to you. Because security futures products can be traded either through a futures commission merchant (FCM) on the futures side or through a broker/dealer (B/D) on the securities side, you have some options. Within those two categories, there are traditional full-service brokerage firms and a wide array of discount brokers available. If you are electronically savvy and already familiar with the markets, you may wish to look for a firm that offers computer-based order placement systems, where you can directly place your orders online. This chapter will guide you through safeguards for investors that apply to FCM and B/D accounts, offer some brief guidelines on what to look for in a broker, and highlight customer application forms and account statements. It also will touch on your FCM's or B/D's margin responsibilities and, finally, clearing—how your trades are guaranteed.

A FUTURES COMMISSION MERCHANT OR A BROKER/DEALER?

Securities futures products are unique because they are the first products created that span the futures/securities divide and, as mentioned, can be traded either through a futures commission merchant or through a broker/dealer. No matter what type of firm through which you trade, you will be protected by stringent industry standards. However, you should know that industry regulations do not insure your account against losses due to market movements. The following excerpt from *SFO* magazine will give you some insights into how account regulations *do* protect both securities and futures accounts.[1]

---

[1] From Debra Earnest, "Who Is This Broker Anyway? A Guide to Finding Your Partner in the Investing World," *SFO* magazine, August 2002.

FCMS

In the futures business, all customer funds must be segregated from the FCM's operating funds. Even though the FCM may commingle funds belonging to separate customers trading on U.S. futures exchanges, it cannot use the funds of one customer to margin transactions of any other customer. FCMs are also required to "gross up" customer funds by adding their own company funds to cover customer debits and deficits. And, the firms have the responsibility to calculate their segregation and add additional funds on a daily basis, if necessary.

This segregation requirement (in the trade, known as "seg funds" rules) was developed to meet particular needs and characteristics of the futures industry, including daily settlements, possible rapid moves in the value of open futures positions, and small insolvency losses. The gross-up and daily calculation requirements help protect customers against the possibility that trading losses incurred by one customer will draw down the funds available to another customer. It also makes up for the lack of the securities markets' SIPC-like (Securities Investor Protection Corporation) protections that would be inefficient in the futures markets; according to a National Futures Association survey from a few years back, in the futures industry, just six percent of the trading volume and three percent of the equity comes from the retail customers. Much more, obviously, comes from the institutional side of the pond.

[In the worst-case scenario, you may not be able to recover the full amount of any funds in your account if your FCM goes bankrupt and has insufficient funds to cover its obligations to all of its customers. However, customers with seg funds receive priority in bankruptcy proceedings, and there is no limit on the amount of funds that must be segregated or can be recovered by a particular customer.]

B/DS

In the securities business, there's protection too. The Securities and Exchange Commission's (SEC) reserve requirement ensures that B/Ds don't use customer funds to fund their own business and trading activities.

But, there are two significant differences between the securities' reserve requirement and the futures' segregation requirement. The first difference is the calculation itself. While the segregation calculation requires that futures firms "gross up" the funds that are segregated by and to customer debits and deficits, the reserve requirement formula nets the obligations to customers against the obligations from customers. The second difference is the frequency with which FCMs and B/Ds calculate and maintain the funds. Most securities B/Ds have a week to make calculations and adjust funds, while futures firms have a daily segregation requirement [meaning they must make calculations daily].

>*While it looks on the surface as if the reserve requirement may not provide as strong a protection as the seg requirement, when combined with the Securities Investor Protection Corporation (SIPC) coverage in the securities industry, the protections in the two industries are equivalent. SIPC is a nonprofit membership corporation that provides coverage for insolvency losses by securities customers of its members, which consist of B/Ds. If customer funds appear to be at risk, SIPC institutes a proceeding to liquidate the B/D. Secondly, SIPC provides coverage against customer insolvency losses—$500,000 per customer, except that claims for cash are covered only up to $100,000.*

Researching an FCM or B/D

Although there are safeguards in each industry, you should know the history of your FCM or B/D as thoroughly as possible. If you are interested in opening a futures account, a good place to start your research is the web site of the National Futures Association (NFA), www.nfa.futures.org. All FCMs or their introducing brokers (IBs) must be registered with the NFA, so you can obtain company information through this self-regulatory organization. At the NFA's web site you will uncover any disciplinary action taken against an FCM.

If you are interested in opening a securities account, you can research your prospective B/D through the National Association of Securities Dealers (NASD), at www.nasd.com. All companies that trade securities in the United States must be registered with the NASD. At this site, you will find information similar to the information provided by the NFA, except that it is for B/Ds.

FINDING A GOOD FIRM AND A GOOD BROKER

If you choose to trade through an online account, as discussed in Chapter 9, you will want to research the firm's electronic order entry systems. In that chapter, we detailed a variety of key items to look for in a reliable and efficient electronic trading system. If you have some experience in trading or you have your own ideas about a trading methodology, you may want to check out a discount brokerage firm that will allow you to place your orders directly, either online or through a representative on the phone, at a reduced commission rate.

If you're new to trading and are interested in opening a traditional account, in which you place your orders through a specific broker who will help guide your trading, we've outlined some key questions to ask and the qualities to look for in a broker. You need to be sure that your broker fulfills your personal financial goals and needs.

To meet those needs, you will need to communicate comfortably with this person. Remember that you will not only put money into an account, but also pay commissions on your trades, so you should be able to communicate with your broker in a way that suits you and your trading needs. To find a broker suited to your needs, research firms and brokers thoroughly. That research should include reviewing at least seven attributes of the prospective broker: experience, reliability, receptiveness, trustworthiness, trading style, discipline, and composure.

Experience

The first question that you will want to ask is, "How long have you been a broker?" You will want someone who knows the markets, and one of the ways to assess this is to ask a prospective broker how long he or she has been a broker. You'll also want to reassure yourself that your prospective broker knows more than you do. After all, the broker is there to help guide *you*, not the other way around.

In addition to getting a general feel for a broker's experience, find out some of his or her past history. You don't want a broker who has jumped from firm to firm. Again, you can learn more at the NASD and NFA web sites.

Reliability

The reliability of both your broker and your brokerage firm is essential in today's fast-paced, 24-hour markets. Reliable brokers are available to their customers whenever the customers want to place a trade or ask a question (within reason, of course). Reliable firms will employ knowledgeable associates who can place your trades and answer your questions quickly and completely if your broker is not immediately available.

Receptiveness

Your broker must be receptive to your ideas and concerns. Only then can he or she get a feel for your goals and aid you in achieving them. The broker's receptivity will also give you a good indication as to whether he or she wants you as a long-term client. You want a broker who will stick with you in the long run, not one who simply wants a way to make a quick buck.

Trading Style

Does the broker use fundamental research, technical analysis, or a combination to help analyze the markets? Does her or his style mirror your own trading style, if you have one? If you have not yet developed your own style of trading, do the broker's reasons for trading in this style seem credible and well thought out? You want to learn how well the prospective broker will present and explain an opportunity to you.

Discipline

Good brokers are very disciplined and develop trading styles through thoughtful market research and experience. How well does your broker execute his or her trading style or plan? Does he or she appear to follow the plan in a disciplined manner? Less-than-disciplined brokers' trading styles, on the other hand, may fluctuate more than market prices. These brokers will rely on emotions more than price charts when trying to sell you a trade, which, in both the short and the long run, will do you little good.

Trustworthiness

If you are going to place thousands of dollars in a broker's hands, there must be a certain level of trust. As with all trading, there are risks in futures trading, and your prospective broker should outline for you the nature of those risks. A broker should not gloss over these risks or evade a discussion about the risks of futures trading with you. If she or he does, you may want to start searching elsewhere for a broker.

Composure

With risk, of course, comes the potential for loss. You will need a broker who maintains her or his composure even after placing money on the losing side of the market. Even if money is lost, the broker's composure shouldn't be. Good brokers, like good traders, don't let losses unsettle them, because incurring losses as well as making profits is a part of trading. Good brokers will maintain contact even when your trades are losing money. When you begin searching for a broker, this attribute may be difficult to detect, so you should try to obtain references from current or former clients.

If you require little or no assistance in selecting trades, tracking them, managing money, understanding technical and fundamental analysis, placing orders, understanding exchange floor reports, and the like, you might consider using a discount brokerage firm or trading online. If you cannot do these things yourself, you will probably need a broker who can offer you more services.

UNDERSTANDING A FUTURES ACCOUNT APPLICATION FORM

Once you've found a broker with whom you think you'll be doing business, you will be sent account forms to read and complete. If you have not traded futures before, be sure to read through these documents carefully. Even if you *have* traded futures before, you should at least do a thorough scan, because some policies may differ from firm to firm.

Before you can trade single stock futures, your broker will need to obtain personal information about you. This will include your name and address, your principal occupation, your age, and your previous investment experience. It also will include, under new regulations, whether the account is for speculative or hedging purposes, your employment status, your estimated liquid net worth, your marital status, and the number of your dependents.

Once you have given your broker this information, you will need to read the two main components of a futures account application: the account agreement and the risk disclosure statement.

Account Agreements

Account agreements cover the following areas: order entry, margining, commissions and fees, commodity options, delivery and short sales, security interest, liquidation, foreign exchange rates, customer representations and warranties, market recommendations and information, communications, credit, recording, terms of the agreement, and miscellaneous provisions. All parties to the account must sign and date this document, indicating that they have read and understood it.

Risk Disclosure Statement

The risk disclosure statement, required by the CFTC, informs you of the risks of futures trading. Read this information, particularly if you are new to futures trading. If you want to protect your investments, inform yourself thoroughly. The NFA and the NASD have outlined the risks of trading security futures as follows:

- *Trading security futures contracts involves risk and may result in potentially unlimited losses that are greater than the amount you deposited with your broker.* As with any high-risk financial product, you should not risk any funds that you cannot afford to lose, such as your retirement savings, medical and other emergency funds, funds set aside for purposes such as education or home ownership, proceeds from student loans or mortgages, or funds required to meet your living expenses.

- *Be cautious of claims that you can make large profits from trading security futures contracts.* Although the high degree of leverage in security futures contracts can result in large and immediate gains, it can also result in large and immediate losses. As with any financial product, there is no such thing as a sure winner.

- *Because of the leverage involved and the nature of security futures contract transactions, you may feel the effects of your losses immediately.* Gains and losses in security futures contracts are credited or debited to your account, at a minimum, on a daily basis. If movements in the markets for security futures contracts or the underlying security decrease the value of your positions in security futures contracts, you may be required to have or make additional funds available to your carrying firm as margin. If your account is under the minimum margin requirements set by the exchange or the brokerage firm, your position may be liquidated at a loss, and you will be liable for the deficit, if any, in your account.

- *Under certain market conditions, it may be difficult or impossible to liquidate a position.* Generally, you must enter into an offsetting transaction in order to liquidate a position in a security futures contract. If you cannot liquidate your position, you may not be able to realize a gain in the value of your position or prevent losses from mounting. This inability to liquidate could occur, for example, if trading is halted as a result of unusual trading activity in either the security futures contract or the underlying security; if trading is halted as a result of recent news events involving the issuer of the underlying security; if systems failures occur on an exchange or at the firm carrying your position; or if the position is on an illiquid market. Even if you can liquidate your position, you may be forced to do so at a price that involves a large loss.

- *Under certain market conditions, it may also be difficult or impossible to manage your risk from open security futures positions by entering into an equivalent but opposite position in another contract month, on another market, or in the underlying security.* This inability to take positions to limit your risk could occur, for example, if trading is halted across markets as a result of unusual trading activity in the security futures contract or the underlying security or as a result of recent news events involving the issuer of the underlying security.

- *Under certain market conditions, the prices of security futures contracts may not maintain their customary or anticipated relationships to the prices of the underlying security or index.* These pricing disparities could occur, for example, when the market for the security futures contract is illiquid, when the primary market for the underlying security is closed, or when the reporting of transactions in the underlying security has been delayed. For index products, it could also occur when trading is delayed or halted in some or all of the securities that make up the index.

- *You may be required to settle certain security futures contracts with physical delivery of the underlying security.* If you hold your position in a physically settled security futures contract until the end of the last trading day prior to expiration, you will be obligated to make or take delivery of the underlying securities, which could involve additional costs. The actual settlement terms may vary from contract to contract and exchange to exchange. You should carefully review the settlement and delivery conditions before entering into a security futures contract.

- *You may experience losses as a result of systems failures.* As with any financial transaction, you may experience losses if your orders for security futures contracts cannot be executed normally as a result of systems failures on a regulated exchange or at the brokerage firm carrying your position. Your losses may be greater if the brokerage firm carrying your position does not have adequate backup systems or procedures.

- *All security futures contracts involve risk, and there is no trading strategy that can eliminate it.* Strategies using combinations of positions, such as spreads, may be as risky as outright long or short positions. Trading in security futures contracts requires knowledge of both the securities and the futures markets.

- *Day-trading strategies involving security futures contracts and other products pose special risks.* As with any financial product, persons who seek to purchase and sell the same security future in the course of a day to profit from intraday price movements ("day traders") face a number of special risks, including substantial commissions, exposure to leverage, and competition with professional traders. You should thoroughly understand these risks and have appropriate experience before engaging in day trading.

- *Placing contingent orders, if permitted, such as stop-loss or stop-limit orders, will not necessarily limit your losses to the intended amount.* Some regulated exchanges may permit you to enter into stop-loss or stop-limit orders for security futures contracts, which are intended to limit your exposure to losses due to market fluctuations. However, market conditions may make it impossible to execute the order or to get the stop price.

- *You should thoroughly read and understand the customer account agreement with your brokerage firm before entering into any transactions in security futures contracts.*

- *You should thoroughly understand the regulatory protections available to your funds and positions in the event of the failure of your brokerage firm.* The regulatory protections available to your funds and positions in the event of the failure of your brokerage firm may vary, depending on, among other factors, the contract you are trading and whether you are trading through a securities account or a futures account. Firms that allow customers to trade security futures in either securities accounts or futures accounts, or both, are required to disclose to customers the differences in regulatory protections between such accounts and, where appropriate, how customers may elect to trade in either type of account.

ACCOUNT STATEMENT

Unlike many of the rules regarding security futures products, which are based on securities rules, the account statement format will follow the outline and frequency of statements for traditional futures accounts. If you are unfamiliar with futures account statements, here is a summary of what you will see.

Futures account statements will have the same format and frequency that they have always had. You will receive a statement every month and every day on which you make a trade—much more frequently than for securities accounts. The statement will include all the typical information, such as date, whether you're long or short, transaction description, profit and loss, debits and credits, fees or commissions, currency code, exchange, and balance.

Your account statement will reflect gains and losses in security futures contracts at least on a daily basis. Each day's gains and losses are based on a daily settlement price distributed by a regulated security futures exchange or its clearing organization. The daily settlement process is called *marking to market*. As a result, you may be called on to settle your account daily. For example, say trader A buys a single stock futures contract at $150 today, and trader B sells the same contract. If the next day's daily settlement price is either $145 or $155, the effect would be as shown in Table 10.1.

As you can see from this example, when the daily settlement price rises, trader A gains and trader B loses. If the daily settlement price declines, trader A loses and trader B gains. Also, notice that the one-day gain or loss is determined by calculating the difference between today's settlement price and the previous day's settlement price.

Securities account statements, on the other hand, will change somewhat. If you hold single stock futures positions in a securities account, you will receive statements much more frequently than you're accustomed to when you are trading securities (unless you are a day trader). Generally, stockholders receive an account statement quarterly or whenever they have bought or sold stock. Because trading in security futures occurs on a short-term basis, you will receive an account statement every day that you trade, or, at the very least, once a month. Account statements must show the market price of a security futures contract, the mark-to-market value of the security futures position, and the nominal value [number of contracts × market price × numbers of shares per contract (probably 100)]. Statements also must show the nominal value used for computation of margin requirements. This information was not previously required for securities accounts.

YOUR FCM'S OR B/D'S MARGIN RIGHTS

When you trade single stock futures, you will have minimum margins that you must maintain. The minimum margin for single stock futures is generally 20 percent of the current market value. In addition to understanding

TABLE 10-1

Daily Settlement Value	Trader A's Account	Trader B's Account
$155	$500 gain (credit)	$500 loss (debit)
$145	$500 loss (debit)	$500 gain (credit)

One contract represents 100 shares.

your end, you should know the rights that your FCM or B/D has as the holder of these accounts. First, individual brokerage firms retain the right to set margin minimums above the exchange requirements, and therefore specific margin requirements vary from firm to firm. In addition, firms can increase "house" margin requirements at any time without notifying customers in advance, potentially leaving you with requests for additional margin, or margin calls.

So, before trading single stock futures, you should know your FCM's or B/D's policies on how and when it accepts margin deposits. Such policies can and often do vary from firm to firm, so read your customer agreement thoroughly. For example, brokerage firms may require margin calls to be met in a certain way, such as through a wire transfer from a bank or the deposit of a certified or cashier's check. In addition, some firms may require deposit on the same day that a deficiency occurs, whereas others may give you a little leeway and require a deposit on the following business day. As an extra precaution, some firms may require margin to be on deposit in the account before they will accept an order for a single stock futures contract. Should losses cause your deposited funds to fall below the maintenance margin level (or the firm's higher house requirement), your brokerage firm will require you to deposit additional funds.

If you do not deposit funds as required by the firm's policies, the firm can liquidate your security futures position or sell assets in any of your accounts at the firm to cover the lack of margin. Do not incorrectly assume that a firm cannot take action to meet a margin call unless it has contacted you first. Generally, your firm reserves the right to liquidate assets or offset positions as necessary without contacting you. Be assured, however, that most firms notify their customers of margin calls and allow some time for deposit of additional margin, although the law does not require them to do so. Even if your firm has notified you of a margin call and set a specific due date for a margin deposit, the firm can still take action, as described earlier in this paragraph, to protect its financial interests.

Unfortunately, you cannot choose which futures contracts, securities, or other assets are liquidated unless this is dictated by your customer agreement or applicable law. Furthermore, should any of your assets be liquidated or sold, you remain responsible for any deficit in the account.

CLEARING ORGANIZATIONS AND MARK-TO-MARKET REQUIREMENTS: ENSURING YOUR TRADES AND THE INTEGRITY OF THE MARKET

So, you've found a good broker, and you're successfully placing trades. How do you know that your trades will go through correctly? How can exchanges guarantee that a buyer will take delivery of a product or that a seller will make delivery as promised? Moreover, with contracts changing hands many times before delivery, how can a trader keep track of who is on the other side of the transaction?

That's where the clearinghouse comes in. Every regulated U.S. exchange that offers security futures is required to have a relationship with a clearinghouse. The purpose of the clearinghouse is to guarantee trades on each exchange. It does so by performing the following functions: matching trades, effecting settlement and payments, guaranteeing performance, and facilitating deliveries.

Clearinghouses consist of brokerage firms that are also exchange members (although not all exchange member firms are clearing members). Nonmember clearing firms must have their trades verified by a clearing member.

Clearing members submit trades to clearinghouses for matching. Trades that are *not* matched, either because of inconsistencies or because the other side of the trade is missing, must be sorted out on or before the opening of trading the next morning.

Once the necessary trade details have been confirmed, the clearinghouse assumes the legal and financial responsibilities of each customer in the transaction. Think of the clearinghouse as the "buyer to every seller and the seller to every buyer." Furthermore, because the clearinghouse acts as the counterparty to every transaction, you can liquidate a security futures position without regard to what the other party to the original security futures contract decides to do.

For example, suppose trader A sold a December Microsoft single stock futures contract to trader B. At the end of the day, the clearinghouse would stand between the two traders. Essentially, the firm that represents trader A would be short a Microsoft contract against the clearinghouse, while the firm representing trader B would be long a Microsoft contract against the clearinghouse. If trader B sold the contract to trader C, then the firm representing trader C would be long against the clearinghouse, and the firm's representation of trader B's obligation would be canceled. Meanwhile, trader A doesn't need to worry about keeping track of trader C. And trader C can sell the Microsoft contract, transferring the obligation to yet another participant, without seeking trader A's approval. Trader C can act without concern for what trader A does because the clearinghouse keeps track of all the trades.

The clearinghouse also completes the settlement of gains and losses from security futures contracts transactions between clearing members. At least once a day, the clearinghouse will pay to or collect from clearing members the change in the current price from the price earlier in the day or, for a position carried over from the previous day, the change in the current price from the previous day's settlement price. Whether a clearinghouse completes settlements daily or intraday depends on clearinghouse rules and market conditions.

Clearinghouses perform an important function, one that is critical to the marketplace. As a trader, you can have confidence that your trades will be honored and backed by your and opposing traders' clearinghouses. It is this system that allows the trading arena to run smoothly. A market won't function without integrity. Buyers and sellers will abandon or at least be unwilling to use markets where losers don't pay up and winners can't collect. Clearinghouses uphold market integrity.

This chapter has given you some background on how to go about looking for a brokerage firm and what will be required of you throughout the application process. Just as there are many different trading methodologies, there are many different brokerage firms and types of order-entry systems. It is important that you take the time to do due diligence in finding a broker, a firm, and an order-entry system that work for you.

PART 2

Before Learning from More Industry Pros about Single Stock Futures...

Are you looking for a way to hedge your 401(k) portfolio? Are you looking for a new product that you can use to speculate on the ups and downs of daily market action? Look no further. Security futures products, launched in the United States in late 2002, are gaining volume and open interest every day and offer individual investors unique opportunities for their personal risk management. Part 2 of this book includes over a dozen articles, published in *SFO* magazine, that will introduce you to some basic concepts of how to use single stock futures and other security futures products. The days of "buy and hold" may be over for now. The roaring bull market of the 1990s has faded into distant memory. Individuals now have to sit up and take a more active role in managing their personal portfolios. Single stock futures have arrived at a crucial time for the individual investor, as they offer new opportunities to profit and also a method to protect capital already achieved.

BASICS OF TRADING SECURITY FUTURES PRODUCTS: A QUICK REVIEW OF PART 1

To start trading single stock futures, you must deposit funds, usually at least 20 percent of the current market value of the contract, with your brokerage firm, in either a securities or a futures account. The amount deposited may vary depending on the exchange, the brokerage firm, and the type of trading you do. The minimum initial margin required by law is 20 percent; however, exchanges and firms may require more than the legal minimum as an extra guard against losses. For clients trading large volumes or trading with specialized strategies, exchanges may also lower the margin requirement.

The purpose of margin in futures trading is different from its purpose in stock trading. (See Table II.1 for definitions of different types of margin.) When you deposit initial margin to buy stock, you are essentially making a down payment on the stock, and your brokerage firm loans you the rest. For that loan, you also pay interest to your broker. To short a stock, you borrow stock from your broker and pay your broker the broker loan rate plus any dividends due.

In futures trading, the margin you post is considered a "good faith" deposit that assures your brokerage firm that you can meet the obligations of the contract should your position move against you. It is not a type of down payment, as it is in stock trading, so there is no loan to repay or interest charges.

TABLE II.1

Types of Margin

Margin (futures): The amount of money or collateral deposited by a futures client with a broker, or by a clearing member with the clearinghouse, as required by the exchange and/or clearinghouse for open futures positions.

Margin (securities): (1) The purchase of securities on credit extended by a broker/dealer; (2) the deposit made to a broker/dealer by a securities customer in order to sell securities short; (3) the type of securities account in which such purchases and short sales are made.

Initial margin: (1) The minimum initial payment or deposit required to buy or sell short securities; (2) customers' funds put up to guarantee contract fulfillment at the time a futures or options position is established.

Maintenance margin: The minimum amount of equity per contract that must be maintained at all times a futures or options position is open or a loan to purchase or sell short securities is outstanding.

Once you have posted margin for a security futures contract, you may settle the contract or offset it upon expiration, as noted previously. When you have an open position, either long or short, you offset it by entering an opposite position. For example, if you were long one December GM single stock futures contract, you would offset your position by selling one December GM single stock futures contract. Generally, futures contracts are closed prior to expiration, and holders are not obligated to either receive or deliver the stock. As of this writing, both NQLX and OneChicago settle their contracts through physical delivery. With physical delivery, if you are long the contract, you must pay the final settlement price set by the regulated exchange or the clearing organization and take delivery of the underlying shares. Conversely, if you are short the contract, you must deliver the underlying shares in exchange for the final settlement price.

On the other hand, non-U.S. exchanges may specify cash settlements. In this case, if you were long a security futures contract, you would pay the value of the shares. If you were short, you would receive an amount of cash determined by the exchange or clearing firm. The amount is usually based on the value of the shares at the end of trading on expiration day. Once this transaction takes place, neither party has any further obligations on the contract.

NOW ON TO THE FUN STUFF

Now that we've defined what these new products are, we can delve into their many uses and benefits. This anthology will walk you through strategies for trading single stock futures and narrow-based indexes, methods of analyzing the markets, and how to develop trading skills and styles that work for you.

11

What Do I Do with These Things? Part 1: Trading Strategies for Single Stock Futures

Security futures products began trading in late 2002 and are now gaining volume and open interest every day. So how can you get into this new market? Security futures products can be used in a variety of ways, with strategies ranging from opportunistic to risk-averse. This chapter will focus on the uses of futures contracts on individual stocks. The next chapter will focus on the uses of futures contracts on narrow-based stock indexes.

The first article by Chad Butler offers ideas on one of the most evident uses of single stock futures, hedging, as well as giving a basic definition of what hedging is: a way to protect your positions in the market by securing a desired price. You can protect either straight stock positions or positions in funds, such as a 401(k), by securing a desired price with single stock futures.

But protecting existing investments is not the only use of these instruments. David Floyd's article expands on strategies for single stock futures. In addition to hedging, traders can speculate, or anticipate price movements and profit from those movements, on single stock futures. Stock traders can watch the price movements of single stock futures as indicators of where stock prices will head, and veteran traders can capitalize on these products by spreading between the single stock futures market and the cash market.

Finally, if you have ever traded stock options, you may be asking, "Can't I already speculate and hedge with stock options?" In the final article, Chad Butler details the advantages of single stock futures over options. For example, you can exercise a single stock futures contract at any price, whereas with options, you have to wait until the underlying instrument of the option reaches the strike price. Single stock futures, then, may offer traders more flexibility.

A PRIMER TO HEDGING STOCKS USING SINGLE STOCK FUTURES (MAY 2002)

By Chad Butler

A helping hand in the initial success of single stock futures (SSFs) will be the ease of using them as a hedging tool. Previous attempts to market products geared toward the individual investor as hedging tools have been relatively unsuccessful. Why? Hedging can, at least initially, be a complex and confusing subject. In fact, entire volumes have been written on the subject. A full and complete discussion of hedging individual stocks using SSFs would be well beyond the scope of this article. I intend, rather, to give an overview specific to the individual investor, a beginner's introduction, if you will.

Hedging seems complex and esoteric to the majority of the investing public. And most people don't feel at all comfortable doing things with their money that they don't understand. Not to mention that to hedge an individual's stock portfolio with a broad-based index like the S&P 500 requires complex adjustments and mathematics. It is difficult to match a portfolio to the index.

If you add in the huge bull market of the last few years, most investors have no interest in being a short hedger. (If you don't know what a short hedger is, however, we will cover that momentarily.) With stocks coming off of a brutal bear market, the economy in recession, and the general public concerned about the safety of their retirement plans in the wake of the Enron debacle, there is a definite need for a hedging tool accessible to the individual investor. Single stock futures can fit that need. They will allow for a direct hedge against a given stock without the complexities of an indirect hedge of a stock index future.

Hedging Isn't Just for Landscaping

"But all I know about hedging is how to trim the ones in my front yard," you say? No fear, it's not that difficult to understand. And as luck would have it, the individual investor can benefit from long hedging as well as short hedging, so we will discuss both. First, though, let's review hedging in general.

Hedging is nothing more than protecting your position in the market by locking in today's prices. Let me say that again. You can protect your cash market position by locking in *today's* prices. To make this a little clearer, I like to use the grain market as an analogy.

Joe Farmer has acres of wheat growing on his farm. He feels that as of today, prices are very good for his wheat. What is his concern? Obviously, Mr. Farmer worries about prices coming down. Mr. Farmer is afraid of wheat prices dropping below what he considers to be a fair price. What can he do about that? Hedge! Mr. Farmer can sell one futures contract now for every 5000 bushels (the contract size) of wheat he has in the ground. By doing this, he has sold at today's prices a contract for future delivery of a product that he will harvest in the future.

Mr. Farmer is a short hedger. He utilizes a sell hedge to protect his long cash position. If prices stabilize and look to head higher, he can lift his hedge by buying back his futures contract and simply wait for harvest to sell his grain. But if prices drop, he can either deliver on his contract with his harvest or he can take profit in the futures and a loss on the cash crop. Either way, he locked in the price when he placed the hedge and any money he loses on one side of the hedge will be offset by a gain on the other side.

So what is a long hedger? A commercial interest, such as General Mills, is concerned about prices of wheat going up. They know how much they can sell a box of Shredded Wheat for, and they are concerned about profit margins getting squeezed by rising costs of grain. They would place a long hedge by buying a futures contract against their future need for wheat. This is exactly the opposite of Mr. Farmer's hedge. But like the short hedger, they are protected against losses on one side of the hedge by gains on the opposite side. They have locked in today's prices.

But What Does That Have to Do with Stocks?

Commercial entities have had the ability to transfer their risk to the speculator for years. With the advent of SSFs, there will now be a tool for hedging individual stocks within reach of the individual investor. You will have the same opportunity to hedge your portfolio as commercial players.

As I mentioned in the beginning of this article, broad-based index futures have been around for quite some time, giving commercial institutions the opportunity to hedge their large stock positions by transferring their risk to the speculators in the futures market. The problem for the individual was that the contract was too broad and too large to hedge an individual portfolio. The individual was confined to hedging with options, which are not the ideal hedging vehicle due to the huge time premium typically factored into an "at-the-money" option and the subsequent decay of that premium over time. Don't get me wrong; there is a time and place to use options, but now with futures available on individual stocks, options will not be the best, or the only, hedging tool available.

Fear and the Retiree

In the wake of accounting scandals and bankruptcies such as Enron and Global Crossing, a great many of you are concerned about the safety of your retirement funds, so I can think of no better example to use for a short hedge than a 401(k).

Think of your 401(k) just like Joe Farmer thought of his wheat in my analogy. You have a crop of stock in the ground that you will not harvest for quite some time. But you believe the market is shaky and are concerned about prices going forward a year or two. Or, maybe you are being notified that your 401(k) plan is changing administrators and you will be locked out for 2 weeks.

Let's say you have 1000 shares of AT&T in your 401(k). Because your plan is changing administrators, you can neither buy nor sell any positions in your portfolio during the lockout. During this time, the price of AT&T starts to drop. You wish you could sell, but you can't. Enter the single stock futures contract. You can hedge your position by selling 10 contracts of AT&T futures. You have now sold at today's price. In this case, you will need to lift the hedge by buying back your short position, as you won't be able to deliver the physical shares from your 401(k), but the net result is the same. Whether you make money or lose money on your stocks, the opposite will be true with your hedge. One will offset the other. You locked in the price when you placed the hedge.

What if, on the other hand, the price looked as though it would break out during your lockout? You wish you could participate in the rally, but you can't buy or sell any stock in your plan. You'd like to buy 1000 shares, but the cash is tied up in your 401(k) as well. You only have enough to buy about 250 shares. In this case, you would be a long hedger. Since the anticipated margin on SSFs could be 25 percent of the contract value, the margin for 10 contracts of 100 shares will be roughly the same cost as buying 250 shares of stock.

In this hedge, you buy 10 contracts with your available cash and participate in any rally as though you had bought 1000 shares. You can lift the hedge prior to expiration and buy the stock in your 401(k). Any part of the rally you missed out on will be offset by the profit in the futures contracts. Alternatively, you can take delivery of the shares at expiration, knowing you have purchased them at a cheaper price.

Getting Down to Fundamentals

By now, you should have a basic understanding of the mechanics of both long and short hedging. Let me give you a couple of working examples of each type of hedge. To keep the concepts simple, I'm going to leave out some of the complicating factors such as tax implications, dividends, and interest-rate computations. Remember, this article is meant to be a beginner's guide to concepts, not an advanced course on hedging. Be aware, however, that these factors do exist and must be calculated into any real-time hedge plan. It will be up to you, once you understand the basics, to learn how to fine-tune your hedging strategy.

First, let's further examine the short hedge with a real-world example (note: the futures contract in the example is purely hypothetical, as there is no contract available at press time). You own a 1000-share position in GE in a taxable account purchased in 1997 for an average price $20 per share. It is now late December 2000 and, after trading to a high around $55, the stock looks as though it will break its trend line to the downside and is trading at about $50. There would be a substantial long-term capital gains implication on a sale of stock, so you choose to protect the profit you have with a direct hedge using GE stock futures.

You sell 10 contracts of GE futures at $50. Your required margin for the trade is roughly $12,500. The stock trades down to about $40 in February 2001, where you choose to cover your hedge. You cover your short position by purchasing 10 contracts of GE futures at $40 and also, at the same time, sell your cash position in the stock. The profit on the hedge is $10 per share × 100 shares per contract × 10 contracts for a total of $10,000. This will offset what you gave back on the stock during this time. You had considered selling your stock at $50 but weren't sure, so instead you hedged and were correct about the market direction giving back $10 per share of profit, or a total of $10,000 in the stock. This $10 was recouped on your short hedge in the futures.

When you placed the hedge, you locked in the price of $50 per share. If you were wrong about market direction and the stock had actually gone up $10 instead, you would have gained $10 per share on your stock position while losing $10 in the futures. The net result is the same—your resulting total profit in the stock is the same—$30 per share.

Now let's look at the long hedge. After September 11, 2001, Michael Dell announced that he was going to buy a large block of his own stock, DELL, at an average price of $18. You consider purchasing the stock for your own account. The problem is, you do not expect an influx of trading capital until January. You hedge with a buy of the futures at $18, intending to either cover your hedge when you buy the stock or take delivery of the shares.

January comes around, your capital comes in, and you purchase DELL at an average price of $28. At the same time, you lift your hedge in the futures at $28. Do you own the stock at $28? Well, technically, yes. You purchased the stock at $28 and missed a $10 move in the stock. Or did you? Your hedge in the futures gained $10 (bought at $18, offset at $28), gaining the full amount of the rally you missed in the stock.

Hedging a Short Position

You can also use the long hedge if you are shorting the stock. Using DELL from the previous example, you are actually short the stock from $26 in August 2001. After September 11, 2001, you feel the market will continue to trade lower. Michael Dell makes his announcement, but you consider he may be wrong. The stock has bounced a little from a low of about $17, and you would like to see if the downtrend continues. Just in case, you buy DELL futures at $18 against your short position in the stock.

As we know from the previous DELL example, in January, DELL was trading at $28. Your short position is taking a beating by giving back $8 of profit and tacking on a loss of $2 per share! However, even though you were wrong about the continued downtrend in the market, you can still sleep well at night knowing that your hedge covers your position all the way from $18! Not only does your hedge cover your loss of $2, it is also protecting $8 of profit that you had when you placed the hedge. Furthermore, because futures are marked to market daily, there is available cash in the account to cover margin calls that may be received from your short stock position.

Hedging Equity Options Positions

SSFs will also provide an easy and cost-effective method of hedging for option traders utilizing short options techniques. While this would actually be a subject for an entire book geared toward the advanced options trader, I feel it is worth mentioning. If you are familiar with short option positions and spreads, you should be able to see the fact that utilizing a futures contract that provides physical delivery of the underlying instrument (in this case, the stock) would provide you with a method of hedging your position less capital-intensive than buying or selling a block of shares.

A Word of Caution

With the ability to enter and exit a direct hedge with ease as well as the ability to take or make delivery on a contract, SSFs offer a wealth of possibilities to the individual investor well beyond mere market speculation. While this article is by no means the be-all and end-all of hedging, I hope that maybe the road is a little more clear, and perhaps you have gained some insight into a subject that can, at first, be a little confusing. Or, maybe you have gotten some other good ideas on how you may better utilize the derivatives that are available to you as an investor and trader. In either case, should you decide that hedging may be suitable for your situation, I would highly recommend that you get your hands dirty doing your due diligence.

Do your homework! Get books and brochures on hedging. While not all of the mechanics of all types of hedging are the same, you will find the concepts to be similar. The exchanges currently offer some good brochures on hedging with their existing products and most certainly will offer similar material on single stock futures. Check these out, as well. Last, but certainly not least, if you intend to hedge, please, consult a professional! All too many investors fancy themselves savvy enough to go it alone. Don't increase your risk by jumping headlong into something you may not totally understand. Good luck and good trading!

SINGLE STOCK FUTURES: TRADING STRATEGIES TO GET YOU AHEAD OF THE GAME (JULY 2002)

BY DAVID FLOYD

Given that my background since 1994 has been trading stocks professionally, many of you may ask, "Why the switch to futures?" First off, I am not abandoning stocks. Single stock futures (SSFs) will merely complement my existing approach to trading. My style would be described by some as incredibly intense and perhaps just a bit too short-term in nature. However, I firmly believe that the short duration of my average trade (less than 5 minutes) offers me the best possible risk/reward relationship. SSFs will be one additional tool that will not only offer more trading strategies, but more importantly, be yet another indicator for the underlying stocks that I already trade.

For those of you who are not familiar with my trading style as it relates to individual stocks, I am a listed stock trader who makes several, sometimes upwards of 100, trades per day. Some would call this style "scalping." While that is a bit of a misnomer given the classic definition of a scalper, it will suffice for illustrative purposes.

Now let's back up for just a moment. The whole idea behind scalping is to make as many high-probability trades during trading hours as possible, making a few cents on each trade, but trading a relatively large size (1000 to 5000 shares per trade). Based on just that, you have to have a very high win/loss ratio in order to overcome commissions and losing trades. My rule of thumb is that if your commissions are more than one-third of your gross profit on a given day, chances are you took some trades that were marginal, and simply were not worth the effort.

How do I identify setups that offer the best risk/reward ratio? Simple, trade with the trend. That being said, let's define what I mean by the "trend." The moving average on the 1-minute chart is how I define the trend. Is the moving average sloping up or down?

As Figures 11.1 and 11.2 clearly show, trying to short tops in uptrends offers far less reward than does waiting patiently and buying the pullback. The same can be seen on the downtrending chart, trying to pick bottoms is more trouble than it is worth.

A scalper's world lies in seconds and minutes. As a result, I feel the 1-minute chart offers the best time frame to identify entry points.

My approach, while simple in theory, is a bit more difficult in practice. I initiate my entry and exit points based on the S&P and NASDAQ futures. I also use technical setups on 1-minute charts, in both the stock I am trading as well as the futures.

My lead indicator is the futures. Without the futures, I can't possibly expect the stocks that I trade to move. As a result, if the futures do not generate the signal, I do not trade.

With the introduction of SSFs, I will have one additional tool at my disposal to determine my entry and exit points. Before I discuss some other benefits of SSFs and possible strategies that I may employ, I want to put into context where the markets currently stand to illustrate the potential SSFs have to introduce some much-needed intraday volatility back into the market.

FIGURE 11.1

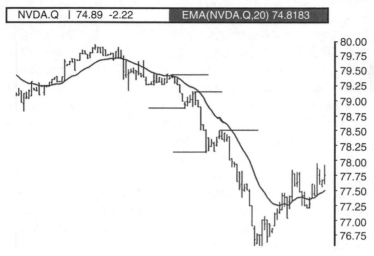

Chart created with AT Financial.

FIGURE 11.2

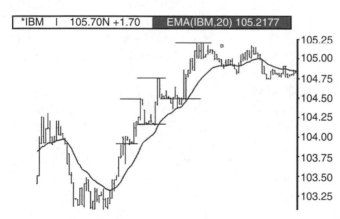

Chart created with AT Financial.

The game has changed. While this is no surprise to anyone who has been actively involved in the markets over the last 18 months, it does warrant a discussion as it relates to intraday trading. Traders now find themselves in the position of adjusting to the dynamics affecting the market currently, most notably, the erosion of stock prices. However, other factors are at work that make trading challenging, and at times quite baffling. This lesson, however, needs to be prefaced with an ample dose of recent history.

When I first got involved with day trading back in 1994, the markets were in the midst of embarking on yet another leg of the bull market. (The economy was coming out of the recession from the early '90s.) At the time, mutual funds were the rage and the latest en vogue financial product, as espoused to us by every financial journalist and marketing guru within the industry. "Save for retirement" was the mantra, and Americans dutifully drained their once beloved FDIC bank accounts to latch on to the 10 percent Total Return Train. This reallocation of capital from savings accounts to portfolio managers only further strengthened the bull market with massive infusions of capital. Add to this all the 401(k) money, and in retrospect, you have a bull market driven more by fear of being the unfortunate portfolio manager left behind by your fellow peers, as opposed to one driven by fundamentals.

Fast-forward a few years. Suddenly, online direct-access trading was appearing on the horizon. This not only occurred at a time when technological advances made it possible to offer this to retail customers, but it also occurred when many portfolio managers were having a difficult time beating the S&P 500 on an annual basis (not an easy task when you need to deploy large amounts of capital). Combine this with the early stages of Internet mania, and it was an easy decision for individuals who wanted to get in on the action via discount brokerage accounts versus the now disdained common stock fund. Publications and financial news channels only added to the desire for individuals to get involved.

While the concept of individuals changing their savings and investing habits due to demographic changes is admirable and well intentioned, it set many up for a rude awakening when reality set back in, or, as many call it, the reversion to the mean. Things in life go on for only so long before unforeseen events, or the "randomness" of the market catches everyone off guard. Suddenly, the song is over and there are no chairs.

With all the money that was being thrown at stocks during this time, it made the whole notion of intraday trading a whole lot easier.

First off, you had massive share purchases and sales by large institutions, which not only provided large intraday price swings, but also the volume to navigate in and out with ease. In fact, many trades during this time were "shoot from the hip" trades, as opposed to trades that are stalked and executed with absolute precision, which is the way the game is again being played.

Second, you had rampant speculation in tech stocks, further adding to the market being awash in liquidity.

The point is that everyone in the world was trading stocks. Everyone was an expert. And by the returns some people put up, it was hard to say otherwise. However, the market has a nasty habit of testing one's resolve. The current period is one such time. Gone are the times of picking up half and whole points with a couple of mouse clicks, at least for now. Sure those trades still exist intraday, but they seem a bit more elusive then they were, say, just 6 months ago. Today, as day traders, we are forced to dance in and out of the market, picking up small amounts each time.

I hear a few rumblings in my office about the futility of trading for 5 and 15 cents per trade. This is a sure sign of one's unwillingness to adapt. It also indicates that perhaps the trader's intention for trading is for entertainment, rather than for income stream. I will trade for 5 and 15 cents all day, provided the setups are there. This approach will get me through the lean times and allow me to further refine my skills. Sure, I'll admit this is not the most exciting approach, but I am still here after many have either been wiped out or simply gave in when it came to down to brass tacks.

Add to the mix the introduction of decimalization, the seemingly overnight disappearance of billions of stock market capitalization, and, unfortunately, an economy heading into, or already in, recession combined with a looming Middle East crisis. The result is truly epic. Those who adapt will surely survive; those who continue along without making some adjustments will surely be tested and may not survive.

This is where I see SSFs playing a pivotal role in shaking up the landscape. Whenever there is an introduction of a new product, you can be reasonably assured that there will be some inefficiencies as well as extreme volatility in the early going as the new players adapt to new and somewhat unfamiliar surroundings. These are certainly not characteristics that describe the current marketplace for individual equities.

What Are SSFs and What Are the Benefits?

A SSFs contract is simply a standardized agreement between two parties to buy or sell 100 shares of a particular stock in the future at a price determined today. Futures contracts are bought and sold on federally regulated exchanges, and for SSFs, regulation is by both the Securities and Exchange Commission (SEC) and the Commodity Futures Trading Commission (CFTC).

The advent of SSFs has the potential to reintroduce some of that sorely needed volatility. First and foremost, it will introduce a completely new trading arena. That alone will create substantial opportunities and volatility. Secondly, the increased leverage afforded by SSFs will offer a nimble and proficient trader excellent potential, while tying up less capital intraday.

Not since the introduction of the QQQs has there been so much buzz surrounding the launch of a new trading product. The SSFs are sure to change the trading landscape forever. They will not only be a product that can be traded exclusively, but they will be a wonderful complement to what I already do as an intraday stock trader. This second aspect is what I find most intriguing.

The fact that you will able to sell short without an uptick is a major plus. For those of you who have had the good fortune of using married puts (bullets) and conversions as a way to circumvent the uptick rule, SSFs will offer the potential to further reduce your cost of doing business. For those of you who have been establishing shorts by waiting for the uptick, your world is about to be turned upside down. Let's take a look at the potential savings, using my trading activity as a guideline.

I typically trade in 2000- and 4000-share lots, and on some days may trade two to three different stocks. Given that I will go short just as easily as going long, I need to have a bullet or conversion on in order for me to sell short effectively. I am able to get bullets and conversions electronically and will usually put them on when I am seeing a trade develop shortly after the opening. At 3 cents per share, it is quite easy for me to run up a daily total of between $60 and $120 or more, just for bullets. Given that a bullet expires at the end of each trading day, you always need to reestablish them each day.

$$2000 \text{ bullets in IBM: } 0.03 \times 2000 = \$60$$
$$4000 \text{ bullets in IBM: } 0.03 \times 4000 = \$120$$

On a monthly basis, it adds up to anywhere from $1000 to $2000. SSFs give the potential to remove this expense.

A conversion can make more sense simply because it does not expire until the next options expiration (third Saturday of each month). The drawbacks of a conversion are:

- Pay margin interest on outstanding balance.
- It is not cost-effective to remove the conversion if you do not end up trading the stock again.

If you trade the same stock every day, and know you will continue to do so, a conversion is far more cost-effective.

At the time of this writing, it appears as though the margin requirement for SSFs will be 20 percent. Whatever the initial margin level is at any given time, remember that margin can be your best friend or your worst enemy. For the sake of example, let's assume an initial margin level of 20 percent in our examples of (1) going long a single stock futures contract on ABC Company at a $50 trade price and closing your long position at $55, or (2) going short a single stock futures contract on ABC Company at a $48 trade price and closing your short position at $57. The margin level represents 20 percent of the value of the contracts traded for calculating the return on initial margin in these two trades.

Example of going long and closing the position at $55:

Initial margin at $50: (20% $\times$ $50) $\times$ 100 shares $\times$ 5 contracts = $5000

Gain on position if closed at $55: $2500

Return on margin: $2500/$5000 = 50%

Example of going short at $48 and closing the position at $57:

Initial margin at $48: (20% $\times$ $48) $\times$ 100 shares $\times$ 5 contracts = $4800

Loss on position if closed at $57: $4500

Return on margin: $4500/$4800 = 93.75%

The importance of this illustration cannot be emphasized enough: In futures trading, you can lose more than your initial margin deposit. Never base the number of contracts you trade on the level of the initial margin. If you have not traded futures before, consult your broker or financial adviser about the risks involved.

The one aspect that still remains unanswered, although history is an excellent guide, will be the inefficiencies in the way they are traded. More than likely the following traits will be evident:

1.   Large spreads
2.   Futures trading far above or below fair value, offering arbitrage opportunities
3.   Exaggerated moves relative to underlying market movement

I recall fondly back during the time after the QQQs were launched that the intraday moves were just wild. While there was a higher degree of risk associated with trading them at the time versus another stock, the rewards more than compensated for it. Will the SSFs follow a similar pattern? I am betting on it. The bottom line is that nobody knows for sure how it will all play out, but opportunities will exist for those who quickly adapt to this new marketplace.

Strategies

Initially, the most appealing aspect of SSFs will be the potential inefficiencies that will exist. They won't be there for long, so nimble traders will be able to capitalize. From a longer-term standpoint, there will be a few strategies that will fit in quite nicely with the SSF environment.

SSFs have been described as the ultimate financial derivative: an instrument which can hedge just one of the thousands of equity securities that are traded in world markets. How much more refined can you get?

Not much. But this single attribute is what has made SSFs so controversial. SSFs were illegal in the United States until 2001 because regulators worried that they may be used to manipulate stock prices. This is all changing currently. Are SSFs set to join interest-rate, currency, and equity index derivatives as the financial world's biggest hedging and speculative instrument?

A study done in Hong Kong, where SSFs have been trading since March 1995, showed that 70 percent of all trades were for speculative purposes, and 30 percent for hedging. If, as I suspect, this is how SSFs play out here in the United States, the game will be pretty straightforward, and liquidity will also be pretty good. However, given the fragmented nature of SSFs, liquidity is not a slam-dunk. Theoretically, an SSF is as liquid as the underlying stock, but in practice, this is not the case because of various considerations such as hedging and position funding costs. As a result, spreads between the bid and offer on SSFs can be wider than on the underlying stock.

This can be illustrated by looking at current quotes in London, on the LIFFE, where SSFs currently trade. The spread on Vodafone universal stock future (USF), for example, is about 1.5p versus a fraction of 1p in the cash market, though this is somewhat offset by cost savings, i.e., there is no stamp duty on USFs.

Another aspect which may enhance liquidity is the much simpler structure of SSFs. Currently, if an investor wants to hedge a position, they normally turn to the options market. However, unlike SSFs, options as a hedge force one to determine which particular option offers the best alternative. Do I go with the May 55s or the May 50s? What is my time decay?

And so on. For most traders/investors who have little options experience, SSFs may become the clear alternative. However, SSFs only provide market exposure, not insurance, and for some investors/traders, that may not be suitable. SSFs have the potential to be used for a number of purposes:

- As a straight substitute for the cash market when investing or speculating
- As a leveraging instrument for hedging or speculative purposes
- Dampening of volatility in a portfolio ahead of earnings or disruptive geopolitical events
- Arbitrage

Speaking for myself, I plan to embrace pure speculation as my approach to SSFs. For me, it is a fairly seamless way to transition over to these new products with a minimal learning curve. I anticipate not only using SSFs as a leading indicator, but also as a way to take advantage of price discrepancies. I envision instances where the SSFs will be mispriced relative not only to the underlying stock, but also to their corresponding index. These will be the trades which will be around for a relatively short period of time, as speculators and arbitrageurs will quickly sort out any inefficiencies.

The other approach is simply to trade them the way I trade stocks currently. In this case, I may use the corresponding futures index as my leading indicator to establish a position in the underlying SSF. The edge in this scenario will be to know in advance key technical levels for the SSF. As regular readers of my TradingMarkets.com column know, each day I calculate technical levels that I feel will offer possible support and resistance areas for the S&P and NASDAQ futures. I would say overall that they have been a great addition to my "toolbox," and given the response from readers of my column, it appears I am not the only one who benefits.

Naturally, the obvious question when SSFs were introduced was: "Will those same calculations be relevant on SSFs?" In order to make an assessment before the fact, I simply started doing test runs on the underlying stocks. Let's just say that the results have been very encouraging, and I have actually implemented key technical numbers (KTNs) for individual stocks into my daily trading. Figures 11.3 and 11.4 clearly illustrate the advantage that KTNs for stocks and SSFs offer.

It should be noted however, that the number (KTN) by itself might not prove to be meaningful. I typically find these numbers to be helpful when I have already identified an area that looks as though I should be getting long or short. The fact that these levels appear in addition simply gives me further confirmation on the trade, and will sometimes indicate that I should trade more assertively on this trade.

Managing earnings/news volatility: This concept applies more to the investor and portfolio manager. Nonetheless, it illustrates the simplicity of dampening volatility versus establishing an options position.

Let's assume you have a portfolio of oil stocks, like ExxonMobil (XOM), ChevronTexaco (CVX), and Anadarko Petroleum (APC). XOM is due out with earnings after close. Rather than exposing yourself to a bombshell, you could simply sell the equivalent number of shares in XOM SSFs to eliminate a downdraft.

- Sell XOM futures to hedge potential stock price decline caused by earnings announcement.
- Close out hedge position after earnings news has been reflected in stock price.
- Temporary earnings volatility is hedged.
- Equity portfolio kept intact.
- Low transaction costs.

Arbitrage

I can already see some other trading strategies that will evolve due to the introduction of SSFs. The most obvious one being arbitrage. While it is true that this edge will be taken out of the market not too long after their introduction simply due to the level of sophistication of traders and arbitrageurs, the very fact that these are new products and will likely trade haphazardly for some time will allow for arbitrage.

DISCOVER ANOTHER ASSET FOR YOUR TRADING TOOLBOX (AUGUST 2002)

By Chad Butler

In 1973, standardized exchange-listed options began trading at the Chicago Board Options Exchange and revolutionized the trading arena. Soon single stock futures trading will begin in the United States and will have the potential to be equally as groundbreaking. While the full impact of single stock futures (SSFs) may not be known for a number of years, there are some elements of SSF contracts that may make them more

FIGURE 11.3

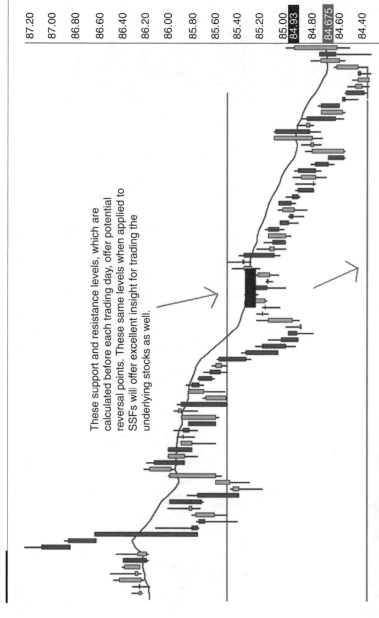

These support and resistance levels, which are calculated before each trading day, offer potential reversal points. These same levels when applied to SSFs will offer excellent insight for trading the underlying stocks as well.

Chart created with QCharts.

FIGURE 11.4

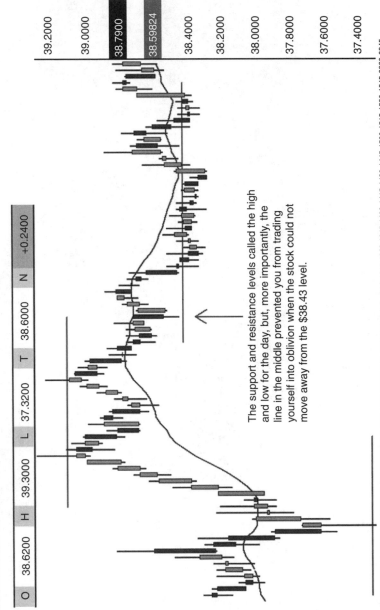

The support and resistance levels called the high and low for the day, but, more importantly, the line in the middle prevented you from trading yourself into oblivion when the stock could not move away from the $38.43 level.

Chart created with QCharts.

appealing than options for market speculation.

Options are very popular with market speculators because there are hundreds of ways to capitalize on market movement, combined with the tremendous leverage of capital. Unfortunately, due to the complexity of option pricing, they can be difficult to trade successfully, even for the seasoned professional. Factors such as days until expiration, market volatility, and hedge ratio (or delta), all affect the price of an option. In short, a trader can be on target on market direction and still lose money on the options.

On the other hand, single stock futures, once they actually appear on market screens, will be more simply priced and will offer advantages of leverage without the disadvantage of complex pricing models that could adversely affect profitability. The equity options trader who employs single stock futures in his trading arsenal will have some substantial advantages over other traders.

While buying an option gives traders a limited-risk position, they lose a number of other advantages. As a result, those traders who buy (or "go long") put and call options to speculate in a particular stock using a large degree of leverage may wish to explore the possibility of using single stock futures instead.

When a trader purchases an out-of-the-money option, or an option that has a strike price away from the current market price, the only value of the option is time premium, or extrinsic value. There is no intrinsic value. The closer an option gets to expiration, the less this time premium is worth. This is the effect of time decay, or theta, on the price of the option.

Because a single stock futures contract is bought or sold at a value representing the price of the stock plus the cost of carry, there is no adverse effect of time decay (cost of carry consists of the value of current interest rates less any dividends paid).

For example, a trader wishes to speculate on Johnson & Johnson (JNJ). His analysis says that JNJ, currently trading at 55, "should" be trading at 65 by the end of 2002. He would like to gain as much leverage as possible, so he will consider using either the January 60 calls or the December 2002 JNJ SSFs.

Calculating the cost of the option is not difficult. Options trade in contracts of 100 shares, so if the options are trading at $2.00, the cost per option would be $200. We know this is all time premium because the stock is trading below the price of the call option.

The basis, or fair value, of the December SSFs 6 months prior to expiration would be expected to reflect the current share price plus interest, less any dividends. In this example, we will use the current price of JNJ at $55 per share, a short-term interest rate of 1.75 percent, and the JNJ dividend yield of 1.49 percent. We would expect then that the futures should be trading at around $55.0715 ($55 plus 6 months short-term interest of 0.875 percent less dividends of 0.75 percent). Full contract value would be $55.0715 × 100 shares, or $5507.15. SSF margins will be about 20 percent of the full contract value, so the margin to hold this contract would be about $1100.

While this calculation may seem a little complex and may be somewhat confusing, it merely gives some background on the fair value of single stock futures. Since hedge funds and large institutions will most likely be taking advantage of price discrepancies between the actual stock and the SSFs through arbitrage, the SSFs will most often trade at or around fair value. It is more important that traders be aware of fair value, not necessarily how to calculate it. [It is likely that the concepts of fair value in SSFs will be similar to those of stock index futures. For an in-depth look at fair value as it relates to stock index futures and concepts of arbitrage, see *Exchange Traded Funds and E-mini Stock Index Futures* by David Lerman.]

The advantage of trading the option in this example is that the total risk on the trade is limited to $200. This is the better trade for those who may be averse to greater risk, but the benefits of trading SSFs outweigh this advantage. First, the only value of the option is time value, so if the market does not move ahead quickly, the value of the option will decrease as time goes on. Time decay will accelerate as expiration approaches. In fact, the profit target needs to be very precise.

In order for the option trade to be profitable at expiration, the stock must be trading higher than $62. How can that be? If the option strike price was 60, wouldn't the option be profitable above $60 per share? Not exactly. The original outlay to purchase the option was $200. To turn a profit, the option has to be more than $200 in the money at expiration. So at $62, we get the initial investment back, but anything less yields a loss. Only above $62 per share will the option turn a profit.

The SSFs, on the other hand, yield a profit if they are trading at a price higher than they were originally purchased. If they were purchased for $55.07, as in this example, any price above that yields a profit. It is that simple. If the stock is at $60 at expiration, where the option would have expired worthless, the SSFs show a profit of $4.93 per share, or $493 for each 100-share contract (the standard contract unit).

Granted, a trader needs to accept more risk in order to gain this advantage. However, in the case of buying the SSFs, the risk is not unlimited. The risk is limited to the stock going to zero. Of course, while recent market events have shown that this can be a real possibility, it is not the "textbook" unlimited risk of loss.

Another advantage to using SSFs is contract expiration. In the case of the option, if the market has not moved into profitable territory, the option merely expires worthless. The trader holding a single stock futures contract at expiration, however, can take delivery of the physical stock and, thus, hold onto the position for an indefinite period of time.

In the case of put options, the reasons to consider using single stock futures become even clearer. Put options are frequently used by the speculator to take a bearish position in the market. Additionally, puts are often used to hedge an existing stock position. Single stock futures may be a better alternative vehicle in both scenarios.

In the case of taking a bearish position in the market, the put option has been popular mainly because it is an easier position to enter than shorting the stock. In order to short stock, a number of events must all come into alignment. First, the brokerage firm must have the stock to loan the trader. Once the stock can be obtained, it can only be sold short when the last trade in the market is an uptick. Margin must be posted and interest is charged on the margin. If any dividends are to be paid, the trader is responsible for those costs as well. By purchasing a put option, the trader is able to speculate on the stock going down without these hindrances.

The same disadvantages arise for the put option trader as were apparent in the call option example. The time decay is working against the position, and the trader must be fairly precise in both market direction and time in order to make a profit. An additional disadvantage in options trading that we can explore in this example is an overpricing of the option due to an increase in volatility.

If the market is moving down already, the price of the put option is going to reflect that market sentiment in the volatility. The actual calculation of these numbers involves complex mathematics. Suffice to say that the option premium is going to be high in this trade due to an increase in volatility. [For more information on this and other factors of option pricing, see *Option Volatility & Pricing* by Sheldon Natenberg.] In higher volatile markets, the opportunity for profit decreases because the cost of the option becomes too high relative to the potential gain.

Using single stock futures will provide the trader with an easier and more efficient way to capitalize on downward price movement in stocks. As we examined in the call option example, the price of the futures is not affected by the various factors that affect the premium cost of the options. Furthermore, there is no restriction on selling the futures short. The required margin is the same and there is no borrowing cost associated with the posted margin. Because the dividends already are calculated into the cost basis of the futures, the trader does not need to worry about paying dividends either.

Continuing on with the JNJ example, we will assume that a trader has decided that JNJ will be trading lower in 6 months. With the stock at $55 per share, the trader considers the put option versus the single stock futures. He considers the January 2003 50 put, which is trading at $3. The risk on trading the put is then $300, so the stock must be trading lower than $47 for the trader to be profitable at expiration.

Using the single stock futures, however, the trader will be profitable if the SSFs are trading at a price lower than what they were sold. The ease with which a trader can speculate on bearish stock price movement using single stock futures makes this product a powerful tool for the speculator.

Another popular use of the put option is not necessarily to speculate on bearish market moves, but rather to protect a current position by hedging. Single stock futures will definitely be the better product to use in contrast to put options. A hedge is used to protect and lock in profits for a future transaction at today's prices.

If the trader owns JNJ at $55 and is concerned about price declines in the future, he could hedge either by buying a put or selling the JNJ SSFs. Using the put option does not provide a perfect hedge for the trader. For example, let's say the trader purchases the January 2003 50 put for a total of $300 per contract. The position is only profitable at expiration if the stock is lower than $47 due to the $3 per share option premium that was paid.

Let us assume that at expiration, JNJ stock is trading at $50 per share. Using the put option did not protect the trader. The stock is sold for a $5 per share loss, and the $3 per share that was paid for his hedge is sold, resulting in a total loss of $8 per share. The trader hedged his position in the stock to protect from losses, yet he managed to lose $800 for every 100 shares.

Compare that with the use of single stock futures for this hedge. Using the estimated fair value as previously discussed, the trader is able to sell the December 2002 SSFs for $55.0715 per share. As time continues to expiration, the cost of carry in the fair value decreases until, at expiration, the cash price and the futures price converge. At expiration, if the stock is trading at $50 per share, the $5 loss has been fully covered by the hedge. The stock lost $5 per share while the hedge gained slightly more than $5. This makes single stock futures a clear winner in terms of choosing an effective hedging tool.

With any trading plan, the risk versus reward needs to be fully evaluated. Due to certain limited risk features, purchasing options may be a better choice for the risk-averse trader. However, for the trader willing to take on a greater degree of risk, the potential for profit with SSFs can be greater. The trader himself is the only one who can determine exactly how much risk he is willing to take. Risk management and money management are important keys to any successful trading program. Do not leave them out of yours.

As with any new investment product, there are nuances and issues that will need to be discovered, studied, and tested over time before a clear trading plan can be developed. By initial investigation, however, it appears that there will be clear advantages in the single stock futures camp.

Since SSFs have yet to commence trading in U.S. markets, there is a great deal of speculation on the possible success of this new product. As is often the case with a new product, there are a number of vocal rivals that are actually calling for the demise of single stock futures. While the use of options trading should not be disregarded for the market speculator seeking to leverage a position, single stock futures may, in some cases, be a better alternative to trading options.

What Do I Do with These Things? Part 2: Strategies for Trading Narrow-Based Indexes

There may be instances where you want to hedge with more exposure than a single stock future could offer. Or, sometimes you may prefer to trade an instrument that has tempered volatility. In those situations, futures on narrow-based indexes (NBIs) could fit the bill. Futures on narrow-based indexes are the second part of the security futures products category. They are groups of nine or fewer stocks in an industry, and they can be used for basically the same purposes as single stock futures, except that they provide greater exposure and more diversification.

Christopher Krohn outlines the construction of indexes and their many uses. Like any futures contracts, futures on narrow-based indexes will be a cost-effective tool for risk management. For example, trading one narrow-based index is more cost-effective than trading several stocks and trying to keep track of multiple trades. Like single stock futures, futures on narrow-based indexes can also be used for hedging, for example, to over- or underweight a sector in a portfolio.

Not only do futures on narrow-based indexes allow you to bet on the direction of a sector or protect current investments, but they are, as previously mentioned, cost-effective. For example, a OneChicago narrow-based index will generally include more than 1000 shares of stock, yet its trading price will usually be under $100, because OneChicago uses a divisor of

1/500 of the contract's value to calculate the price at which the contract is likely to trade.

If Krohn's extensive article doesn't convince you of the advantages of trading futures on narrow-based indexes, read on. Kira McCaffrey Brecht highlights more advantages of trading these futures. For example, indexes, because they represent the price movement of several stocks, tend to reflect the trend of an overall sector more accurately than a single stock or single future. That being the case, you can use them as price signals for stock trading or index trading or use them to make sector bets. Also, you may be able to hold the indexes longer than individual stocks or stock futures because they take longer to move in one direction or the other. Futures on narrow-based indexes only increase the opportunities that security futures products offer the individual trader.

DOLLAR-WEIGHTED NARROW-BASED INDEXES: TRADING THE ECONOMIC SECTORS (NOVEMBER 2002)*

BY CHRISTOPHER KROHN

Over the past few years, many investors have become terribly accustomed to electronic trading of futures on broad-based stock indexes, such as the popular "e-mini" contracts based on the Standard & Poor's 500 index, the NASDAQ 100, and the Dow Jones Industrial Average, among others.

The popularity of these products stems in part from the fact that investors can use mini-sized index futures to handle both sides of the investment coin—both as a hedge for their stock positions and to make outright trades. The contracts feature futures-style portfolio margining, making them highly capital-efficient instruments. And given the increased popularity of electronic trading, they can be accessed easily right from an investor's PC at home.

Futures on narrow-based stock indexes will debut for trading this fall, giving investors even greater market flexibility than before. By themselves and in combination with single stock futures, these new security futures products will enable market participants to efficiently execute a variety of trading strategies for specific sectors of the stock market.

Simplifying the legal definition to its essentials, a narrow-based index contains nine or fewer stocks. OneChicago, the all-electronic joint venture of the Chicago Board Options Exchange, Chicago Mercantile Exchange Inc., and the Chicago Board of Trade, will offer at least 15 narrow-based indexes when security futures trading begins. Representing key economic sectors such as biotech, computer networking, and defense, OneChicago narrow-based index futures will enable an investor to take a long or short position in a focused area of the stock market with a single trade.

How Are These Indexes Constructed?

The specific stocks in OneChicago's narrow-based indexes have been selected based on a number of considerations, the most important of which are their historical price correlation to the performance of the sector they represent as well as input from investors regarding the products in which they are most interested in trading. Unlike most broad-based indexes, such as the NASDAQ 100, which contain many stocks and are weighted by market capitalization, these narrow-based indexes contain only four to six stocks each and are modified equal-dollar-weighted indexes rounded to the nearest multiple of 100 shares of each underlying stock.

In the NASDAQ 100, for example, there are 100 different stocks in the index, yet Microsoft (MSFT) alone represents about 13 percent of the index's value. It has recently been trading at about $48 a share, and its market capitalization is a whopping $257 billion; thus, the price movements of Microsoft have a disproportionately larger effect on the performance of the overall index relative to other index components with smaller market capitalizations.

By contrast, take a look at OneChicago's investment banking narrow-based index in Table 12.1, which includes just four stocks: Goldman Sachs (GS), Lehman Brothers (LEH), Merrill Lynch (MER), and Morgan Stanley Dean Witter (MWD).

To create a modified equal-dollar-weighted index of these stocks, OneChicago adjusts the number of shares of the index components so that each company represents roughly 25 percent of the total value of the index. There are, therefore, twice as many shares of Morgan Stanley (recently trading around $35 a share) as shares of Goldman Sachs (recently trading around $70 a share). In this way, a 10 percent move in Morgan Stanley will have approximately the same effect on the index as would a 10 percent move in Goldman Sachs, even though Morgan Stanley is trading at half the price.

Why use a modified equal-dollar-weighted methodology rather than the more common market-cap-weighted approach? The exchange's narrow-based indexes are designed to provide a risk transference vehicle that

TABLE 12.1

OneChicago Investment Banking Narrow-Based Index

Index Component	Shares in Index	Recent Trading Price	Value % of Total	
Goldman Sachs Group, Inc. (GS)	100	$67.48	$6,748	26%
Lehman Brothers Holdings (LEH)	100	$49.88	$4,988	20%
Merrill Lynch & Co., Inc. (MER)	200	$33.98	$6,796	27%
Morgan Stanley Dean Witter & Co. (MWD)	200	$34.69	$6,938	27%
Total Value of Index			$25,470	100%

Note: The number of shares in OneChicago's indexes is subject to change.
Component values will vary as market prices fluctuate.

approximates the performance of a given economic sector, not that of a single company. With equal-dollar-weighted indexes, the performance of the index should more closely mirror the performance of the overall sector rather than primarily reflect only the performance of the higher-market-cap stocks in that industry.

As with all indexes, the composition of those in the narrow-based category is subject to change and periodically will be rebalanced. Please check the OneChicago web site at www.OneChicago.com for the most updated listings.

Risk-Averse Strategies Are Number One

The classic purpose of futures contracts is to provide a cost-effective tool for risk management, and narrow-based indexes are no exception to this rule. Just like single stock futures, investors generally will be required to put up 20 percent of the notional value of the contract to trade narrow-based indexes. Margin requirements may be lower than the 20 percent standard if the investor also holds certain offsetting positions in cash equities, stock options, or other security futures in the same securities account. This makes narrow-based indexes a natural tool for cost-effective hedging.

For example, let's say an investor has recently invested in a range of biotech stocks, based on a belief in the long-term growth potential of the sector. He, of course, is concerned about short-term price volatility of biotech stocks, however, and wants to hedge his biotech portfolio. By initiating a short position in OneChicago's biotech narrow-based index, he essentially could protect himself against a short-term dip in the industry in a highly capital-efficient manner.

A similar approach could be used by an investor with a diversified portfolio concerned about short-term volatility of a specific economic sector. For example, an investor with large holdings in an index fund that tracks the S&P 500 who is uneasy about the near-term outlook for the gold mining industry could take a short position in the exchange's gold mining narrow-based index. With a margin requirement of only 20 percent, he can cost-effectively protect against a potential downside in gold stocks—without redeeming shares in mutual fund holdings.

Trading Strategies for Narrow-Based Indexes Abound

The following examples highlight potential uses of security futures products to execute various trading strategies. Trading security futures, like all futures, involves risk, including the potential risk of losses greater than a trader's initial capital investment. It is, therefore, important for an investor to consult his broker or financial adviser before trading these products to determine if they are appropriate to his financial circumstances and investment objectives.

Strategy 1: "The Directional Trade"

Consider a hypothetical investor who believes that the retail sector will rebound as the economy improves, but is not sure which retailer will lead the way up. One option for this investor is to try to determine which retailer has the best potential and buy that company's stock; however, this approach risks being right about the sector's overall performance but picking "the wrong horse to ride." Will Best Buy (BBY) outperform Circuit City (CC), or vice versa? Will Wal-Mart (WMT) continue to recover from its July 24 low (See Figure 12.1), or will it struggle to break $60 a share?

If the investor is concerned about the risk associated with picking a single retailer in which to invest (economists refer to this risk as the "idiosyncratic risk" of a firm), an alternate approach would be to purchase multiple stocks in the retail industry, thus diversifying the investor's risk within the sector. While in principle there is nothing wrong with this method, in order to execute this approach the investor would, of course, need to pay multiple commissions to his broker to make the various trades, as well as be subject to the bid/ask spread for each stock he buys.

FIGURE 12.1

Wal-Mart 2002 YTD Stock Price: Leader of the Retail Pack?

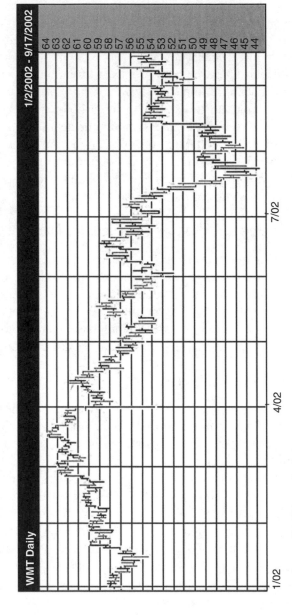

Source: OneChicago Analytics

To achieve the dual objectives of reducing idiosyncratic risk associated with individual stocks and, also, avoiding the transaction costs associated with buying and selling multiple instruments, this investor could now choose a third option: buying futures contracts on OneChicago's retail narrow-based index. This index, which includes Best Buy, Circuit City and Wal-Mart, along with Autozone (AZO) and Home Depot (HD), provides exposure to the performance of the overall retail sector with a single, efficient trade execution.

Strategy 2: "Fine-Tuning the Directional Trade"

As time goes on, let's say the same investor determines that Wal-Mart's upside potential relative to the other retailers is not as great as he originally had estimated. To reduce the impact of Wal-Mart's stock price on his narrow-based index holdings, the investor could simply sell short single stock futures contracts on Wal-Mart. Depending on the number of contracts he sells, he could either reduce the effective weighting of Wal-Mart in his position or eliminate it altogether.

Or, perhaps, the investor remains generally bullish on the retail sector, but also believes that an increasing percentage of consumer transactions are migrating to the Internet. To further fine-tune the narrow-based index, he could then buy single stock futures contracts on e-Bay (EBAY) to add an e-commerce component to his position.

When this type of portfolio construction is compared with trading cash securities, the transactions cost advantage of using narrow-based indexes is striking (see Table 12.2).

The two sets of transactions in Table 12.2 result in essentially equivalent positions in the market with respect to price risk, yet the execution approach with security futures requires only three transactions, whereas the cash securities equivalent requires seven. Exiting the security futures positions will require just three additional transactions, for a total of six transactions, compared to six additional transactions to exit the cash equities positions, for a total of 13 transactions. The transaction cost savings from using narrow-based indexes are, therefore, likely to be significant, and the OneChicago customer margin requirements for these security futures top out at 20 percent of the notional value of the contracts.

Strategy 3: "Sector Underperform/Outperform"

Earlier in this chapter, we considered an investor with a long position in an S&P 500 index fund that used the OneChicago gold mining narrow-

TABLE 12.2

Comparison of Transactions

Narrow-Based Indexes and Transaction Efficiency	
Security Futures Transaction	**Cash Equities Equivalent**
1. Buy Retail narrow-based index futures	Buy Autozone stock
	Buy Best Buy stock
	Buy Circuit City stock
	Buy Home Depot stock
	Buy Wal-Mart stock
2. Sell (short) Wal-Mart single stock futures	Sell Wal-Mart stock
3. Buy e-Bay single stock futures	Buy e-Bay stock

based index to hedge the short-term performance of gold stocks. This type of trade is sometimes referred to as an "underperformance" trade, because the investor is expressing an opinion that a particular sector will underperform the broader market.

The converse of this strategy, a sector "outperform" approach, is consistent with the viewpoint that a particular sector will outperform the broader market. For example, if an investor believes that oil services stocks will outperform the overall market in the near term, he or she could purchase futures contracts on the OneChicago oil services narrow-based index to overweight that sector within the portfolio.

If this long oil services position is accompanied by an opposing short position in a broad-market index such as the S&P 500, and these opposing positions are weighted appropriately, the investor may be able to create a so-called market-neutral portfolio. The idea behind this approach to investing is to attempt to profit from the differential in performance between a sector and the broader market rather than just on the directional performance of the sector.

The moniker "market neutral" comes from the fact that if the entire market does well, the investor will make a profit on the long oil services narrow-based index holding, but lose money on the short S&P 500 position. And if the entire market does poorly, the investor will lose money as the oil services futures fall in value, but make it back up on the increased value of the short S&P 500 position. So, if the positions are balanced appropriately, movements in the broader market will have limited impact on the trader's portfolio ("neutral" to the overall market). Instead, the trader is likely to make money if the oil services sector outperforms the market and lose money if the industry underperforms the market, regardless of overall market direction.

A similar market-neutral approach can be executed with narrow-based indexes on two subsectors of a given industry. For example, a long position in OneChicago's computer software narrow-based index and an opposing short position in the exchange's computer networking narrow-based index may also create a market-neutral trade. This is because movements in the broader market may have limited impact on the net value of such a position to the extent that networking stocks and software stocks are equivalently correlated with the broader market.

As Figure 12.2 shows, the overall value of this portfolio is not affected by the performance of the overall market. In a bull market, the value of the investor's position in the narrow-based index A would increase, but would be offset by losses in the short position in the narrow-based index B.

FIGURE 12.2

Theoretical market-neutral portfolio with opposing long and short positions in two perfectly correlated narrow-based indexes.

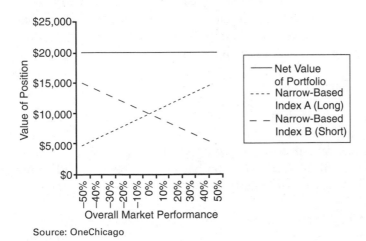

Source: OneChicago

Conversely, if the market turns bearish, losses in narrow-based index A would be offset by gains in narrow-based index B. Thus, the net value of this portfolio would remain constant at $20,000 regardless of market direction. Any profits or losses in this example would derive solely from the relative performance of the two indexes.

Of course, this is a theoretical example and, in reality, narrow-based indexes are not likely to be perfectly correlated with the market. In fact, most market-neutral trades executed in the actual market by professionals are not completely market-neutral. But the principle of opposing positions in correlated instruments points the way toward minimizing the impact of the broader market in a trade to approximate a market-neutral position.

In fact, this principle may also point the way toward limiting the impact of an overall industry's performance in addition to the market's movements.

Let's return to our example of the long computer software narrow-based index position and simultaneous short of the computer networking narrow-based index. If the broader movement of technology stocks affects software companies and networking companies in an equivalent manner, this position may be neutral with respect to the overall movement of tech stocks. By taking opposite positions in these two narrow-based indexes, the trader is, therefore, expressing the view that regardless of market direction and the general performance of technology stocks, software firms will outperform computer networking companies.

In fact, a number of professional fund managers have expressed interest in this use of narrow-based indexes for what they call "double-alpha, zero-beta" trading. This simply means that with a long position in a sector expected to outperform a benchmark index and a simultaneous short position in a sector expected to underperform, the fund manager has two opportunities to outperform their benchmark (double-alpha) while remaining market-neutral overall (zero beta).

Strategy 4: "Sector Rotation"

Given the sector-focused orientation of OneChicago's narrow-based indexes, it is fairly straightforward to then take this concept of industry underperformance/outperformance to the next level for active sector rotation strategies. The concept of sector rotation has become popular with some investors in recent years, particularly as the overall market has become increasingly volatile.

This can be a difficult strategy to execute, however, because many mutual fund companies are now restricting active switching among funds, and the transaction costs in cash equities are often too high to make this a profitable approach. With the low transaction costs and capital efficiency of narrow-based indexes, however, active sector rotation may become a more realistic trading opportunity for active market participants.

NBI Trading Mechanics

The Price, the Price, the Price

A typical OneChicago narrow-based index will contain more than 1000 shares of stock, yet the price at which the index trades will usually be under $100. How is this possible? With all indexes, OneChicago uses a "divisor" of the contract's value to calculate the price at which the contract is likely to trade.

The divisor OneChicago has selected is 500, meaning that the price of the narrow-based index will be 1/500 of the total value of the index. Put another way, the value of the overall index is 500 times the price at which it is trading (this is why an index's divisor is also often called the index "multiplier").

Let's return to the investment banking narrow-based index as an example. The total value of the contract at recent price levels of the component stocks is $25,470. With a divisor of 500, the price of the index itself would theoretically be $50.94 ($25,470/500 = $50.94).

But let's not forget that we are discussing a futures contract on the index, not trading the index itself. The price shown in Table 12.3 is the likely cash price of the index. To calculate the theoretically correct price of the futures contract, it will likely be necessary to adjust for interest rates and dividends.

Specifically, the price of the futures contract will usually trade at a higher price to the cash index value due to the premium investors are willing to pay to put down a 20 percent margin requirement rather than the full value of the index. This premium would be adjusted downward by the present value of any dividends expected to be paid to holders of the component stocks prior to expiration of the contract, as expressed in the following formula:

Cash Index Price+ Interest Rate Premium - Dividends=Theoretically Correct Futures Price

Of course, futures may not always trade at the theoretically correct price due to short-term supply and demand for the contracts as well as a variety of other market conditions.

TABLE 12.3

OneChicago Investment Banking Narrow-Based Index

Index Component	Shares in Index	Recent Trading Price	Value
Goldman Sachs Group, Inc. (GS)	100	$67.48	$6,748
Lehman Brothers Holdings (LEH)	100	$49.88	$4,988
Merrill Lynch & Co., Inc. (MER)	200	$33.98	$6,796
Morgan Stanley Dean Witter & Co. (MWD)	200	$34.69	$6,938
Total Value of Index:			$25,470
Divisor:			500
Price:			$50.94

Managing Expiration Dates

As with all futures contracts, there are three ways to manage contract expiration dates:

- Offset the position to complete the trade;
- Roll the position forward to another contract month; or
- Hold the contracts until expiration.

OneChicago's narrow-based indexes are physically settled at expiration. So, if an investor is long at expiration, he will be required to take delivery of the component stocks of the index. Conversely, if the investor is short at expiration, he will be required to make delivery of these stocks. Remember that brokers may charge additional fees for delivery of these contracts, so you should talk with your broker first if you are considering holding a narrow-based index position to expiration.

Margins at 20 Percent

The 20 percent margin requirement for a narrow-based index is calculated on the value of the index, not the price at which it is trading. If, for example, an investor wants to estimate the margin required to trade a narrow-based index trading at $50, he needs to first multiply the price by 500 and then calculate the 20 percent margin requirement. In this example, the margin requirement would be approximately $5000 ($50 × 500 × 20% = $5000).

Also, note that while OneChicago and its clearinghouses permit certain margin offsets that may reduce an investor's margin requirement for certain trades, some brokerage firms may choose not to offer these offsets to their customers, or may mandate higher margin deposits than required by exchange rules. For those who want a list of margin offsets permissible for positions in OneChicago's narrow-based indexes, check OneChicago's web site. It's recommended that investors should also contact their brokers to determine which, if any, of these offsets will be applied to their specific positions.

No Limit to the Possibilities

Marketplace innovations often beget even further innovation, and this is to be expected with narrow-based indexes. Risk management applications and trading strategies that employ narrow-based indexes will expand quickly once trading begins. The potential uses of these products, by themselves or in conjunction with single stock futures and the existing line-up of popular stock index futures, will, in the end, be limited only by two factors—the creativity of market participants and the careful consideration of the risks of trading these products and their suitability to each market participant's investment objectives.

FUTURES ON NARROW-BASED INDEXES OFFER OPPORTUNITIES TO MAKE SECTOR BETS (OCTOBER 2002)

By Kira McCaffrey Brecht

Do you think gold stocks are going up? Do you expect drug stocks to tank over the next several weeks? Or, are you willing to play the beaten-up biotech sector from the long side? If the answer to any of these is "yes," the new narrow-based index futures, which will be offered by OneChicago, LLC, within what may be just a few weeks, may well be worth a look-see.

This product is pretty straightforward. It's just a futures contract on a basket of stocks in key economic sectors. In August, OneChicago topped off their previous list of proposed indexes, bringing it to 15 the various narrow-based index futures contracts being offered. And the range is broad: commercial banking; computer networks; computer software; drug companies; gold mining; pharmacies; semiconductor circuits; airlines; biotech; computer hardware; defense; investment banking; oil services; retail; and semiconductor components. So, there's virtually something for everyone.

Narrow-based means just that. Each of the indexes is comprised of just four to six stocks, which offers a very narrow and extremely concentrated sector view. So, for example, under the investment banking index, four stocks make up the total: Goldman Sachs, Lehman Brothers, Merrill Lynch, and Morgan Stanley Dean Witter.

The futures indexes are approximately equal dollar weighted and are physically settled.

Peter Borish, senior managing director at OneChicago, cited the physical delivery of these futures contracts as a major advantage, which actually should increase liquidity in the product. "They are perfectly arbitrageable," he said. "At expiration of the futures contract, you get shares of those four to six stocks in the index."

For example, the computers narrow-based futures index contract is comprised of Apple Computer Inc. (AAPL), Dell Inc. (DELL), International Business Machines (IBM), Research in Motion (RIMM), and Sun Microsystems (SUNW). Borish offered the example of Dell trading at $25 per share and IBM trading at $80 per share. In order to approximately equalize the dollar weighting, "for every 100 shares of IBM, 300 shares of Dell" would be included in the index.

He also highlighted the very concentrated nature of the indexes as an advantage. "You want to eliminate event risk, but at the same time have a concentrated view," Borish explained. Pointing to the retail investor, he added, "If you are a trader with a futures-oriented account who is trading e-minis, you now have the ability to trade sector futures, which you've never had before."

Liquidity Will Be Key, Says Raschke

While these products offer potentially interesting trading opportunities for the individual investor, liquidity will be the key to their success, Linda Bradford Raschke, independent futures trader and president of the LBR Group, Inc., said. "The success of this product really depends on the market maker on the other side willing to make tight markets and provide market depth. Ultimately, the large players and the hedge funds have to be able to get in and out in size. It's really going to be dependent on the big boys,"

she said. However, if these new products do prove themselves after several months with tight bid/ask spreads, Raschke sees some potential trading
opportunities.

Catch the Move on a Sector

"The narrow-based indexes could be a nice product because there are a
number of advantages to being able to catch a move on a sector. And, traditionally, the sectors can have a higher degree of 'trendiness' than an
individual stock," Raschke noted. "An individual stock is subjected to
news, individual earnings, and announcements that can cause more noise
in that stock. The theory is that a sector really helps eliminate some of that.
You are buying a basket, so if you have ten stocks and one of them comes
out with a news item—it's generally going to be buffered by the rest of
them. There is not as much risk trading a sector as there is in trading one
individual stock," she explained.

Also, Raschke believes that sector futures may offer slightly longer
trading opportunities than individual stocks. "I think you'd be able to hold
these for slightly longer periods than if you were just day trading stocks."

Volatility Breakouts with the Indexes

One potential trading strategy that retail investors might be able to employ
with futures contracts on narrow-based indexes is a volatility breakout
type of trade. Raschke, who focuses on shorter-term and intraday types of
trading in her work, thinks that the indexes "could be a great product on
which to do a breakout strategy from congestion areas or classic chart formations. But a strategy like this is only viable if there is good liquidity and
a reasonable spread between the bid and ask," she says. "If I want to execute a basket of ten stocks and I'm buying at the market, it's really hard in
stocks if you have to pay the offers on ten different shares. Of course,
somebody has to be willing to take the other side of my trade, and that is
going to be the tricky issue with this product."

What type of technical setups would identify trading opportunities?
Raschke says that breakout strategies can be created to take advantage of low
volatility points when there has been a period of several days of range contrac-
tion in the market. Traditional strategies such as buying breakouts from bull
flag formations or extended bases can also be used. "Since there is no uptick
rule necessary to establish a short position, as there is in individual stocks,
indexes are great vehicles that can be used to capture downside breakouts, too."

In-Vogue Sectors Can Have Some Profitable, if Short, Moves

"What we've seen with the individual sectors is that they can quickly go in and out of vogue. For example, let's say everyone loves the biotechs . . . there's very much a herd mentality among some of these institutional funds. If they see the relative strength is in drugs, they say 'oh, we've got to own drugs in our portfolio.' So, they all 'dogpile' into the drugs for 2 days; the minute they back off there is no support for drugs, and drugs fall back a bit. And then gold stocks are in vogue and they rush into gold stocks—so you do get these nice 2- to 3-day moves," Raschke added.

Raschke advises that when backtesting breakout strategies, test for what an optimal holding time might be. For example, with a majority of short-term breakout opportunities, a large percentage of the gains often are captured in only 1 to 3 days.

Another potential type of trading opportunity, if these narrow-based index futures deliver on their "promise" of being liquid markets, would be a play on rotation—taking advantage of plays in strong sectors as leadership rotates. "You can play a relative strength game in a momentum environment," Raschke says. "In that kind of environment, you can get away with holding a relative strength leader of the sectors for a longer period of time. Keep in mind, though, that we are not currently in a momentum type of environment."

Advice on Use

What advice does she have for individual investors interested in trading futures on narrow-based indexes? "Any time you test a new market, do it with the smallest size possible. Be extremely conscientious about liquidity," she said. "And treat each index as an individual market. For example, semiconductor futures will be totally different from biotech futures. If you want to do general market timing, you are better off just using S&Ps or the Dow futures. But, if you feel strongly about a particular group or sector when you are in a momentum environment—perhaps the biotechs are particularly strong for 2 to 3 days, for example—just go in and treat them as another market to trade," Raschke advised.

What about the reverse situation? "If you think the overall market is going to sell off—consider selling the weakest group. For example, over the last couple of weeks, the semiconductors were underperforming, so contemplate using that vehicle to play to the downside since they are already weak. Likewise, if you think the overall market is poised for a large up move or you want to express an upside opinion on the market, and let's say the drugs have been holding up the best, use that as the vehicle to express your opinion to the upside," Raschke added.

However, Raschke warned that narrow-based index futures might not be nimble enough for intraday trading. "I would not try to use them as an intraday trading vehicle, because there is a good chance you will get eaten alive by the vig [bid/ask spread plus commissions]," Raschke said.

Other uses? Sure. Says Raschke, "There could be individuals out there who have longer-term holdings and don't want to liquidate for tax reasons or whatever—this could prove to be a viable hedge as opposed to doing individual options on a stock where you are most likely to experience decay in the premium. Perhaps you own Intel and the market is a little weak, but you don't want to sell your Intel and you don't want to buy puts on it—you could trade from the short side, with the purpose of it being a hedge."

Final thoughts that Raschke offered surround the constant concern of "how easy is it to get in and out?" What is the depth of the market—how tight is the spread? Anybody can make a tight spread and have it two up. But, you need to have a market where you can buy 20 and sell 20. The better volume and the tighter the spread, the more players you ultimately will attract into the game," she concluded.

What Does the Sector Environment Look Like Heading into the Fourth Quarter?

For thoughts on trading the current sector environment heading into the final quarter of 2002, *SFO* spoke with Christopher Hendrix, CMT (certified market technician), senior technical analyst for H&R Block Financial Advisors based in Detroit, Michigan.

When asked about his views on sector trading, Hendrix harkened back to an old market adage, "the purpose of investing is to make money, and there is a saying in the markets—'to make money you have to be where the action is.'" That, of course, is what sector trading is all about—identifying which sectors of the equity market are hot and which are not.

"When you do sector analysis, you are looking at a top-down approach," Hendrix explained. "You want to find a group and sector that is coming into favor." In his analysis, Hendrix relies on a variety of technical tools, including moving averages, trend lines, the relative strength indicator, and MACD momentum indicator (moving average convergence/divergence) on the weekly and monthly charts. Every Monday morning, Hendrix issues a report summarizing the weakest and strongest sectors in the market.

"The point of sector analysis is to focus on strength within strength. You want the strongest stock, within the strongest group, within the strongest sector," he said. "There's a saying that 'there's always a bull market somewhere.'"

Generally, when the economy begins to emerge from recessionary conditions, the basic materials sector traditionally shows improvement first and often is a leader as industrial production begins to increase. However, this is not currently the case, Hendrix said. "Basic materials is stuck in a range and is lacking a buy signal. The weekly MACD is moving down."

Looking at the current market environment (late August at the writing of this article), Hendrix pointed to the technology sector as an area in which investors could realize "more bang for their buck," in part because that area of the market is so oversold.

Hendrix highlighted the DJ Technology Index as a potentially bullish area currently. "It has given positive signals for the aggressive investor," he said. "For my more aggressive style, it's formed a bottom and it's been moving up for the past 2 weeks. For those that are less aggressive, there are not yet enough clues for a true bottom even though it may be working towards that signal." (Investors can view this index at bigcharts.com.)

The DJ Technology Index has plummeted from its high at 1578 in March 2000 to the August low at 293. However, Hendrix said the bulls are showing some signs of life at these depressed levels. Most importantly, at the writing of this article, Hendrix highlighted a bullish divergence on the weekly momentum charts for the DJ Technology Index. A "bullish divergence" is a positive technical environment in which price makes a new low, but the momentum reading does not "confirm" this with a new low in momentum.

Hendrix noted that the DJ Technology Index made new lows in August, but the weekly MACD indicator did not make a new low—hence the bullish divergence. The Computers group within the technology index appeared to be the strongest group, at this writing, the analyst added.

Another sector investors might want to keep an eye on is the DJ Consumer Non-Cyclical Index, Hendrix said. This sector includes such items as cosmetics, tobacco, soft drinks, and food products. While this sector tends to perform well during more defensive times, Hendrix said, "the MACD is shifting out of negative and is starting to turn up. But, it still has to cross through its moving signal line" in order to confirm a bullish turn.

Hendrix advised investors to look at weekly charts when trying to gauge sector opinions. "When you are looking at a top-down approach— you are trying to get a bigger picture." He also suggested using trend lines on the relative strength indicator. "Put a trend line on a relative strength chart. When the relative strength breaks above its trend line—then it lets you know you have leadership" and a potential trading opportunity, Hendrix concluded.

(Readers interested in learning more about sector analysis may want to check out www.bigcharts.com. That web site offers charts on the ten Dow Jones sectors, which break down into additional groups and subgroups, for analysis.)

Goldman Sachs Analysts Upbeat on Prospects for Narrow-Based Index Futures

Some final thoughts from the big boys.

In an article written by Matthew Boucher and Joanne Hill, analysts in the Goldman Sachs derivatives and trading research group, the firm was "optimistic" about the success of futures on narrow-based indexes. "Potentially useful applications of narrow-based index futures include managing cash flows, taking active views on industries, industry or sector hedging, managing concentrated portfolios efficiently, and managing long/short (market-neutral) strategies," the analysts wrote.

They also highlighted the concentrated nature of the contract as a plus. "Note how narrow-based index futures can focus on the leading stocks in an industry. For certain industries, like many of those selected for first launch, this narrow focus could be attractive to active investors. Past products could not deliver this type of exposure because of the regulated structure under which they came to market," the analysts concluded.

*Editorial Note: At the creation of this anthology, OneChicago was in the process of developing changes to its narrow-based indexes, and those changes had not yet been released. These particular articles should not necessarily be construed as an ongoing trading guide.

13

What Do All Those Charts Mean, Anyway? Basic Technical Analysis

We see line graphs and bar charts in newspapers, on financial networks, and on market web sites. But what do they really mean, and how can they help you in your trading? In Chapter 11, David Floyd's article relied somewhat on technical analysis, the study of price charts, to explain his strategies. Chapters 13 and 14 will build on that to provide you with an overview of what analysis is as a way to examine the market. The articles in this chapter will highlight several aspects of technical analysis.

To begin, Kira McCaffrey Brecht summarizes the major points of technical analysis, such as the noticeable chart patterns of the trend, resistance and support, and tops and bottoms. While these patterns clearly indicate price and price movement, they also indicate investor sentiment, or what people think of the current market. For example, when the price of a stock future sharply hits a low, creating a bottom, investors are selling and are generally fearful of losing any more money. Technical analysis can help you cut your losses, as it quickly reveals price movement. Although technical analysis can be as complex or as simple as you choose to make it, virtually anyone can conduct technical analysis, as many charting tools are available for every type of investor.

In the second article, Christopher Terry reviews the revered Dow theory, which states that averages—or indexes—must confirm the market trend. Currently, the major indexes are the Dow, S&P, and NASDAQ, and these are used for confirmation and nonconfirmation. When all three indexes trend together, there is confirmation. When one index does not move in sync with the other two indexes, there is nonconfirmation. In terms of chart analysis, the theory concentrates on three types of trends: primary, secondary, and minor, or the tide, the wave, and the ripple. Terry also explains how to identify these trends in charts and confirm price movements.

Just as important as identifying primary, secondary, and minor trends is identifying pivot points in trends, or the place where the price begins to buck the trend, going down instead of up or up instead of down. In the third article, Clif Droke will explain how to pinpoint pivot points in the market. As Droke notes, "Your chances of profiting from stock price trends will be greater if you can quickly identify these turning points and jump on board just as the new trend is beginning." Droke explains that you need to study historical charts in order to get a feel for how a financial instrument trends. Then, you can begin looking for pivot points on charts and breakouts in trends. The bottom line is that pivot-point analysis is about finding significant areas and trend reversals and observing price reaction to these area reversals.

Barbara Rockefeller next explains how to use channels, the highs and lows connected on a price chart, to develop exit strategies. These channels provide a clear visualization of the trend and enable you to confirm what you *think* you're seeing in the chart. Developing an exit strategy is just as important as developing a buy strategy, Rockefeller reasons. As with all technical analysis, knowing how to use channels enables a trader to make greater sense of charts and thus to have the ability to determine future price moves.

WHY DOES TECHNICAL ANALYSIS WORK? LOOKING FOR ENTRY/EXIT POINTS? "IT'S ALL IN THE CHARTS" (MARCH 2003)

BY KIRA MCCAFFREY BRECHT

"The principles of successful stock speculation are based on the supposition that people will continue in the future to make the mistakes that they have made in the past."

—Reminiscences of a Stock Operator, Edwin Lefèvre

Most investors are familiar with concepts such as the price/earnings ratio or quarterly profit reports, but if the terms double bottom, Fibonacci levels, or head-and-shoulders top sound a bit more foreign, you are not alone. While cash flow analysis and the price/earnings ratio fall under the category of fundamental analysis, the latter fall under the category of technical analysis. If you are a beginning trader, this article is a basic introduction to the subject of technical analysis. Perhaps, after reading these few pages, you'll be interested in learning how to trade breakout points for yourself!

To the average investor, technical analysis may not be standard cocktail hour conversation, but it is a methodology that market players have utilized for hundreds of years. In recent times, with the advent of the personal computer and the Internet and as more day traders have become active in the financial markets, technical analysis has "come out of the closet" and is becoming more well known even among individual investors.

But, what exactly is technical analysis? Before attempting to define and explain technical analysis, it is probably worthwhile to briefly define fundamental analysis, as these are the two major forms of analysis that market watchers utilize in an attempt to determine future direction of price. Fundamental analysis relies on the use of economic numbers, including supply/demand figures, production and consumption numbers. Or in the case of individual stock analysis, analysts examine the financial books of a company, evaluate management and cash flows and dividends, and consider new product launches and overall competitiveness in the marketplace.

"Fundamental analysis deals with companies and economies, while technical analysis deals with stocks and markets. They are not the same thing," said Philip Roth, chief technical analyst at Miller Tabak & Co. "The company and the stock are not the same thing. Fundamentalists look at the company—is the management good, are the products good? But, we are not buying the company. We just buy one teeny bit of the company. One hundred shares can trade off the psychology of the marketplace. The technician analyzes supply/demand relationships in the market and the psychology of the participants. The charts have memories. They represent actions of investors in the past."

Price Is the Key Indicator—"It's All in the Charts"

The technical analyst will say there is no way that one person, or perhaps even a team of researchers, can identify and pinpoint every known fundamental supply and demand factor in the marketplace. Therefore, a major tenet of technical analysis is that "it is all in the charts." The current price of a stock index future, or a commodity, or an individual stock reflects the current opinion of all of the players in the marketplace. In other words, all currently "known" fundamental information is reflected by buyers and sellers to push the security to the current price—"it's all in the charts."

Technical analysis, simply put, is remembering prices. It is the study of prices and price history, in an effort to gauge current and future trends. Technical analysts rely on three major tenets—the first is that all news is discounted in the price, and, secondly, that price moves in a trend and that history tends to repeat itself.

In his book, *How Technical Analysis Works* (New York Institute of Finance, 2003), author Bruce Kamich says, "The prices of goods and raw commodities—silk, spices, gold, rice, horses, cattle—have been followed for centuries. People remembered the prices of last season, the extreme highs and lows, and more. For centuries, farmers have had a vital interest in following prices; the result of a whole season of sweat and toil will come down to the price they are able to get in the marketplace. If your livelihood depends on being paid for one crop of tobacco, coffee, or rice, you will have a strong interest in price."

Price Resistance and Price Support

One basic element in technical analysis is the concept of price resistance and support. Miller Tabak's Roth explains it as "if I buy a stock at 50, but then it goes down to 40—I'm thinking—please just get back to 50 so I can get even—that becomes a resistance area. Or, if I buy a stock at 40 and then it goes to 50, I'll remember that 40 was an attractive price. If it goes back down to 40, I may buy it again, which becomes a support level. Support and resistance are basically established because of the psychological component. People remember past successes and failures."

Technical Analysis Is the Oldest Form of Market Analysis

Technical analysis, or analyzing price, is the oldest known form of market analysis, originating back to the rice markets in Japan in the seventeenth century. Even here in the United States, early technicians were simply "tape readers," or those who watched prices go up and down on the ticker tape, which was introduced in 1867. The point-and-figure type of charting can be traced back to the 1880s here in the United States. It wasn't until the 1930s that fundamental analysis first emerged as a market discipline.

The basic tool of the technical analyst is the price chart. One of the most widely used types of charts is simply a bar chart. In the case of a daily bar chart, the line will represent the price high, low, and close for the day. Depending on the trading or investment time frame, you could utilize an intraday chart (such as an hourly or 15-minute) if you are a very short-term trader, or a weekly or monthly chart if you are a longer-term investor.

The Concept of Trend

The idea of trend is pivotal to developing a basic understanding of technical analysis. There are many old market expressions that you may have heard, "the trend is your friend" and "never buck the trend." A basic definition of trend is simply the direction in which prices are moving. While many people tend to think of the market in two directions—a bull or a bear—there are actually three types of trends: an uptrend, a downtrend and a sideways or a range-trade trend. Looking at a price chart, a technical analyst would need to see a series of higher price highs in order to confirm an uptrend. On the flip side, a series of lower price lows reveals a downtrend. Trend can also be classified in terms of time frame. For example, the longer-term trend could be down, but the shorter-term trend could be up, which would be called a corrective upmove in a downtrend.

John Murphy, long-time market technician and author of what many consider to be the "bible" of technical analysis, *Technical Analysis of the Financial Markets* (New York Institute of Finance, updated 1999), said that "all technicians are trying to do is measure the trend of the market."

Murphy, currently the chief technical analyst at Stockcharts.com, adds, "Technical analysis tells you what the market is actually doing, as opposed to what people think the market might be doing. The market is always looking to the future. If the market is telling us what is going to happen 6 months in the future, if you don't look at the charts, you'll always be behind the curve." (Economists tend to believe that the stock market is a leading indicator of the economy and that current stock market prices tend to reflect expectations for the economy and companies 6 months out.)

Fear and Greed Make Tops and Bottoms

If you've ever done any trading or investing, you may have experienced some of the common feelings of fear and greed. Market bottoms tend to be made during extreme periods of investor and trader fear, while market tops tend to occur during times of extreme greed. A case can be made that the bubble-like top in the NASDAQ index, scored in March 2000, was made amid investor greed. More and more individuals bought into tech stocks because they had seen a brother-in-law double his money in a matter of months—and they wanted in on the game too. Miller Tabak's Roth explains it as, "A long-lasting market advance will eventually lead to feelings of greed. Tops are made from buying excesses. Conversely, market bottoms occur amid panic, when people can't take the pain [of losses] anymore."

Human psychology really hasn't changed much over the centuries. Markets move from greed at a top to fear at a bottom, and unless people learn to control those emotions, markets will continue to move up and down.

Within the field of technical analysis, there are hundreds of different indicators and tools. However, in the early days of technical analysis, price and volume were the two main factors that traders analyzed. Now, with the advent of calculators and computers, traders have devised mathematical formulas which automatically measure such things as how fast a market moves up or down—is it "overbought" or "oversold." There is pattern recognition, which simply is a visual read of a chart looking for certain patterns, such as double tops or double bottoms.

One long-time market technician explained the likely evolution of the "double top" pattern as this: "Somebody was watching the tape and they'd see General Motors rally to 110 and pull back. Then they'd see it rally again, but fail at 110. By empirical observation, the trader can say that after it fails the second time and closes under the intervening low price, there are good odds that a top has formed."

Relating to the human psychology and emotions, technical analysis offers tools to gauge investor sentiment. Stockcharts.com's Murphy notes, "Markets tend to overreact in both directions. Like, right now—everyone is very pessimistic (on stocks). Traders can use technical indicators, such as the put/call ratio, to measure sentiment. When the put/call ratio gets too high—generally a reading over 1—that means that people are too pessimistic, and this is often associated with market bottoms. Or when the put/call ratio gets too low, under 0.5, it means people are too optimistic, which tends to occur around market tops."

Many "innovations" in technical analysis actually evolved from the futures side of the markets, not the stock trading side. Murphy estimates that 80 to 90 percent of futures traders rely on technical indicators in their trading, as "futures trading tends to be very short-term-oriented and is very highly leveraged. It's all timing. If you are 90 percent leveraged, timing is extremely critical, and you have to be right. The shorter term you are, the more you have to rely on technicals. If you are buying and holding for 3 years into the future, it doesn't matter as much."

Technical Analysis Offers Tools to Tell You When You Are Wrong

You may have heard the old market saying, "Let your profits run and cut your losses short." Getting out of losers—and getting out quickly—is key to capital preservation, especially in fast-moving and highly leveraged futures markets. A major advantage that technical analysis offers over fundamental analysis is that "it tells you very quickly when you've made a mistake," says Murphy.

How does this work? One traditional "buy" type of signal in technical analysis is when a single stock futures contract rallies above a previous peak, or resistance point on the chart—that is considered a "breakout to the upside," or a buy signal. Traders could use that breakout to initiate a long position. However, the charts offer a clear "I'm wrong" level with that breakout point. If the single stock future retreated back below the "breakout" point, the trader would know that something had gone awry—it had been a false breakout—and the trader could quickly exit the position, thus preventing serious losses.

Cut Your Losses Short

Murphy notes a key to success in trading is "never let a small loss turn into a big loss," and the charts offer specific price levels that let you know when you are wrong. Many profitable futures traders actually say that they have more losing trades than winning trades. How is that so, you ask? It goes back to the old saying, "Let your profits ride and cut your losses short." If you rely on technical price points to get out when you are wrong, thus keeping losses to a minimum, and on the flip side—when you are right—let a winning position ride a trend, you can be profitable.

Murphy notes that when a fundamental analyst recommends a stock as a "buy," the stock may actually lose 50 percent of its value before the fundamental analyst changes his outlook. "With fundamentals, there is no fail-safe mechanism for getting out."

Technical analysis can be as simple or as complex as you make it. While there are sophisticated computer programs and books that burgeoning technical traders can read and study, the experienced market watchers say, "Keep it simple." Murphy says, "All of technical analysis is extremely simple. If a line is moving up, that is good and you want to participate. If the line is moving down, that's a negative sign for a market."

Many "old-timers," or traders who were active several decades ago before the heavy reliance on computer trading, actually recommend charting by hand. BC (before computers), traders would compile their own daily bar charts, or point-and-figure charts, by hand. The actual physical act of drawing the line on a piece of graph paper or putting in a number every day after the close offered a type of "feel" for the market that may be missing in the computer-dependent trading world of today. While computer charts are clearly easier, it may not be as easy to catch the innate feel or momentum of a market without the touchy-feely process of yesteryear.

If you are interested in learning more about technical analysis, there are a variety of books and seminars available. Or you may want to check out the Market Technicians Association at www.mta.org. This organization offers the Chartered Market Technician (CMT) accreditation program. There are three different exams which need to be passed, and studying for the exams is an excellent way to learn about the field.

Overall, it is important to remember that technical analysis is the study of market action mainly through the use of price charts, in order to identify future price trends. Patterns on the charts can offer price objectives and clear stop-out points. Momentum tools can measure "overbought" and "oversold" status, and investor sentiment gauges can help determine when a major trend may be nearing an end. No method of analysis is perfect. No method of analysis is right all the time. But, technicals can be valuable tools to a trader, especially one who is active in the fast-moving futures arena.

THE OCEAN'S TIDE AND MARKET'S TREND . . . THE DOW THEORY STILL HOLDS WATER (DECEMBER 2002)

BY CHRISTOPHER TERRY

The challenge of the stock and futures markets is multifaceted. Each trader has his own interpretation of the trend, individual reasoning as to what support and resistance levels may be, what continuation patterns and reversals are, and what constitutes a meaningful chart formation versus what does not.

The "Dow theory," which came to light around 100 years ago, offers an incredible wealth of information for the technical trader, and these concepts and rules are truly as valid today as they were back at the turn of the twentieth century.

The intention of this article is to educate the reader on some of the basic concepts of the Dow theory, a philosophy that has defined the foundations for technical analysis since the early 1900s. The goal here is really quite simple—to help improve the reader's work by applying multiple-time-frame analyses to the rules of the theory and, in essence, to give a good feel for timing important turning points in a trend.

Dow Theory and Technical Analysis

Charles H. Dow in the late 1800s and until his death in 1902 wrote editorials in the *Wall Street Journal* outlining his theories by observing that averages of both the primary industrial and the rail stocks acted as a barometer for the nation's economy.

Dow's successor, William P. Hamilton, for the next 27 years continued the development of Dow's theories and principals and crystallized them into his own version of what we know today as "the Dow theory."

The pioneering work of Dow and Hamilton became the foundation of the discipline that led to the groundbreaking work that helped launch the "technical analysis" revolution. Richard Schabacker's *Technical Analysis and Stock Market Profits* (1934) paved the way for Edwards and Magee's *Technical Analysis of Stock Trends* (1948). Their books have stood the test of time and are considered to be the some of the most important work ever on technical analysis.

Technical analysis in its purest form, of course, is the study of price and the use of charts as a tool to discover patterns and to learn the trend of a market. When using the term *technical analysis,* some of the first visions that come to mind would be various types of chart patterns, both continuations and reversals. Some of the more popular are triangles, wedges, head and shoulders, flags, and pennants.

The Theory and Foundation of Trends

Realizing the prices of stocks and futures quite often trade in trends, a basic understanding of what makes up those trends will be the foundation necessary for a trader to identify the type of market in which he is trading. By gaining a broad understanding of the Dow theory and technical analysis, a trader will gain confidence in chart reading and, ultimately, will enhance his ability to spot and trade trends successfully.

The Dow theory concentrates on three types of trends: primary, secondary, and minor. Below is a description of each type of trend with a subsequent chart that visually simplifies the concept. The most easily understood definition of trends, of course, is that an uptrend exhibits "higher highs" and "higher lows," and a downtrend exhibits "lower lows" and "lower highs."

The Primary or Major Trend

When each intermediate rally (advance in price) rises above the high of the prior rally (higher highs), and each "correction" down or "secondary" reaction stops above the low of the previous correction and price reverses back up (higher lows), the primary trend is up. This is bullish.

When each intermediate decline (decrease in price) takes prices below the low of the previous decline (lower lows), and each "rally" or "secondary" reaction stops below the high of the previous rally and price reverses back down (lower highs), the primary trend is down. This is bearish. Figure 13.1 shows this very clearly.

The original theory refers to the primary trend on a very large time frame, but today traders can and do utilize multiple-time-frame analyses to qualify a primary trend. For example, a primary trend could be on a daily chart, with the secondary trend on a 60-minute chart. Or a primary trend could be on a 60-minute chart, with the secondary trend on a 15-minute chart. There is ample flexibility to determine a trend using multiple-time-frame chart analyses.

The Secondary or Intermediate Trend

Secondary trends are significant reactions that disrupt the development of the primary direction. These reactions are the declines in a bullish trend and rallies in a bearish trend, also known as "retracements."

An intermediate trend is also considered a smaller segment of the primary trend. For example, if you break down a primary trend into two components, each of those intermediate-term segments—whether primary or secondary in direction—is an intermediate trend.

Typically, the "retracement" levels for these secondary trends are a minimum of 38 percent to a maximum of 62 percent, and many times they stop at around 50 percent (see Figure 13.2). These retracement levels are just probabilities because, for instance, there are times in which prices never reach the 38 percent level and also times in which prices correct more than 62 percent.

FIGURE 13.1

As seen, the primary bearish trend for this tracking index is down, with lower highs and lower lows.   Credit: TradeStation.com.

SPY SPDRs Trust Series—60-Minute Chart Primary and Secondary Trends

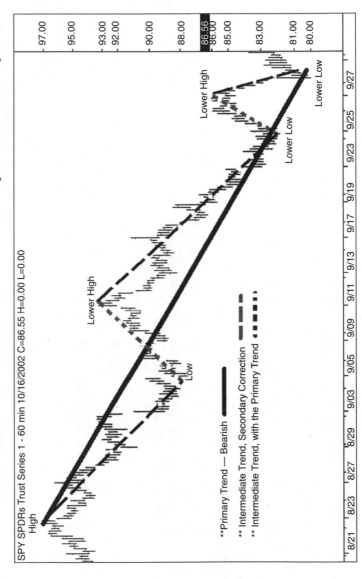

SPY SPDRs Trust Series 1 - 60 min 10/16/2002 C=86.55 H=0.00 L=0.00

**Primary Trend — Bearish

** Intermediate Trend, Secondary Correction

** Intermediate Trend, with the Primary Trend

FIGURE 13.2

This chart clearly shows two examples of secondary corrections of a primary trend; note how one example retraced all the way to 62 percent, and one example just touched 38 percent. Credit: TradeStation.com.

SPY SPDRs Trust Series—60-Minute Chart Secondary Corrections of a Primary Trend

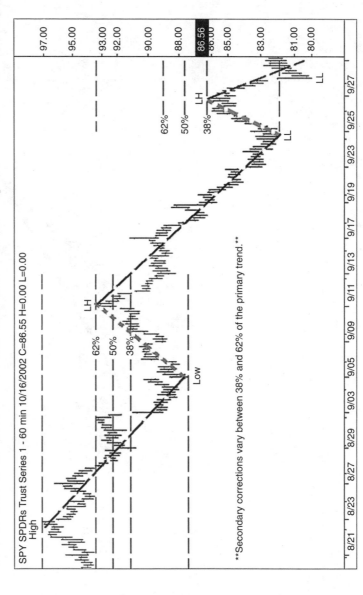

SPY SPDRs Trust Series 1 - 60 min 10/16/2002 C=86.55 H=0.00 L=0.00

Secondary corrections vary between 38% and 62% of the primary trend.

The Minor/Short-Term Trend

Very simply, minor or short-term trends are a series of three or more "distinguishable" short-term waves that make up an intermediate swing, within either the primary or the secondary trend.

Figure 13.3 shows that the minor trends within the direction of the primary trend have lower lows and lower highs and, conversely, that the minor trends within the secondary trend have higher highs and higher lows.

A trader would generally assume that a minor-trend rally within the scope of a down primary trend would have a high probability of failing and continuing lower, and, thus, minor trend retracements in the secondary trend would have a high probability of failing and continuing higher.

A trader must also be aware of the primary trend when trading the minor trends. Also in Figure 13.3, one can see that trading minor waves in the direction of the secondary trend holds greater risk, as the primary trend can resume at any time.

The Theory Compares the Ocean's Tide and the Market's Trend

"The tide, the wave and the ripple represent, respectively, the primary or major, the secondary or intermediate, and the minor trends of the market."

"THE DOW THEORY", TECHNICAL ANALYSIS OF STOCK MARKET TRENDS, 7TH
EDITION ROBERT EDWARDS AND JOHN MAGEE

Though this may be a bit trite, it's nonetheless apropos of market trends in their various states of importance. If we take a close look at the market's primary trend, it is similar in respect to the ocean's tide. The bullish market can be compared to a rising tide, where the waves continue to push further up the beach each time the water rises until a high tide sets in. The reverse is true for a bearish market or an ebb tide, where the ocean's tide continues to recede, and each push of waves onto the beach falls short of the mark of the last preceding wave.

The intermediate or secondary trend is compared to waves. Each wave is an intermediate trend, either primary or secondary depending on whether its movement is with or against the direction of the tide. And, finally, a minor trend, the shortest type of trend, can be likened to the surface water being constantly agitated by wavelets, ripples, and "cat-paws" moving with or against or across the trend of the waves.

FIGURE 13.3

The dashed lines on this chart indicate the primary trend of the market. The dotted lines indicate the secondary trend, which is considered a corrective price retracement within the primary trend. The solid lines on this chart indicate minor trends, which are typically a series of shorter-term waves that occur within both the primary and secondary trends. See Figure 13.4 for a 15-minute-time-frame example detailing a segment from Figure 13.3. Credit: TradeStation.com.

SPY SPDRs Trust Series—60-Minute Chart Primary Trend, Intermediate Trend, and Minor Trends

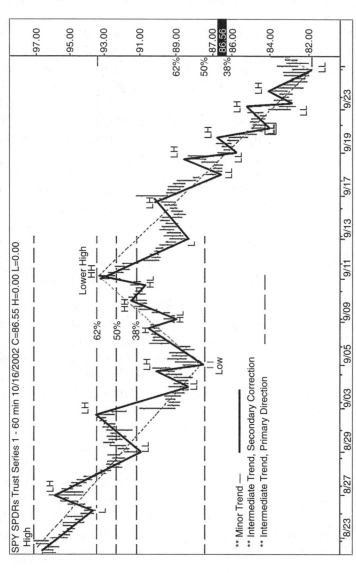

FIGURE 13.4

This example shows a segment of the intermediate trend from September 12 to September 25, 2002, detailing the minor trend with a series of lower lows and lower highs. Credit: TradeStation.com.

SPY SPDRs Trust Series—15-Minute Chart The Minor Trend

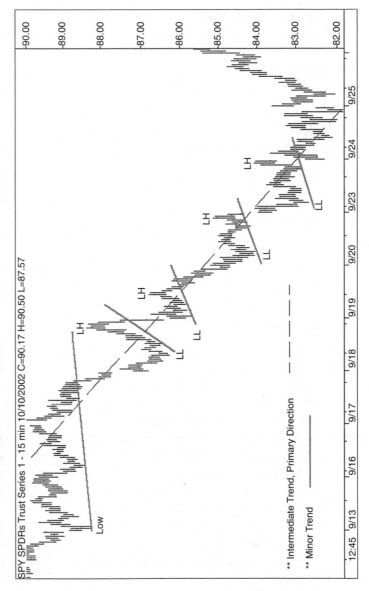

SPY SPDRs Trust Series 1 - 15 min 10/10/2002 C=90.17 H=90.50 L=87.57

** Intermediate Trend, Primary Direction

** Minor Trend

Tools of the Trade for Today's Technical Chart Analyst

> *"Like a carpenter who uses blueprints and a wide assortment of tools to properly build a house, a trader also needs the proper tools to do his job correctly. A trader uses these tools to determine recognizable chart patterns and spot trends across multiple time frames as short as a one-minute chart or as long a weekly chart."*
>
> "THE DOW THEORY", *TECHNICAL ANALYSIS OF STOCK MARKET TRENDS, 7TH EDITION* ROBERT EDWARDS AND JOHN MAGEE

Pivot highs and pivot lows are important chart points. The time frame the trader watches will determine that chart's pivot high or low. Twenty-day highs and lows are considered important chart points, as well as weekly highs and lows for showing major chart point support and resistance levels. A basic example is shown in Figure 13.1, in which each high/higher high and low/lower low are pivot highs and lows.

Regarding retracement levels, today's charting program trend-line tools allow the trader to plot a "support/resistance"; these are 38-50-62 percent lines plotted on the chart from significant highs and lows. (Figure 13.2 shows the use of these retracement levels.)

Patterns, Volume and Confirmation

The trader's toolbox includes a good variety of tools, and they can be used in combination or individually. Some are used more than others. The theory considers trading volume and its relationship to price, indexes and their relationship to each other, reversal and confirmation patterns, and chart patterns to help analyze the trend. In later charts, we'll put all of these tools into play, but initially, let's take the four of them one at a time.

You've heard that *"volume goes with the trend,"* and it's true. Trading volume is one of the best tools to help confirm a trend, but also is one of the more misunderstood areas of technical analysis. In a bullish trending market, as prices rise, volume activity increases to confirm the advance in prices for the direction of the primary trend. The reverse is true for a bearish trending market. As prices decline, volume will rise to confirm the bearish trend. In a secondary correction of a bullish trend, prices decline against the primary trend and volume typically dries up. In a bearish trend, secondary recoveries or rallies in price will see the same decrease in volume. (Figure 13.5 shows this very vividly.)

FIGURE 13.5

This figure shows a detailed view of how volume "goes with the trend." The increased volume with the primary trend is shown between points A and B and between points C and D. Volume dries up on its secondary reaction (B to C). Credit: TradeStation.com.

SPY SPDRs Trust Series—Daily Chart Volume as an Indicator

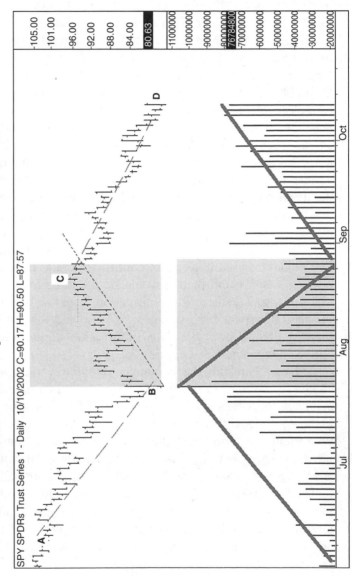

"Lines may substitute for secondaries." A *line* in terms of the Dow theory is considered a sideways movement in which prices trend in a narrow range for an extended period of time. For instance, a daily chart may trend sideways in a line from as little as 2 weeks to as much as 3 months. If using a shorter-term time frame, a 15-minute chart, for example, the time frame of the line would be hours sideways in a narrow range. The longer and narrower the line is, the greater the possibility for a more substantial breakout. Lines may occur at tops or bottoms, but typically they take place during consolidation areas in the progress of an established primary trend. A line may form in lieu of a normal secondary reaction. One average, the NASDAQ for example, may form a line while the S&P has a normal secondary reaction. A breakout up through the line is bullish, and a break down though the line is bearish. It's hard to predict in most cases the direction of the breakout of the line in advance. (See Figure 13.6.)

"The two averages must confirm." This theory was based upon the primary industrials average and the railroad average around the turn of the century. The present day primary indexes are the Dow, S&P, and NASDAQ, and are used in terms of confirmation and nonconfirmation of the primary trend. Confirmation would be the three indexes all making new highs or lows together. Nonconfirmation would be one index not confirming the other two. For example, the Dow and the NASDAQ make new highs and S&P does not. Nonconfirmation of indexes is also called a "price divergence." (See Figure 13.7.)

Then there are the continuation and reversal patterns. *"A trend should be assumed to continue in effect until such time as its reversal has been definitely signaled"* is perhaps one of the most important lynchpins in the entire Dow theory. Many a trader has heard the phrase "the trend is your friend" or "don't buck the trend." Therefore, a trend with momentum has a greater probability of continuing, as opposed to failing and reversing sharply. Some examples of continuation patterns are bull flags, bear flags, bull pennants, bear pennants, and rising and falling wedges. Some examples of reversal patterns are broadening, head and shoulders, and double tops and bottoms. These will be discussed in greater detail in a subsequent article. (See Figure 13.8 for a continuation pattern and Figure 13.9 for a reversal pattern.)

Basic Examples of the Dow Theory at Work

Figures 13.10, 13.11, and 13.12, will show how the reader could improve his market timing using the concepts we have discussed.

FIGURE 13.6

The thick black line crosses through almost all of the bars in a sideways line, indicating a narrow range on the time frame that lasted from early November 2001 until early June 2002. The eventual breakdown from the "line" was a bearish signal that led to an eventual loss of nearly 20 percent of its value in less than two months. Credit: TradeStation.com.

SPY SPDRs Trust Series—Weekly Chart The Sideways Line

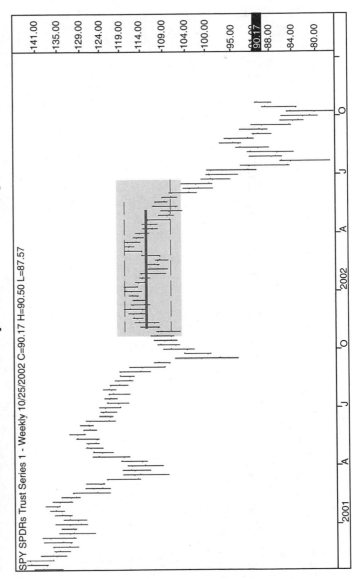

SPY SPDRs Trust Series 1 - Weekly 10/25/2002 C=90.17 H=90.50 L=87.57

213

FIGURE 13.7

This daily chart shows that the new lows in the QQQ were not confirmed by the SPY and DIA, as they made higher lows. Credit: TradeStation.com.

SPY SPDRs, QQQ, and DIA—Daily Chart Confirming Averages

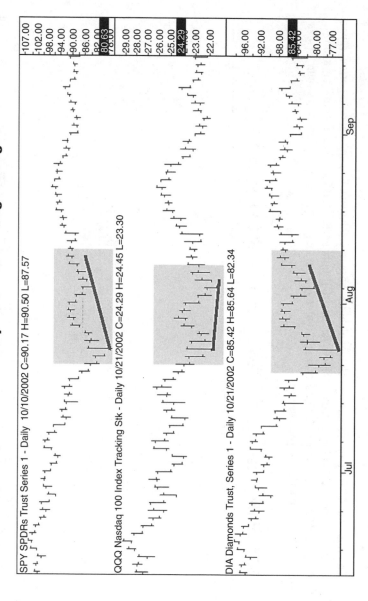

FIGURE 13.8

These continuation patterns, also considered "secondary and minor trends," confirm the direction of the primary trend. The figure shows a rising wedge at point A and a bear flag pattern at point B.

Credit: TradeStation.com.

SPY SPDRs Trust Series—Daily Chart Continuation Pattern

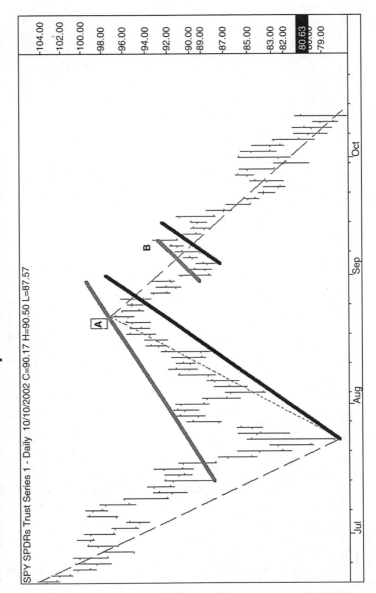

SPY SPDRs Trust Series 1 - Daily 10/10/2002 C=90.17 H=90.50 L=87.57

FIGURE 13.9

A head-and-shoulders (H&S) pattern is a reversal pattern and can be used for both tops and bottoms of a trend. H&S patterns forecast a measured move, for a topping pattern, using the high of the head (in this case using 97.15), subtracting the value of the neckline (93.50), with the resulting number, in this case, 3.65. Subtracting that number from the neckline will give a "measured move" objective; in this case, it is 89.85. Credit: TradeStation.com.

SPY SPDRs Trust Series—60-Minute Chart Head-and-Shoulders Pattern

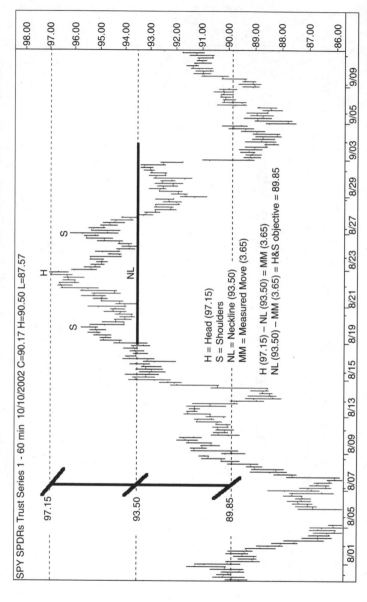

SPY SPDRs Trust Series 1 - 60 min 10/10/2002 C=90.17 H=90.50 L=87.57

H = Head (97.15)
S = Shoulders
NL = Neckline (93.50)
MM = Measured Move (3.65)

H (97.15) − NL (93.50) = MM (3.65)
NL (93.50) − MM (3.65) = H&S objective = 89.85

FIGURE 13.10

This figure shows the larger-term primary trend from May 2002 to October 2002. The dashed lines indicate that the primary trend was down, and the dotted line indicates that the secondary trend was up. Figures 13.11 and 13.12 illustrate an even more detailed view of this chart. Credit: TradeStation.com.

SPY SPDRs Trust Series—Daily Chart Larger Picture of Primary Trend from May 2002 - October 2002

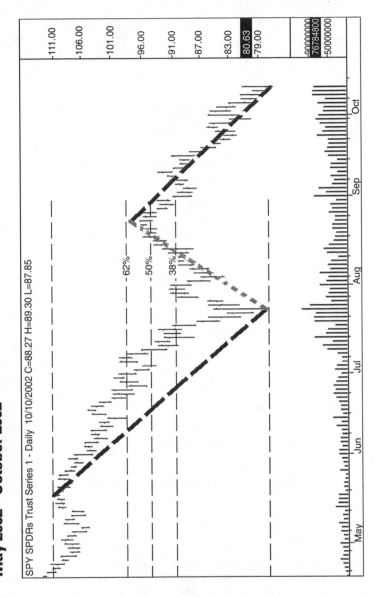

SPY SPDRs Trust Series 1 - Daily 10/10/2002 C=88.27 H=89.30 L=87.85

Putting It All Together

By combining a few tools, such as a retracement zone of 38 to 62 percent, volume, a bearish chart pattern, and a shorter-term reversal pattern, the trader will have an easier time of effectively timing the market turning points with increased accuracy, or it will allow him to enter into the direction of the trend properly once the market turns in favor of the primary trend again.

In Figure 13.11, the letters "A" through "C" illustrate chart points from which the chart reader can take away a wealth of information. A reference to each chart point with the notes below will help give the reader a detailed breakdown, based on the tenets of the Dow theory.

A few notes on Figure 13.11:

- "A" to "B" is a secondary correction against the primary trend; "B" to "C" is an intermediate trend in the direction of the primary trend.

- "A" is an important "pivot low"; leading to that low, there was increased volume that confirms the primary trend, and the price low also had the highest volume day in months.

- "B"—Market retraces up to around the 50 percent retracement level of its previous secondary trend high.

- "A to B" shows a rising wedge pattern (from Figures 13.8 and 13.11), and the highlighted area "B" is a head-and-shoulders topping pattern on a 60-minute chart (from Figures 13.9 and 13.12).

- "C" shows the retest of the pivot low, support from "A."

- "D"—Volume increased into pivot low "A," subsequently dried up as prices rose into "B," and again increased as prices tested into "C."

- "H-1" shows a segment of the primary trend, as originally detailed in Figures 13.1, 13.2, and 13.3.

It would be a massive undertaking to give a chart example and an explanation for each and every rule of the Dow theory. My intention, though an abbreviated one, was simply to give an overview of the Dow theory and to educate the reader on its basic concepts, as well as to give various examples of some of these rules and show how they can be applied in multiple time frames. In essence, these principles should assist traders in their chart analysis. Credit for the analysis of these time-tested technical principles is given to *Technical Analysis of Stock Trends*, 7th edition, by

FIGURE 13.11

This chart pulls a number of the pieces of the Dow theory together and details how the various tools are used to help confirm the trend and reversal zones. (Also see Figure 13.12, showing reversal patterns on a shorter-term time frame.) Credit: TradeStation.com.

SPY SPDRs Trust Series—Daily Chart Putting the Tools Together

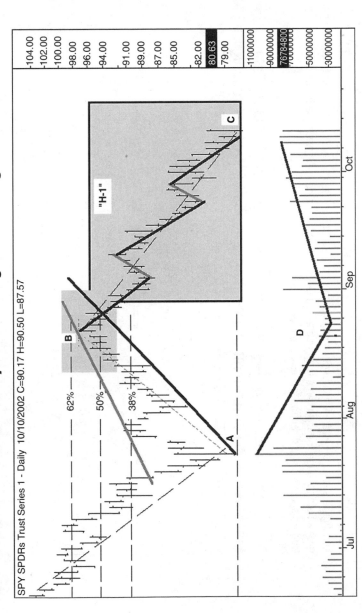

219

FIGURE 13.12

This figure shows a head-and-shoulders topping pattern, a reversal pattern, on a shorter-term 60-minute chart. Combine this with a rising wedge (bearish) on a larger time frame—daily—and see how the two time frames and patterns mesh to give traders some market direction. Credit: TradeStation.com.

SPY SPDRs Trust Series—60-Minute Chart Head-and-Shoulders Pattern (from Figure 13.9) Combined with Larger-Term Chart Pattern and Rising Wedge (from Figure 13.8)

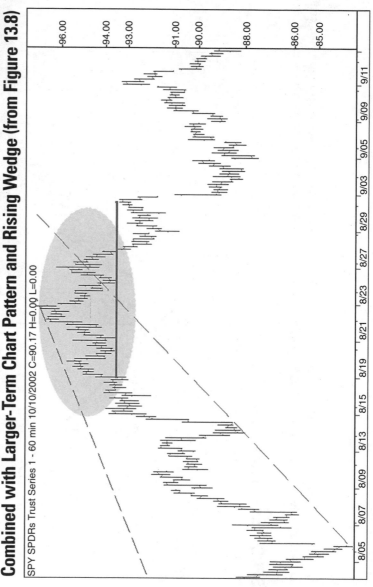

SPY SPDRs Trust Series 1 - 60 min 10/10/2002 C=90.17 H=0.00 L=0.00

Robert D. Edwards and John Magee, the book that outlines "the Dow theory." These theories serve for the basis of my trading and for the trading of countless others.

In closing, readers should understand that before applying any of these concepts and risking trading capital, they must have a full understanding of the tools they are using, the time frame or frames involved, and a feel for market conditions. Armed with that knowledge, they should have a considerably easier time making sense of their charts and what those might portend.

(This article includes text from "The Dow Theory" from Technical Analysis of Stock Trends, 7th Edition by Robert Edwards and John Magee.)

GET A JUMP ON NEW TRENDS BY IDENTIFYING MARKET TURNING POINTS (NOVEMBER 2002)

By Clif Droke

An integral part of trading the markets is the ability to locate and trade off of "pivot points" in stock charts. The object of trading in stocks and stock futures for the average trader is to realize capital gains by following price trends. Price trends in technical analysis are identified in a number of ways utilizing a variety of technical tools, most notably the trend line. But equally as important for the stock or index trader is the identification of significant turning points, or pivot points, when price trends reverse course and change from up to down, or from down to up. Your chances of profiting from stock price trends will be greater if you can quickly identify these turning points and jump on board just as the new trend is beginning. In this article, we'll be focused on two basic, yet extremely effective, ways of finding pivot points in stock charts.

A pivot point, classically defined, is the price at which the direction of price movement changes. [Gopalakrishnan, Jayanthi, "Pivot Points," *Technical Analysis of Stocks & Commodities,* copyright 2001]. By looking at the high, low, and closing values of a stock's price, you can calculate the next day's (or hour's) pivot point as well as identify potential support and resistance levels.

Potential (as distinguished from actual) pivot points can be easily seen on stock charts by even casual observers. It is important to note this distinction, because if all potential pivot points became actual changes of trend, then anyone could make money in stock trading easily. As anyone experienced in this business knows, nothing comes easy when dealing with stocks. Therefore, it will do well to keep in mind that most potential pivot points are just that—just dips or blips on the price chart until an actual trend reversal takes place.

Shadowing the "Masters"

The great trading past masters, including W. D. Gann, Richard Wyckoff, et al., always emphasized the importance of beginning stock price analysis with the longest time frame possible (within reason). For instance, if your objective in trading stocks is the very short term (defined as a few days to as many as 3 months), you will be tempted to ignore the longer-term time frames in stock charting. This is a normal reaction among traders, yet one that has led to a great many downfalls and missed profits. Let's pick a random stock as an example, one that few have ever heard of, yet one that has a reliable trading history and adequate liquidity. For this article we chose Aviall, Inc. (AVL: NYSE), an airplane manufacturer. Aviall is a rather low-priced stock, yet not so low that it classifies as a "penny" stock or micro-cap. It actually has a small institutional following and is fairly reliable for trend-following purposes as well as short-term swing trading.

The Presidential Cycle

It is this author's personal opinion (bolstered by experience) that the starting point for this type of stock trading should go back at least 4 years. I am a firm believer that the 4-year, or "presidential," cycle should be the starting point for short-term support/resistance and pivot-point analysis, since it is always important to know where a stock stands within the context of the 4-year cycle. All stocks respond to this emphatic cycle to some degree or another, and it is probably the smallest of all long-term cycles that has great significance to most actively traded stocks. Since the 4-year cycle bottoms in late 2002, let's go back to the previous 4-year bottom in late 1998. In doing so, we bring up the 4-year weekly chart of Aviall (Figure 13.13), and already we see some things worth noting.

First, notice in Figure 13.13 where Aviall bottomed (point A) in the previous 4-year cycle bottom in 1998 (November is typically when the 4-year

FIGURE 13.13

Aviall, Inc. [AVL: NYSE], Aug. 1998–July 2002

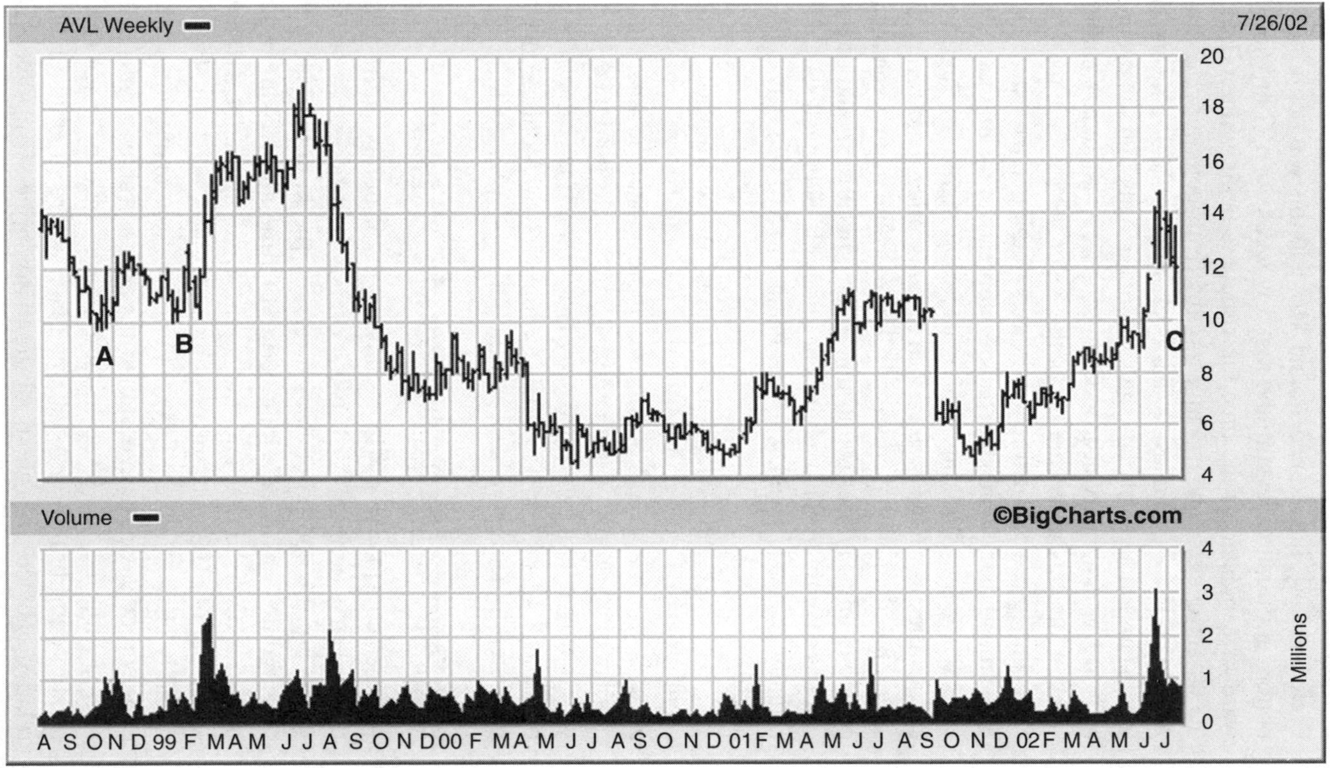

AVL Weekly ▬   7/26/02

©BigCharts.com

Volume ▬   Millions

cycle bottoms). It bottomed around $10, and this was confirmed by a double bottom at this same level in the first few weeks of 1999 (point B). Fast-forward 4 years later. At the time this article is being written (late July 2002), the 4-year cycle is about 3 to 4 months from bottoming, and notice where Aviall is relative to the last 4-year cycle floor of $10. It's very close to testing that important level once again (point C). Although Aviall currently trades near $12, it came very near to testing the $10 benchmark earlier during the week in late July and is not out of the water yet, as there may still be another decline to test $10 before a bottom is in. Notice the extremely heavy volume around the $14 area that had developed over the previous several weeks, even as Aviall was making a run on its 3-year highs. This high-volume reversal qualifies as a pivot point, since Aviall's price trend reversed below $14 after a failed attempt at crossing it. The extreme trading volume that accompanied it only confirms the turning point. This area should be marked on the chart as a legitimate pivot point, since not only did Aviall stall at this area, but actually reversed as well. A further decline to $10 will only confirm the pivot at $14.

The fact that Aviall has a history of declining into the final few months of the 4-year cycle (known as the "hard down" phase in cycle parlance) is worth noting. Not only was there a steep decline from the second quarter of 1998 to when the last 4-year cycle bottomed later that same year, but Aviall also declined heavily into the final 2 quarters of 1994, the previous 4-year cycle. True to its trading history, Aviall is once again being pressured under the influence of the falling 4-year cycle.

Don't Forget the Less Obvious Reversals

Another consideration when studying pivot points is this: Not only are those clearly-defined "V-shaped" reversals considered as pivot points, but so too are the not-too-obvious reversals, the kind that can only be noted when going back over a long period of time and looking at levels where price has reversed time and time again. Once again, the $10 level takes on added significance as a pivot point in Aviall. Take a look at the 10-year monthly chart (Figure 13.14), and notice how many times price reversed either up or down, or else stalled for considerable lengths of time, when approaching the $10 level. In fact, a case could be made that $10 is the level of equilibrium for Aviall, the place where supply and demand are in relative balance. Just about all the major price swings have come off of $10 over the past decade.

FIGURE 13.14

Aviall, Inc. [AVL: NYSE] 1994–July 2002

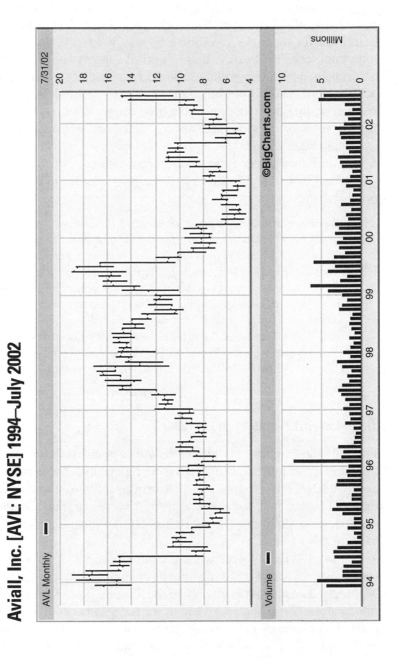

So now that Aviall is currently under pressure beneath its most recent price pivot of $14 and apparently is headed for another test of $10, it will be critical for the trader to observe how Aviall reacts upon reaching this important technical level. A failure to find support above $10 (preferably accompanied by heavy volume) should be viewed as a potential point for selling short, and an outright failure of $10 to hold in the weeks and months leading up to the November time frame should be treated as a confirmed sell short entry point. Thus $10 becomes an important pivot point in Aviall once again.

The famed trader Jesse Livermore made note of the importance of going back over the past history of a stock in order to locate its pivotal points when he wrote:

> *"It is when you set down prices in your [chart] and observe the patterns that the prices begin to talk to you. All of a sudden you realize that the picture you are making is acquiring a certain form. It is striving to make clear a situation that is building up. It suggests that you go back over your records and see what the last movement of importance was under a similar set of conditions. It is telling you that by careful analysis and good judgment you will be able to form an opinion. The price pattern reminds you that every movement of importance is but a repetition of similar price movements, that just as soon as you familiarize yourself with the actions of the past, you will be able to anticipate and act correctly and profitably upon forthcoming movements."*

> How to Trade Stocks, Jesse Livermore

Trend-Line Breakouts as an Identifier

Probably the simplest way to identify pivot points is to use some form of the basic trend-line breakout. This is technical analysis in its purest sense and, when performed properly, will bring profits to a trader more times than not. Of course, the classical trend-line penetration method requires patience and discipline, virtues that all too many traders lack. Let's explore this method.

Using Aviall's 4-year weekly chart (Figure 13.15), we have drawn four basic trend lines off its all-time price high of July 1999 at around $19. Major price peaks should always be the starting point for long-term trend-line analysis. From the long slide in mid-1999 into 2001, we can draw at least three distinctive downward trend lines, all starting from the 1999 high. Granted, there may be slight variations in how one trader draws a trend line compared to another, but the rule that should be followed by all is (a) start with the highest point in terms of price, and (b) connect as many

FIGURE 13.15

Aviall, Inc. [AVL: NYSE]—Trend Lines from All-Time High

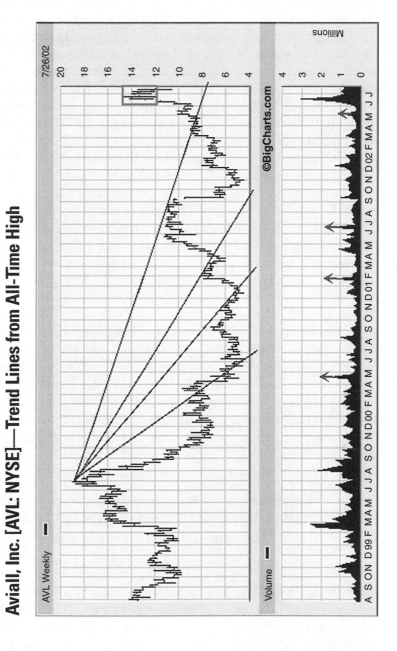

secondary highs as you can; the greater the number of times the price line touches the trend line without breaking it, the more legitimate it is.

From 1999 through January 2001, Aviall traced out what is known in technical parlance as a triple or "fan-line" retracement, breaking through three consecutive declining trend lines. It is important to note that each time a trend line was broken, there was a conspicuous increase in trading volume, which is essential for confirming a trend-line breakout. These trend-line breakouts and high-volume spikes, when taken together, constitute pivot points.

A fourth trend line can also be drawn off the 1999 high to the trend-line penetration in March-April 2002, which was also accompanied by a volume spike. From there, Aviall rallied impressively up into early July before meeting with heavy resistance around $14 and then reversing. As we mentioned earlier, the $14 area also constitutes a pivot point based on the trend reversal and extremely heavy trading volume. All that remains for the trader to watch is how Aviall responds between its current price and the critical $10 pivot. How Aviall responds to this pivot point will likely be the basis for how it trades for the remainder of 2002.

Pivot-point analysis also works equally well for stock indexes, the widely followed S&P 500 being one such example. Note the pivot point at the 1050 area in the SPX chart (Figure 13.16). The S&P tested this important pivot twice between November 2001 and May 2002 before eventually falling beneath it in June. The fact that this pivot was violated provided a strong indication that the short-term trend had turned down sharply for the S&P.

In a nutshell, this is really what pivot-point analysis is all about— locating significant chart areas and trend reversals and observing how price responds to these levels and to previous trend reversal areas.

SANITY CHECK: USING CHANNELS OFFERS REALITY FOR PRICE TARGETS (OCTOBER 2002)

BY BARBARA ROCKEFELLER

Some things never change, or at least they shouldn't. Whenever you buy a security, you should have a price target before you pick up the phone. You should have a stop-loss limit, too. Then you need the courage of your convictions to actually execute the other side of the trade—the sale—according to your plan. Buying is easy and selling is hard, and that's because we tend not to formulate an exit strategy in advance.

FIGURE 13.16

S&P 500 Index (October 2001 to September 2002)

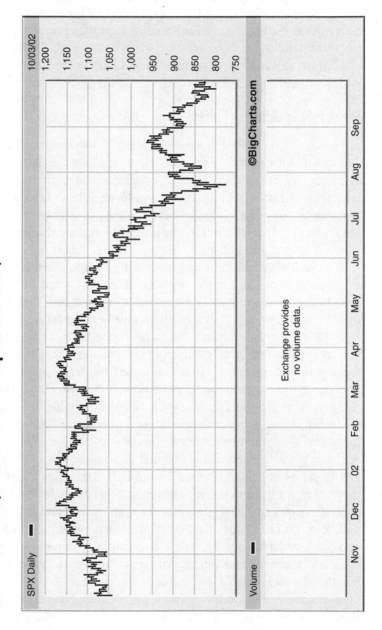

©BigCharts.com

The key excuse for not having an exit strategy is a lack of tools to make realistic estimates of the probable upper and lower price limits that a security is likely to reach. Forecasting securities prices is as complex and (so far) unattainable as forecasting the weather and, for the same reason, has too many variables that change too fast. People throw up their hands in despair and say, "Nobody can forecast the price."

We're Not Looking for Perfect

This is a cop-out. Just because we can't forecast the price perfectly doesn't mean that we shouldn't try to make a realistic estimate. The estimate will always be a work in progress that requires revision. That's why they call it "work." Just as it would be silly to forecast a tornado in Iceland, we shouldn't forecast that Security X is going to triple over the next 3 weeks. It might, but it's improbable in the extreme. So how much is realistic and probable?

A useful technique is to look at a trend-line channel on a chart. Not every security has an identifiable trend line at all times, but usually we can eyeball the recent moves and imagine the trend line. Better yet, we can draw one and extend it out hypothetically into the future.

Linear regression channels can be applied to any price series, whether it is an index, a futures contract, or an individual stock. We tend not to apply them to options prices, but that's because historical options prices are hard to come by (or expensive unless you collect data yourself). There is no reason a linear regression and its channel can't be applied to options prices or any other series. A linear regression is a pure trend line—pure because no judgment is required to calculate it—only to pick a logical starting point. And while a linear regression channel is a valuable tool for picking profit and stop-loss targets, it is not a crystal ball. The outer limits are often not met, or (as we'll see in this article's examples) exceeded by a little. The linear regression channel is general and rough, not precise and specific. But it will help you keep your sanity by providing perspective when you feel that you don't understand price action. Sometimes you get a surprise, too. You think a new uptrend is in place until you try to draw a channel—only to find that the old downtrend is still the dominant pattern.

Before looking at the examples presented, let me say that you don't have to go hog-wild for all the folderol of technical analysis. Charting has a bad name in some circles because a few practitioners promise too much for it—multiyear cycles and the like. There is sometimes an air of religious fanaticism about the field, not to mention the specialized lingo, which is annoying. But there is no inherent conflict between fundamental and technical analysis. Don't be misled. They are both just tools. A stock is not the company—the stock is what the market says it is. So instead of measuring where a security "should" go on its true value, why not look at what the market is saying about it? The price action on a chart can speak volumes about what the market really thinks in the only way that counts—are they buying or selling?

Lines Aren't Fancy

Let's accept that a trend line can be identified. In Figure 13.17 showing the QQQ, we drew a gray trend line from the September 21, 2001, low, which was the obvious low within a few days of the date. We drew it using a linear regression, which sounds fancy but is nothing more than the straight line that minimizes the distance between itself and every closing price in the selected data.

We know from experience and common sense that a flat trend line (nearly horizontal) means the market doesn't have a strong view of the security. Buyers are not so numerous and determined that they are driving the price up. When the line is upwardly sloping, as it is in the gray line from the 9/21/01 low, buyers are overwhelming sellers. They are hot to trot. They are demanding as much as the market will supply and are not discouraged by higher prices.

Up to a point. By the first week of December, they want to take profit on their winning positions, now up 59 percent from the lowest low to the highest high. The price starts to drop as sellers overwhelm the latecomers to the party. Another effort to rally fails, and the price starts to deteriorate. On February 19, it opens gap down from the close the day before and, at the same time, it breaks the channel line.

What is this channel line? Clearly it is a line drawn parallel to the linear regression line in the center. Formally, we say it is drawn two standard errors away from the linear regression. As with a standard deviation, this means that the probability of a price falling outside of the channel is very, very low—less than 5 percent. It is statistically abnormal for the price to exceed the channel by this much. It is an extreme. Therefore, it means something. We don't know exactly what it means sometimes, but we do know that market sentiment has changed if the price goes beyond the line.

We are going to name it a "downside breakout," since it broke the trend-line channel to the downside (see, not all specialized lingo is obnoxious). If we had been drawing this channel at the end of every day to incor-

FIGURE 13.17

Data courtesy of Reuters Data Online.

QQQ [NASDAQ 100], June 2001–August 28, 2002

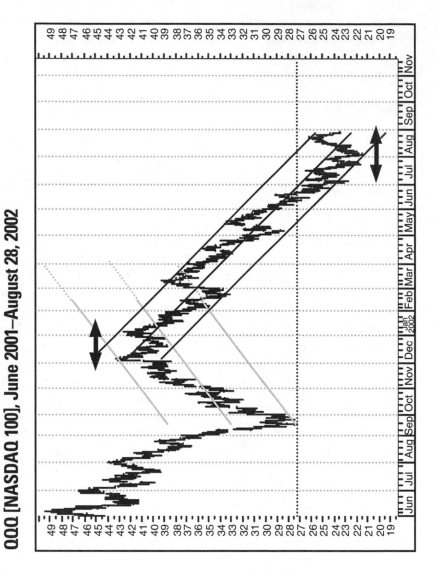

porate today's new price data, we would know exactly where the breakout would occur if one were going to occur. In fact, we would have placed our stop-loss limit at that level and, in this instance, exited a long position.

This gives us a clue to start a new downtrending linear regression and its accompanying two-error channel, this time in black. We start the new channel at what, in retrospect, was the highest high. The price will vary up and down within this channel, but almost never exceed the channel lines by much or for long. Notice that this security made several efforts to break out to the upside—but always fell back.

Then near the end of July and during the beginning of August, we got two lows at about the same level—termed a "double bottom." Suffice it to say that everybody in the universe who looked at this chart saw what looked like a double bottom forming. This pattern predicts a rise, or at least people thought so. The old low was surpassed only a little, and there was no new low after that. They figured, "If you can't sell it, buy it."

The resulting rise produced mostly higher highs and higher lows, the definition of an uptrend. On August 22 (see Figure 13.18), the high rose over the top of the black channel, and it looked like a real rally might be starting. So we drew a new gray linear regression channel from the most recent low and extended it out by hand into the future using dotted lines. This shows that if that channel were the correct new trend channel, we could expect to see a high of about $30 by mid-September. Alas, the "breakout" of the black channel lasted only one day before prices fell back into the black channel. In addition, by August 28, the price had penetrated the bottom of the gray channel. If we were still hoping against hope that this was a real upside breakout, for the price to fall below the bottom of the channel, it should have been the wake-up call not to delude ourselves any longer.

None of the breakouts of the downtrending channel were the real thing. Until we get a valid one, we can use the channel to identify the probable high and probable low going out several days and sometimes weeks. But when a channel is new, it's not stable. You need at least one touch of the top of the channel and at least one touch of the bottom of the channel to have confidence that the range is now a valid estimate. In this case, we have a stable channel that has many touches. The charts indicate that the next move is downward—and we know the maximum move downward, too.

No Excuses

The existence of the linear regression channel leaves us with no excuses for failing to set profit targets and stop losses. This case happened to be neat

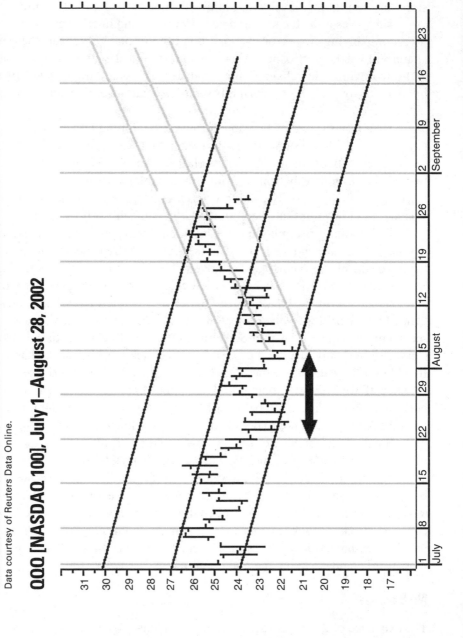

FIGURE 13.18

Data courtesy of Reuters Data Online.

QQQ [NASDAQ 100], July 1–August 28, 2002

and tidy, and that is unusual. There are a number of things that can go wrong using channels. You can start and stop them in the wrong place, for example. The linear regression and standard error channel are tools based on science, but applying them is a craft, if not an art. Using the channels will often get you in too late or out too early—but if you don't know the current probable range, you can't know the probable future range. The purpose of a forecast is not to be perfectly correct—it is to avoid catastrophe.

To use channels, you have to keep in mind that a big news event, whether pertaining to the security itself or the market in general, will always trump the chart. Linear regressions and other tools will catch up to the price action caused by a shock, but with a lag. Very few technical indicators are leading—most of them are lagging. The linear regression channel has both leading and lagging features. As a measurement of the trend, it lags. If we extend the channel out by hand into the future, however, we can see where price is in the process of diverging from the trend by an interesting amount. The human brain has an innate ability to spot when things are alike and when they are different. It's a kind of visual intelligence. The channel helps us make sure that a divergence (or a "breakout") is not a visual delusion.

You wouldn't play a poker hand without some estimate of the probable outcome. We all know that a royal flush will beat a pair. You shouldn't trade securities without having an estimate of the probable outcome, either. At the least, channels are a sanity check. You don't expect a price to double or triple if no channel you can draw will get you there, and you don't hold on to a losing hand after a downside breakout.

CHAPTER **14**

Other Means of Analysis: Looking Beyond the Chart Lines

Bar and line charts are only one form of analysis. Generally, it is best to confirm your outlooks based on technical factors with other analysis or indicators. Marc Gerstein suggests that you confirm your technical analysis with information from fundamental analysis. This can include information such as financial statements and business trends, but fundamental analysis does not end with this information, Gerstein suggests. Behavioral data, or the activities of those in the investment community, can also confirm the movements in price charts, thus boosting your confidence in your trading decisions.

Options can also be a useful indicator of the direction of price movement, if you know how to watch them, according to Lawrence McMillan. For example, you can watch what traders with inside information do with their money in options. McMillan advises, however, that most increases in option trading are due to large daily trades and are *not* necessarily related to corporate events or inside information. More often, increases in option trading are due to a nearing expiration date. Still, both fundamental analysis and options price movement can be used to confirm the direction in which you think the market may move.

In the final article, Kira McCaffrey Brecht reviews how to read the Employment Situation Report, one of the reports many analysts and economists watch, to gauge the direction in which the market may move and the state of the economy in general. According to this article, employment figures reveal people's spending habits as well as investor confidence.

Armed with this information, you can confirm your opinion of which way the market will head.

CONSORTING WITH THE ENEMY: FUNDAMENTAL AND TECHNICAL TRADERS TAKE LESSONS FROM ONE ANOTHER (SEPTEMBER 2002)

BY MARC H. GERSTEIN

I have to make a confession. I'm a fundamental investor. Don't worry, though. I'm not going to pull a Warren Buffett act on you and advocate "forever" as a proper holding period. My idea of long-term stretches are no more than 3 months, based on the corporate reporting cycle, which sets a 3-month ceiling on the shelf life of any item of relevant information. So to my way of thinking, a 5-year investment horizon is really a series of 3-month holding periods that resulted in identical decisions (hold) 15 times in a row, more if, as would probably be the case, relevant information comes out between the ends of quarterly reporting deadlines.

I'm not really here to talk about holding periods. I bring it up only to show that we fundamental types aren't necessarily as stodgy as traders are often led to believe. I may differ in terms of the triggers that cause me to buy or sell, and the way I articulate my goals (along with the related issue of how long I'm willing to wait for them to materialize). But I'm definitely with you when it comes to the importance of staying alert to continuing developments and being willing to turn on a dime if my investment rationale vaporizes. In fact, I recognize the extent to which traders encourage fundamental investors to break free of the "lock-it-in-a-drawer" syndrome.

Actually, your influence on fundamental investing goes way beyond that. Among the things I do when I evaluate a stock is look at charts, not just price and volume, but also moving averages and the rest of the repertoire of indicators that help traders recognize the direction and strength of any trends that might exist. MultexInvestor.com, a site geared toward the fundamental style, includes interactive price charts featuring a wide variety of technical indicators. So, too, do the other fundamentally oriented sites.

The Trend Is Your Friend

I often choose to fight trend, and I have my fair share of success stories in this regard. But I'd have to be crazy to make a decision without knowing what the trend is. After all, stock price movements and all related measures and indicators represent the sum total of the conclusions reached by countless others out there who have studied the situation. And considering how much trading volume nowadays is institutional, chances are that much of this study is the product of far more time and manpower than I can muster on my own.

Examining the charts is like reading reviews before seeing a movie. I ultimately may disagree with the critics, but knowing what they think before I go in provides a useful context for my own viewing experience, especially insofar as it points out to me things (noteworthy scenes, special effects, etc.) I should be watching for. Actually, this example is somewhat hypothetical. Movies are entertainment. I'm often perfectly happy to go in cold even if it means my viewing experience is suboptimal. All it costs me is $15 per person (including refreshments) and a few hours. So the stakes are pretty low.

Investing is a different animal. A lackluster analytic experience that causes me to miss important issues can be far more costly. So I will study the charts, at the very least in order to point me toward the crucial topics of study. (Why did this reversal occur? Why is the stock breaking out now? Why is the support level being established at this price and not some other?)

Fundamentalists Can Offer a Thing or Two

So far, I have presented a one-way street where technical traders influence fundamental investors. But this can actually be a two-way street. Some of our fundamental techniques are relevant to your technical style of analysis. Our approaches won't necessarily show you when to pull the trigger, any more than yours will tell us. But seeing trends through our eyes may help you shed light on issues you face when assessing stock options or the soon-to-commence single stock futures.

Consider the simplified version of the Black-Scholes option pricing model that appears on www.cboe.com (the Cox-Ross-Rubinstein binomial approximation). For equity options, the inputs it seeks are the stock price, the strike price of the option, the option's expiration date, dividend information (amount, date), an assumed interest rate, and the stock's volatility. Most of the information is objectively obvious or subject to a reasonable degree of "forecastability." The challenging aspect of the model is the volatility assumption. Indeed, the on-site documentation cautions users that "professional traders spend a great deal of time and resources developing volatility estimates. In the final analysis, this number is subjective."

Looking at Volatility as a Moving Target

That calls into question the extent to which this model, or other versions requiring comparable input, can serve as a security blanket. Put another

way, telling an option trader that it's easy once you get a reasonable volatility estimate is like telling a fundamental investor that it's easy once you nail
down a correct price/earnings ratio. Data showing historical volatilities is
certainly available (such spreadsheets can be downloaded from the
www.cboe.com site). But volatility changes over the course of time.

Let me use Qlogic (QLGC) as an example in this article. I could use
others, but using one stock will make it easier to track the discussion. By the
way, by using QLGC, I'm not making any—not any—recommendations.
It's just that without a real-life demonstration, examples make no sense.

So, suppose I want to value the Qlogic Aug '02 calls with a strike price
of 45. The most recent volatility spreadsheet, covering May '02, shows this
stock's volatility to have been 90.931. But in April it was 33.839, and in
March it was 41.85. What assumption should I use going forward? If I use
90.391, the call's theoretical price is 1.836. If I switch to a volatility of
33.839, the theoretical price becomes 0.016, and with a volatility of 41.85,
the price jumps back to 0.316. If you download and scan these spreadsheets,
you'll see many stocks with much greater month-to-month variation in
volatility. Obviously, history is a very imperfect guide.

The www.cboe.com tool includes an interesting aid, a volatility estima-
tor. It allows you to work backwards by plugging in a theoretical price and
letting the model tell you what volatility is implied. I plugged the latest (as
of this writing) closing price of 2.40 for the Qlogic option, and the model
tells me that this quote is proper if the stock's volatility is 107.67. Obviously,
documentation's claim regarding subjectivity is right on the mark.

So how might I address the Qlogic option? I notice from the CBOE
Volatility Index that volatilities in general were close in March and April,
moved modestly higher in May, and soared in June and July. The overall
uptrend in volatility makes a case for a Qlogic volatility of at least 107.67,
the number implied in my assessment of the latest option price. But indexes are one thing. Individual observations are something else.

Going back to the CBOE historic volatility data, I notice a lot of
variation in the extent to which individual stocks followed the overall
trend. For example, while volatilities in general were rising between
March and May, some individual stocks marched to their own drummers.
For example, the volatility of JDS Uniphase dropped from 61.616 to
46.791, and Corning's plummeted from 63.181 to 35.201. Even if I'm
willing to assume that the CBOE Volatility Index as a whole will hold its
present high level in the month ahead, what leads me to believe Qlogic
will continue to march in lockstep with the averages, as opposed to going
its own way (as JDS Uniphase and Corning did in the spring)?

Plug in the Fundamentals

Fundamental analysis can help. Note that when I say fundamental analysis, I'm not limiting the field to the sort of classic methods of analyzing corporate financial statements and business trends that investors associate with Graham and Dodd. Although those ideas certainly are still valuable, they are not the be-all and end-all of what I and many other fundamental analysts do.

The modern era presents us with a whole other category of company-related data which can be valuable to those who seek fundamental validation for the work they do analyzing options and the soon-to-commence single stock futures. I refer to this category as behavioral data. It won't necessarily point you toward a forecast of a stock's volatility. It can, however, help steer you toward stocks whose volatilities will more likely than not be high enough to cause the Black-Scholes model to conclude that the current price of the option is attractive. Before going further along these lines, let's see what this behavioral category is all about.

Behavioral data is data that provides a window into the collective thinking of the investment community by examining how they are acting. The best way to grasp this is by considering an example. Let's consider consensus earnings estimates. Suppose I tell you that average Wall Street analysts' estimates for a company's earnings per share (EPS) this year (the consensus estimate) rose in the past month from $1.00 to $1.07. If you think about old-time fundamental analysis, you might imagine revisiting a model and deciding whether a change in the EPS assumption ($1.07 as opposed to $1.00) is big enough to warrant calculating a new target stock price.

When we consider data from a behavioral standpoint, we don't frankly care if the latest consensus EPS estimate is $1.00 or $1.07 or $5.40 or even a loss of $2.50. What we do care about is whether the present number, whatever it may be, is higher than it was in the recent past. By the way, this upward estimate revision is not hypothetical; it reflects a real-world change in how analysts have been assessing Qlogic's earnings potential for the fiscal year that will end in March 2003 (see Table 14.1). I'm not all that interested in knowing that analysts, on average, expect the company to earn $1.07 a share this year. But I am intrigued by the fact that just a month ago they expected the company to earn only $1.00 a share. So, now, I see the present $1.07 estimate as a good thing. If, on the other hand, analysts previously had been expecting Qlogic to earn $1.20 a share, then the $1.07 figure I see today would be a negative factor. In other words, I'm not interested in any particular number per se—only in the way the numbers as a whole work together to help me spot changes in analyst sentiment.

TABLE 14.1

Historical Means Earnings per Share Estimates Trend

In U.S. Dollars			
	As of 7/29/2002	As of Weeks Ago	As of 3 Months Ago
Quarter ending 09/02	0.26	0.24	0.23
Quarter ending 12/02	0.27	0.26	0.25
Year ending 03/03	1.07	1.00	0.97
Year ending 03/04	1.28	1.26	1.24

TABLE 14.2

Earnings per Share Estimates Revisions Summary

	Last Week		Last 4 Weeks	
	Revised Up	Revised Down	Revised Up	Revised Down
Quarter ending 09/02	0	0	18	0
Quarter ending 12/02	0	0	16	0
Year ending 03/03	0	0	18	0
Year ending 03/04	0	0	4	0

In the real-world case of Qlogic, analyst sentiment has changed for the better. And we're not talking about just one or two analysts. Table 14.2 illustrates that 18 analysts raised estimates in the past month (with one having done it as recently as the week of July 22); they also raised estimates for other time periods. They were probably inspired to do this by a "positive surprise" in the June quarter. At the time, the consensus quarterly estimate was $0.23 per share. But Qlogic confounded them. It reported EPS of $0.26. This situation is especially noteworthy considering what Qlogic does; it makes network infrastructure storage products. That sector as a whole has been a mess.

I can't help but add spice to the estimate data by doing a bit of Graham-Dodd and checking some financial ratios (balance sheets, margins, turnover, and returns on capital). When I do that, I see that, generally, Qlogic has been beating its industry averages for a long time.

I haven't gone out and talked with customers, suppliers, and competitors (as if I actually could!). My ratio review took about 10 seconds. I didn't even bother to check relevant industry data, so this isn't exactly hard-core fundamental analysis. But I did use the estimates data to ride piggyback, so to speak, on the efforts of others who did engage in such activities, and I come away with a sense of how I might assess Qlogic's volatility. This can never be a slam dunk, since I'm looking at a call option and prefer to see such volatility as might occur take place on the upside. But if I can satisfy myself that there might be some upward bias in the market in general or, at least, in Qlogic in particular in the coming month, the volatility implied in the recent price of the August call seems acceptable to me. In fact, knowing what I do about the favorable way positive surprises and upward estimate revisions influence stock prices, I can even accept the possibility that Qlogic's volatility might rise above 107.67 if we get some decent (or at least, less rotten) market conditions.

Now please don't be rough on me if, by the time you read this, it turns out that the Qlogic August call expired worthless. Remember, I'm a fundamental guy. My opinion is based on this favorable behavioral data item (upward estimate revision as evidence of improved analyst sentiment based on the latest in-depth company examination). It points me toward a favorable view of the stock, but not necessarily to a belief that the good things will happen quickly enough to make good on an out-of-the-money August call. To address the question of timing, I'd have to borrow from the trader's arsenal of tools and techniques.

Hopefully, though, the estimates data validated by the classic business ratios provide a useful context that can help you interpret your indicators. Looking at the traders' arsenal, I see that a soon-to-expire Qlogic August call appears as a brave course of action, as most indicators are unfavorable. But one indicator, the stochastic oscillator that, as of this writing shows a short-term oversold condition, is aligned with the positive fundamentals. And on four prior occasions in calendar year 2002, when the chart looked very similar (everything except the stochastic pointing south), Qlogic suddenly switched course and rallied. The fundamentals show that these rallies of support in the high 30s were not irrational.

Other Data Can Help Even the Chartists

Even if you are perfectly happy to assess Qlogic based on the charts alone, there is another, perhaps even more important way the data helps you. It can cue you in to the fact that it might be worth your time to consider Qlogic. There are thousands of stocks out there, and you can't look at everything. No matter how great you may be at assessing stocks, either fundamentally or from a trading perspective, you are not likely to succeed if too much of your time is frittered away studying situations that are lackluster or worse.

Stock Screeners Act as a Filter

One way to go is to use stock screeners. These are software applications that sift through databases and create lists of stocks that meet specific tests you create, based on your goals. A requirement that the list be limited to companies for which consensus EPS estimates have been upwardly revised in the past month is an example of a test that can be submitted to a screener. There are, of course, some screeners that are oriented toward technical considerations. But under the two-heads-are-better-than-one theory, you can gain from using a fundamental screener to help you decide which charts you'll want to look at. Screeners are available on the Internet at a variety of price points. You can use NetScreen Pro, Multex's premium application. SmartMoney.com offers a screener that can be very helpful to options/futures traders looking for a fundamental second opinion (about $50 a year). The free MSN.MoneyCentral.com screener, particularly the FYI section (geared toward data items that have experienced recent change), can also provide a helping hand.

Qlogic, the stock used in the example above, would appear on a screening list created by specifying a requirement that estimates be upwardly revised. But if you confine yourself to that single requirement, the list you'd get would probably be unmanageably large. Therefore, you'll often want to add more tests to narrow the field. To make the final list, a stock would have to satisfy each and every one of these tests. If you add a second test requiring that stock's current price be no worse than 10 percent below its 52-week high price, Qlogic would not appear on your screen. In short, your parameters have an effect on the outcome.

The screening angle may be the most interesting way to blend trading and fundamental analysis. You can use stock screens to produce lists of fundamentally strong companies if your trading strategies are such that you benefit from higher prices (i.e., buy call options). Conversely, you can obtain lists of "fundamentally challenged" companies if, for example, you wish to buy puts or sell calls. Either way, you can enhance your probability of success if you can focus your time and effort on lists that are designed to show stocks.

FOR PREDICTING CORPORATE NEWS EVENTS, OPTION VOLUME MEASURES UP AS A TECHNICAL INDICATOR (DECEMBER 2002)

By Lawrence G. McMillan

Option prices and volume can sometimes be used as technical indicators in their own right. That is, one does not necessarily have to be an option trader at all in order to gain some valuable insight from option activity. Once that insight is gained, one could trade the underlying stock if he wanted to (or single stock futures); it would not be necessary to trade the options. In this article, we're going to look at some uses of option trading volume as a way of highlighting what the "smart money" is doing. In particular, when option volume dramatically increases, that may be a clue that "someone knows something." It could be a harbinger of corporate news events—takeovers, earnings surprises, or other significant corporate developments. In addition, it could be a telltale sign of what major momentum players (hedge funds) are doing. We call these situations "volume alerts."

One might rightfully wonder why option activity should be able to predict such things. In the case of momentum trading, it's totally understandable, since momentum traders like to "advertise" what they're doing in order to draw other traders into the same stock. We'll discuss that in more detail later. However, in the case of takeovers, earnings surprises, and so forth, the option market is active because people with (illegal) inside information often trade in advance of the news. They use options because the available leverage can multiply capital quickly on a profitable trade. While their activity may be illegal, it is perfectly legal to look for the footprints of such activity—as you would with any other technical indicator—and trade along with them. Treating options this way is to use them as a direct indicator—not a contrary indicator. Options are useful as contrary indicators when one is observing the activity of the unwashed masses, but, in these cases, we are looking for evidence of insider trading and/or smart money, so we want to go along with them.

Predicting Corporate News Events

We have surely all seen the situation where option activity gets very heated in a stock whose options are not normally very active at all. Perhaps the activity is noticed by the media, in which case a story regarding a takeover rumor might be made public. Occasionally, these rumors turn out to be true, and the stock gaps higher as a takeover bid is made. In a situation such as this, call option activity would be heavy. However, there are also times when put option activity dramatically increases, only to find subsequently that some bad news is released by the company (perhaps an earnings warning). In both cases, someone had information beforehand and traded in the option market to capitalize on that information. This activity is illegal, of course, but the greed of profits sometimes overcomes the better judgment of some traders, and the situation arises.

In order to spot these situations, a trader must do a certain amount of homework. First of all, most situations involving increased option trading volume are not related to upcoming corporate activity. They are often merely large trades conducted in the normal course of trading. For example, an institution may place a large covered call write in a relatively inactive option. That will, of course, generate a "volume alert" to anyone who sees it, but it almost certainly has nothing to do with previous knowledge of an upcoming news event. Or perhaps an arbitrageur established a fairly large position in a stock's options—trading a relatively large quantity of put and calls against the underlying stock.

Again, this increased option activity would have nothing to do with predicting a takeover. Finally, spread traders can be quite active—especially near option expiration day each month—and this may inflate the option volume dramatically as well. Again, it most likely has nothing to do with a news event (for if someone with inside information wanted to profit, he would not bother establishing an option spread). These activities are known as "noise." One has to eliminate the noise if he wants to ascertain the few situations each day where a potential to predict corporate activity exists.

To spot these situations, one simple measure might be to look at situations where total option activity that day in one stock's options more than doubled its average option activity. I use a 20-day average of option volume, but you are free to choose another length average, if you wish. In addition, there should be a minimum activity level—say at least 500 contracts overall. On a given day, there may be 80 or 100 stocks that satisfy these simple criteria. Obviously, most of them do so because of noise. But each must be looked at in order to try to find the few where activity is most likely to be predictive.

The truly predictive situations typically have a common pattern of activity: the near-term options—particularly the at-the-money and just in-the-money options—are most active. Not only that, but the activity propagates out to the other option series. This might be a typical situation.

Assume XYZ is trading at 50, and total daily option volume in XYZ is usually a couple of hundred contracts per day. Also, assume that April is the nearest expiration month. Then, if we saw option activity as shown in Table 14.3, we might conclude that it is possible that a takeover or other corporate news event might lie on the near-term horizon.

You can see that the heaviest activity is in the April 50 call and the April 55 call—the near-term at-the-money call option and the call option that is just out-of-the-money. But, just as important, there is activity in the other series as well. It is important to see activity in the other series. To understand why, consider this. The primary sellers of these options are option market makers or specialists. They are not stupid people. If they feel that the buying is "smart," they will immediately attempt to hedge their sales. That means they will buy up anything else they can find on the book—hence the volume propagates out to the other option series. In addition, these same market makers and specialists will buy the underlying stock if they can't properly hedge themselves with other options. Consequently, an interesting by-product arises: The underlying stock should be rising if there is a serious probability that a true predictive situation exists.

Things would be similar if we were talking about pending negative news and heavy put option activity. But, in that case, we'd expect to see the stock moving down in advance of the news, as market makers and others sold the stock to hedge put sales they made to those with inside knowledge.

While there are other nuances to interpreting this activity, the essence of it has been shown. Look for a sharp increase in trading volume,

TABLE 14.3

XYZ: 50

Strike	April	May	June	July
45	300	100	50	20
50	800	300	100	75
55	600	350	50	
60	200	100		

and make sure that the activity follows a pattern fairly similar to that shown in Table 14.3. If all of the activity is concentrated in just one or two options, then that is probably not a predictive situation. Finally, it is common for the underlying stock to be moving in the direction of the option activity—up if there is heavy call activity or down if there is heavy put activity. If all of these things are in place, then you—as a speculator— should do something bullish if there is heavy call activity. Buy the underlying stock or buy a short-term in-the-money call if the option activity is heavy in the calls.

Alternatively, short the stock or buy a short-term in-the-money put if the option activity is heavy in the puts.

Takeovers have been rare in this bear market, but they will eventually become more frequent. In the 1973–1974 bear market, there were eventually a number of takeovers as companies with good cash positions stepped in to buy companies that had good potential, but were selling at depressed prices. Since there haven't been many takeovers in the current bear market, one might surmise that corporate executives do not think their competitors' stock prices are cheap enough yet. In other words, corporate America may still think stocks are overpriced. They would never admit that in public, of course, but the lack of takeover bids certainly lends credence to the theory. Eventually, though, if the bear market persists, some quality stocks will reach low enough prices to be appealing as takeover candidates. There is a good chance that call option activity will be able to "predict" some of these prospective takeovers.

Detecting Momentum Trades

Predicting corporate news in advance is not the only application of heavy option volume. In addition, it can be useful in spotting what the large momentum players are doing. First, we'll address the situation where call buying is heavy and then look at a similar situation involving put buying.

Momentum trading is the art of "buy high, sell higher" or "sell low, buy lower." It is generally practiced by well-capitalized investors—particularly hedge funds. As mentioned earlier in the article, momentum traders actually want to "advertise" their position, to entice other investors to follow along with them. For example, if the hedge fund has acquired a long position as the stock is breaking out to the upside, they'd want other buyers to follow them and push the stock even higher. Eventually, the momentum trader (who has bought high) will sell his stock to these other buyers, consequently selling higher.

If a stock breaks out to the upside, over a significant resistance level—and perhaps makes a new high in doing so—it is often accompanied by heavy call option volume. That is generally a positive sign, but one other thing is important in these momentum trading situations as well—stock volume. For this purpose, I prefer to use William O'Neill's "up-down" volume indicator. It is a simple indicator, whereby one looks at the last 50 trading days. He sums the stock volume on any day the stock closed up during the last 50 trading days and divides that sum by the sums of stock volume on any day the stock closed down during the 50-day period. Obviously, a reading of 1.0 would be neutral for this indicator, but readings above 2.0 are very positive and indicate that the upside breakout has a good chance of being a true momentum trading situation.

Conversely, there sometimes is heavy put volume, and one's natural reaction is to interpret that as a bearish indicator (perhaps indicating that poor earnings are about to be announced). If that put volume consists of mainly out-of-the-money puts, I have noticed that it doesn't always have predictive value—perhaps because money managers are buying puts for protection. However, if the put volume consists of one or two large blocks of in-the-money puts, then it can often be reliably interpreted as a meaningful negative indicator for the stock. Again, the "up-down" volume indicator can be used for confirmation. In this situation—where we are expecting to see the stock decline—we'd want to see a poor reading from O'Neill's indicator. Readings of 0.8 or lower are poor, and readings of 0.5 or lower show especially negative stock volume patterns in the stock.

There is a strategy that some very large traders use in order to get short stock in a fairly easy manner. Suppose that you had a large amount of capital at your disposal, and you were bearish on the stock, but were having trouble getting an uptick to short the stock. If you could just buy a block of stock and simultaneously buy some in-the-money puts at parity, your problem would be solved. Why? Because you could then just sell your stock, which is long, as sloppily and rapidly as you wanted in the open market. This would leave you with just the long puts, which, of course, would be increasing in value as you pummeled the stock.

After you were done selling your long stock, you would probably have scared other stockholders into selling, so they would be pushing the stock down further and increasing the value of your puts as well. Finally, you could exercise your puts to get short the stock, if you wanted to.

You might say that this all sounds good, but how could the trader just buy stock and buy puts in large size so easily? The answer is that an arbitrageur will take the other side of the trade, in order to earn interest on the credit balance generated by selling the stock and selling the puts. Eventually, when the speculative trader exercises the puts, the arbitrageur will be assigned and his position will disappear. The only remnant will be a large short stock position in the hands of the speculator—and the stock will look "poor" to other traders because it has been sold heavily as the speculator dumped his long stock in a sloppy manner.

Thus, if you notice heavy volume in the in-the-money puts, especially if that volume constitutes the entire open interest of those puts, you can feel fairly certain that someone has established the long stock/long put strategy and is armed to sell stock when he wants. When he begins to sell, you can go along with him by buying puts or shorting the stock. This seller is most likely a momentum trader who, again, wants to advertise his position, and there is no better way to do it than by selling large blocks of stock in a very sloppy manner. This will most certainly attract the attention of other sellers, who force the stock even lower. Eventually, the momentum trader (and you) can cover your short as the other sellers pile onto the stock and drive it down.

Summary

Options are important as a technical indicator, by virtue of their trading volume. In certain situations, traders with inside knowledge of a forthcoming corporate news item are active in the options, and, if we are vigilant, we can spot their activity and trade along with them. In addition, momentum traders often trade options as well. Their increased activity in both the stock and the options can be a good sign for trading in the direction of the stock's momentum.

TRADING THE REPORTS: BE YOUR OWN ANALYST BY UNDERSTANDING THE MONTHLY EMPLOYMENT REPORT
(MARCH 2003)

By Kira McCaffrey Brecht

Whether you've traded futures, stocks, or put money into your 401(k) account, you've surely heard the economic alphabet of the GDP, CPI, PPI, and the ECI, the stuff of financial newscasts. What do all these letters stand for? What do they mean to the economy and the equity futures markets, and how do you trade them? One of the most closely watched and potentially one of the most market-moving economic releases is the monthly employment report. Officially known as the "Employment Situation" report, the Bureau of Labor Statistics (BLS), part of the Department of Labor, releases this mother of all reports on the first Friday of every month. (But, of course, to every rule there is an exception. Every once in a while, the report will be released on the second Friday of the month—if the first week contains a major holiday or is a very short week.)

If you've seen the movie *Trading Places,* with Eddie Murphy, you may remember the scene with all the floor traders huddled around a TV screen, awaiting the outcome of the "Crop Report." Well, it doesn't work exactly like that—but almost. Floor traders, day traders, and position traders do await this report. And, several minutes ahead of the report's release, trading activity in the S&P and Dow futures pits at the Chicago Mercantile Exchange (CME) and the Chicago Board of Trade, respectively, will slow down to only a dull roar. As soon as the big digital clocks flash: 7:30:00, central standard time, the closely watched components of the report—the nonfarm payrolls number, the overall unemployment rate, average hourly earnings, average workweek—all flash across the newswires. Often a roar will emerge in the equity futures pits as traders instantaneously react to the news and, accordingly, adjust positions or take on new positions.

But, now, with the advent of the Internet, more and more individual investors are trading these same equity derivatives contracts from their own homes or offices. The playing field, in terms of access to information and order entry capability, has been leveled, so to speak, with the innovations in technology. Traders have the opportunity to trade off this same information, simply from a screen anywhere—yes, even Hawaii.

Overview of Employment Report

The release of the monthly employment report is considered a crucial piece of economic information to economists and others who gauge the health and activity of the U.S. economy. As the employment data is calculated on a monthly basis and because of the early release date within the month, it is one of the earliest gauges that traders have regarding the previous month's activity. (For example, the report released during the first week of April will contain the March employment data.) Economists rely on the information in the employment report to calculate their estimates of many other indicators, scheduled for release later in the month, including the gross domestic product (GDP) data, industrial production, and personal income reports. This report also is considered to be highly significant because not only does it measure actual labor market conditions, but also because these statistics will play into overall levels of consumer confidence. After all, the more workers that are gainfully employed, the more likely consumers are to spend money, which keeps the economy rolling.

Key Components within the Employment Report

Generally, the first "headline" figure that flashes across the newswire screen is the nonfarm payrolls figure. This reading represents the number of new nonfarm jobs that were created (or lost) in the United States in the previous month. This information is gleaned from the "Establishment survey" conducted by the BLS, for the calendar week including the 12th day of the month. Government workers survey larger businesses in more than 500 industries, not including farming, in every state of the Union to gather data for this portion of the report.

Another key component, of course, is the overall unemployment rate, which is based off the "Household survey" conducted by the BLS. In order to be "counted" as unemployed, according to the BLS, one must be out of work and actively looking for a job. Traders also closely watch the average hourly earnings data in this report. This is considered to be a measure of wage pressure, which can ultimately feed into expectations regarding the overall inflation rate. The average workweek is also included. The report offers a breakdown on the labor market picture, including data on manufacturing employment, construction employment, and mining jobs, as well.

Generally as economic growth begins to slow, the average hours worked will begin to decline, and that tends to be followed by layoffs and a slash in the payrolls rate. This, in turn, will result in a rising unemployment rate. On the flip side, an increase in average hours worked tends to open the door to the hiring of additional workers and a drop in the unemployment rate.

General Equity Futures Reactions to Jobs Data Readings

There are many components within the employment report, and sometimes the markets will actually react in one direction, initially in a knee-jerk response to one of the headlines. But, then, after economists and analysts have had time to digest the actual details of the report, a slightly different picture may emerge.

The general rule of thumb is that a rising unemployment rate is a bearish factor for equity futures, while a declining employment rate is a bullish factor. In general, the thought is that low unemployment is good for the economy and, thus, supportive to the stock market.

Now, let's break down the components of the report further, with a look at the impact from the nonfarm payrolls portion of the data. In general, rising numbers of payrolls (which means that more jobs were created) will cause equity futures to rally, while declining payrolls data (which means jobs were lost) would be considered bearish to the S&P and Dow futures.

Equity- and bond-market players watch the monthly employment release closely, as the components regarding average hourly earnings and average weekly hours worked reflect tightness in the labor markets. This is a factor that the Fed's Federal Open Market Committee (FOMC) monitors closely and factors into its decision making regarding where to set the "target" rate for the short-term interest rates.

You should know, however, that the financial markets tend to place less importance on the overall unemployment rate figure, as that is considered a lagging indicator of economic activity.

Overall, the employment report can actually set the market tone for the month. If the data comes in much stronger than expected or surprisingly weaker than expected, that news can color the market's reactions to other data and events throughout the remainder of the month.

Markets React to Surprises

One of the most important things a novice trader needs to know about the employment report—or any economic or political event—is that markets react the most to unexpected events, or surprises. The S&P or Dow futures contracts will either "scream" higher or plunge lower in the wake of an unexpected surprise in the monthly jobs report.

Days ahead of the report, all the talking heads on Wall Street will be spouting off their various estimates and predictions of what the monthly jobs data will reveal. And, in the days leading up the report, the equity futures markets will factor in the consensus or average estimate. However, come that Friday, if the nonfarm payrolls figure is either substantially higher or lower than expected, that is when you will see the biggest reaction in the futures market, and you as a trader will have to be the most nimble. If the market comes in as expected, sometimes the markets will respond with a type of "ho-hum" reaction and may not even move more than a couple of ticks, because the news was already priced in. However, markets are complex animals (and sometimes they do seem like living, breathing animals that move with a mind of their own!), and the following explains a phenomenon that can occur even if the report comes in as expected.

Buy the Rumor, Sell the Fact

Another characteristic of the S&P and Dow futures markets is that they often will trade according to the "buy the rumor, sell the fact" phenomenon. To the uninitiated, this can sometimes be counterintuitive and, as a result, a market can actually sell off on good news. What, you say? Yes, indeed. Let's say the Wall Street economists are predicting a "bullish" employment report with a healthy 150,000 rise in nonfarm payrolls (What does that component mean exactly? We'll get to that later) and a 0.2 percent decline in the overall unemployment rate to 4.0 percent. In the days heading into the report's release, the S&P market rallies for a couple of days straight—nothing earth-shattering, just decent bullish moves as the market factors in these positive expectations. Then, on Friday morning—boom!—the economists actually got it right and nonfarm payrolls grew by 150,000 and the unemployment rate dropped by 0.2 percent. But, then the market starts to sell off. Hence, the buy-the-rumor, sell-the-fact phenomenon occurs, as traders were "buying the rumor" and bidding the market up ahead of the report's release and, subsequently, "selling the fact" once the Labor Department confirmed the actual news.

Why does this occur? Well, when it does, it usually occurs because the market got a little overly bullish—priced in all the good news, and perhaps even a little more. By then, there were no more buyers willing to push prices to new highs. So, traders took profits on long positions. Sellers gain control, and a short-term move to the downside can be seen. But, overall, these "sell-the-fact" type of reactions tend to be short-lived, and the overall trend in this example—bullish—would quickly regain control. The market would most likely continue on its overall upward path. But, if you are considering trading any of these equity derivatives markets, especially with shorter-term time frames, you'll need to be aware of these types of machinations.

Revisions Can Affect Markets, Too

Beware of the monthly revisions. The BLS at times will upwardly or downwardly revise the nonfarm payrolls figure from the previous month. This is an example of when the "headline" figure could look bullish, but once a trader delves into the details of the report, a revision to the previous month's payroll figure could prove to be overwhelmingly bearish.

This could hold more weight than the initial headlines.

Where to Find Information on Release Date/Prereport Estimates

If you have a software/charting package with a news component, whatever news service is included will offer coverage of this all-important market report. Generally, these news services also will include prereport estimates so you can see what the market is "pricing in." There are many paid web sites that also provide information regarding this and other economic reports. The www.wsj.com site offers an economic calendar. Another paid web site which offers prereport estimates and post-release analysis is www.briefing.com.

The Employment Situation report can be found in its entirety on the Department of Labor's web site at www.dol.gov.

Putting It All Together

The bottom line is that the employment report is a major market mover. When trading equity futures derivatives, you must be aware of the release dates and times of major economic news. Even those traders who strictly trade off the charts—based on technical indicators—need to keep in mind the dates and times that major reports are due out. These reports can spark hefty volatility in prices if they surprise market players with the news.

Novice traders may wish to consider flattening up or booking profits on a position ahead of the report's release, just in case some unexpected volatility occurs. However, to make money, traders do like to see price movement. If volatility is what you seek, look no further than the first Friday of every month.

15

Find Your Trading Style and Your Electronic Trading System

Now you know some techniques that you can use to begin trading, but how do you know that those techniques will work for you and the products you choose to trade? Answer: You have to hone your trading style based on your investment needs. Chris Terry suggests that you can polish your trading style by considering the following: the products you enjoy trading the most, the time frame with which you're comfortable, a time-tested chart pattern and an indicator to confirm what the price tells you, a clear concept of risk, and a profit objective. Once you have considered these, you can begin to develop a trading style that will work for you.

Another step in perfecting your trading style may be finding an electronic trading system that complements that style. Like Chris Terry, Scot Hicks has narrowed down the task of finding an electronic trading system to a few basic steps. According to Hicks, all you have to do is review your objectives and review five attributes of the trading system. After you determine your objectives, Hicks suggests that you research five things in order to find the best trading system: the background of the system developer, the impact of commissions and slippage (in addition to the cost of the system), whether the system includes accurate analysis tools, how much time it will take you to place trades, and whether the system is user-friendly.

THE TRADING GAME: FIND YOUR MATCH (OCTOBER 2002)

By Christopher Terry

When I was asked to write an article for *SFO*, my original thought was to cover some of the more useful technical analysis topics that are so crucial to charting the markets. But as I considered the bigger picture, I felt it should have less to do with technical analysis and more to do with some concepts that merely tie into the technical aspects. Though I will explore various types of stocks that people love to trade, various time frames that can be used, some methodologies, and a few charts, I felt it was important to make an equal balance between personal trading behaviors and the technical side of the market in this article.

We all attempt to play the trading game "correctly," either from buying breakouts or pullbacks, shorting the rallies or fading the gaps, or using our stochastic or MACD indicators and moving averages. That's all fine and good, but the real question we need to ask ourselves is, do we play the *right* game? Does the style we use in our trading really fit our particular profile or personality?

I recently had a pretty frank conversation with one of my close trader friends, Mary, and her "game" is what this article is built around. Mary is quite an intelligent person, but she was really having difficulties making a profit in the markets, buying every gap down, shorting gap ups, taking swing trades, buying bull flags and shorting bear flags, countertrend trading and, also, trading breakouts. She traded anything and everything that she could find, but wasn't having much "luck." She explained to me her criteria for trading, specific trade ideas, why she pulled the trigger to enter, how she placed her stop losses and profit targets, and it all seemed logical to a point. So, how could she lose doing the right thing? Everything sounded right, and yet it turned out to be wrong in her case. Was she over-trading or not trading enough or . . . ?

Of course, there are many others like Mary who want to become good traders and have a rewarding career in this field. And, like her, they do not have a set game plan, a clearly defined road map of what's right for them and what will help them on their journey toward being a successful trader.

Initially, I thought that perhaps there were some very obvious trading errors that I could identify for Mary. I asked myself if it might be possible that Mary was trading NYSE stocks on a 60-minute chart when she should be using a 5-minute chart, and on and on. Each question I asked her led to a series of new questions and, finally (as you'll see), I began to understand what made her tick, what her profile was, and what the "right game" for her was.

Then the light bulb went on—I thought of all the people with whom I have come into contact over the years, and the same identical thread seemed to run through the middle of each of them—that is, they clearly did not know what questions to ask themselves in a very introspective manner to determine what their particular style or game was. Without that, they continued to make errors that could blight what might be a successful relationship with the markets.

As a trader and mentor, I have stayed very close to the trading community over the years. For the last few years, I've been a moderator for a stock chat room that allows me to learn each day what other traders' profiles and personalities are and what makes them tick. I've also been a speaker at various seminars and workshops and, because of that exposure, I've had the good fortune to speak to and learn from those that are "hungry" and willing to travel long distances to become educated about trading. I also make it a point to keep a close watch on the pulse of what traders think.

I previously worked as an assistant to one of the largest stock traders in the nation and currently am a full-time professional trader who has been personally mentored by a New Market Wizard. In fact, I am a partner with that individual. Thus, it might appear that I had it easier than the next person. However, I am no different than Mary in many respects. I have stood in her shoes. I have gone through the same type of growing pains that many traders do. I have questioned my talents and abilities many times, and I chased my tail for years until I found what the right game for me was.

Pablo Picasso, Spanish painter and sculptor, generally considered the greatest artist of the twentieth century, created more than 20,000 works. That does not mean, however, that anybody could use Picasso's brushes and be as great an artist. Just because someone sits at Liberace's piano does not mean he or she will be able to play like Liberace. They had their game, their style, and what works for them, but not for others.

Define Your Game and What Works for You

We hear some of the better traders say that they have a business plan or a game plan. What exactly does this mean? If they want to have a chance, traders have to ask themselves a score of questions before they risk capital in the markets. To start, do they have a sound methodology that has a high percentage of winners to losers?

Do they have the right tools to assess the market environment on a particular day, such as

- Has the market been consolidating so much that it is in a breakout mode? For example, are we looking for a trending market that opens on one extreme of its range and closes on the other extreme?
- Or has the market been trending so much recently that we are looking for a consolidation environment, where volume dries up, leading to a dull sideways trading range, before the cycle begins again in a breakout mode?
- Or are we trading in a holiday environment, an expiration environment, or during a week where the FOMC (Federal Open Market Committee, the board that directs activities of the Federal Reserve Bank) is a factor?
- As well as countless other similar questions.

What Do You Like to Trade?

Speaking to Mary, my questions led to questions that led to even more questions until we were able to define her game. I asked her, what stocks do you like to trade the best? Do you like the Dow stocks or have a favorite index? — the banks, biotechs, oils, drillers, NASDAQ 100? How about the utility stocks or broker-dealer stocks? The list went on and on.

This was the first of several steps in building a plan. Once we got the process going, it became less of the overwhelming task I originally had anticipated.

She finally explained to me that many of her losses came while attempting to get filled properly while trying to enter and exit NYSE stocks. She hadn't been very successful. On the flip side, she loved to trade the more volatile NASDAQ stocks—KLAC, QLGC, BRCM, MSFT, EBAY, QCOM, etc. (in all, 15 to 20 stocks based on their volatility and prices). Other favorites included the QQQ (NASDAQ tracking stock) and SPY (S&P tracking stock), and the DIA (Dow tracking stock). Finally, she indicated "fondness" for the S&P and NASDAQ futures indexes and the E-minis, due to their leverage and hedging benefits. So, there's step one—we defined "her" stocks and also her indexes.

How many of us trade every single stock out there and find that, for us, getting filled on some of the NYSE stocks is not the easiest? Or maybe we feel that the NASDAQ is too volatile for our likes and we like the NYSE ever so much better. So, guts it out and ask yourself the question—what is my stock list or my futures list or whatever? What specific products fit my comfort level? Oils? Drug stocks? NYSE or NASDAQ? E-minis? The Dow? Do I even have a favorite list or do I just trade anything that moves?

And What's the Time Frame?

After we locked in the type of stocks that Mary liked to trade, the goal was to find what particular time frames she liked best. Working a 1-minute chart, for example, is a very short-term time frame, but short-term is a relative term dictated again by a trader's own comfort level. Some traders dislike short time frames and would rather hold for a few hours or a few days. There are other traders who simply cannot be in the markets that long or they will pull their hair out, and Mary was one of those. From experience, she felt that, mentally, she could not hold on to stocks for a few hours or a few days. Yet, she wanted to stay away from an extraordinarily short-term time frame as well.

Her weakness and subsequent losses came from "swing trading" on daily charts or using such large time frames as 60-minute or 120-minute charts. She could not stand the "heat" when a trade went against her. For Mary, those longer time frames were torturous, but scalping on a 1-minute chart was too fast and noisy. As a result, she ended up scalping in and out of the market 50 times a day, and that resulted in paying predictably larger brokerage commissions for her small wins.

We concluded that "her" favorite time frames to trade were 5-minute and 15-minute charts, with the 5-minute time frame the clear favorite. Does this mean she only watches a 5-minute chart? No. In fact, Mary watches a number of time frames across four monitors for support and resistance levels on higher time frames. However, she executes and trades patterns on only the 5-minute chart. That's her comfort level. So, the question is, do you have your "right" time frame defined? What is your time frame of choice? Are you a day trader scalping 50 to 100 times a day on a tick chart or a 1-minute chart, or do you like to put your positions on and wait it out for a few hours to a few days?

With a defined stock list and the chart time frame best suiting her personality well in hand, we moved on to other factors.

Recognizing "Friendly" Price Patterns

Next step? —Identifying price patterns that Mary was able to recognize without forcing herself too much. I asked her if she preferred channels, triangles or wedges, bull or bear flags, head-and-shoulders patterns,

Fibonacci retracements, or breakout plays from a consolidation mode. If the markets wind down to a point of breakout, perhaps she'd like the idea of buying new highs or shorting new lows after the first 30 or 45 minutes of the day. Or maybe not.

Mary felt her eye was best at seeing higher-probability patterns, like bull and bear flags (a "flag pattern" is a continuation pattern in the direction of the trend). Flag patterns have been around since the early days of technical analysis and are considered to be one of the higher-probability trade setups. Simply, a bull flag is a buy pattern in an uptrend, and a bear flag is a sell pattern in a downtrend. Mary felt that since this was a very easy pattern to recognize and that working with the trend is better than fighting it, this would be the best price pattern for her to trade. (See Figure 15.1 for a "bull flag" example and Figure 15.2 for a "bear flag" example.)

At this point, it was time to begin defining risk and profit objectives based on the stocks and futures Mary liked to trade and the time frame and chart pattern she felt most comfortable using. Connecting the dots, so to speak. I explained to Mary that I personally like to use a 20-period exponential moving average on all my charts and felt it would help her as a short-term moving average support in an uptrend . . . and resistance in a downtrend. Thus, we included that in her "game plan." Figures 15.1 and 15.2 show this moving average plotted on the chart examples.

What's your pattern? Have you found one good pattern that repeats itself over and over in a consistent manner that allows you to enter and exit the markets each day? Or do you have many different setups and throw darts until one hits the target? Find your favorite pattern and master it.

Which Indicator Rocks Your Clock?

The next step was to learn if she had a preference for any indicators—an RSI or stochastic or an MACD, for example. With the variety of studies available, we concluded that she felt best using a short-term slow stochastic with a 5,3,3,1 setting for her 5-minute chart time frame. I also needed to explain to Mary that indicators only confirm what the price pattern is telling a trader. For example, the retracement in an uptrend would be a buy, and the slow stochastic would confirm the price pattern when it became oversold (Figure 15.3 shows confirmation of the price pattern when the stochastic went into an oversold condition). She had used several indicators at one time, and I explained to her that if she used more than one indicator, she might find herself facing a buy and sell signal at the same time and not be able to trust either of them. It's similar to wearing two watches, one on

FIGURE 15.1

5-Minute Chart of the S&P 500 E-mini Futures Contract Showing a Bull Flag Pattern

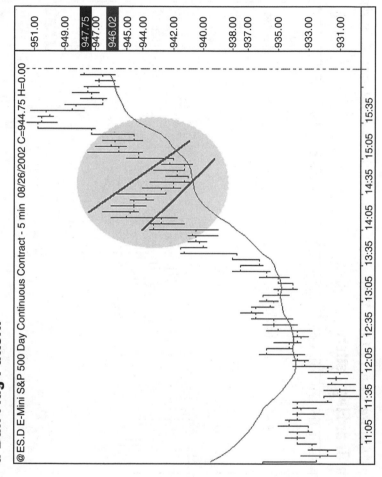

@ ES.D E-Mini S&P 500 Day Continuous Contract - 5 min 08/26/2002 C=944.75 H=0.00

Chart by TradeStation.com

263

FIGURE 15.2

5-Minute Chart of the S&P 500 E-mini Futures Contract Showing a Bear Flag Pattern

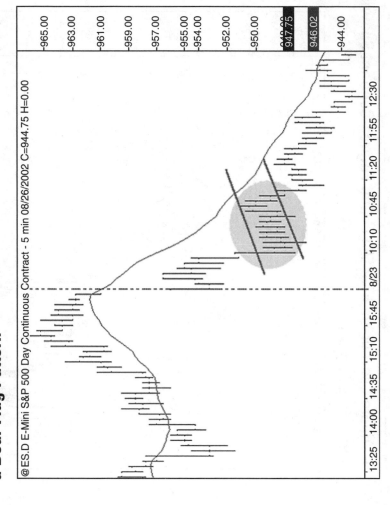

@ES.D E-Mini S&P 500 Day Continuous Contract - 5 min 08/26/2002 C=944.75 H=0.00

Chart by TradeStation.com

each hand; if each tells a different time, one will never know what the true time is. So, a trader should look toward the one particular indicator that he or she feels good about using.

What Can You Afford to Risk?

Next consideration—defining risk levels and target levels, based not just on a dollar value but also on the chart, pattern, and trend of the market. An uptrend is defined by higher highs and higher lows. In Figure 15.4, we see an uptrend. For this trend to stay valid on this time frame, we want to see if the price retracement has a higher low to its last higher low. In this example, the last higher low was 939.00, and the market retraced to 940.75. Therefore, the risk on this trade was around 2 points. I explained to Mary that sometimes the risk of a trade is too high—maybe 4 to 5 points—and sometimes the risk is not as great—maybe 1 to 2 points. That risk, I explained, also will determine the size of the position she will enter. One S&P E-mini futures contract equals $50 per point, and for the larger S&P contract, it would be five times that size, or a point value of $250. And, of course, her risk level would be a factor in her position size. A full position would be five E-minis, and risk would normally be 2 points, or $500 ($250 x 2 points). If, on the other hand, the trade required a 4- to 5-point risk, her contract size would have to decrease to accommodate the dollar value she was willing to risk.

We determined that her account was funded such that she could afford to trade one large S&P contract (or five E-minis), and that the average risk per trade would be around 2 S&P points and, further, that the greater the point risk in the S&Ps, the less contracts she would trade. The same applies to the stock side of the equation if a trader is trading 500 shares with 1 point as the average risk. Intuitively, the greater the risk in price, the less shares the trader can assume for that setup. Have you determined your share or contract size and risk level based on the time frame of your trading?

Another cog in the wheel is in knowing when to get into and out of the market so as to reasonably maximize profit and to avoid undue losses. Those decisions, though, need to be made before Mary puts on a trade, so an exit price is predetermined both for a loss and also for a win. The pattern she felt most appropriate for her trading is based on a trending market environment in an intraday time frame; typically that occurs when an intraday trend exists and, based on other factors, a trader expects the market to open on one extreme and close on the other extreme. Mary's profile

FIGURE 15.3

Confirmation of Bull Flag Pattern When the Stochastic Went into an Oversold Reading

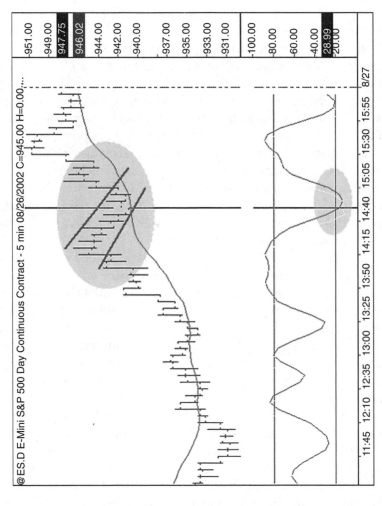

@ ES.D E-Mini S&P 500 Day Continuous Contract - 5 min 08/26/2002 C=945.00 H=0.00....

951.00
949.00
947.75
946.02
944.00
942.00
940.00
937.00
935.00
933.00
931.00

100.00
80.00
60.00
40.00
28.99
20.00

11:45 12:10 12:35 13:00 13:25 13:50 14:15 14:40 15:05 15:30 15:55 8/27

CHART BY TRADESTATION.COM

FIGURE 15.3

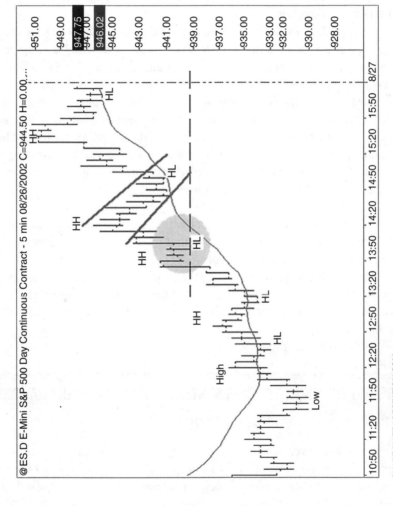

CHART BY TRADESTATION.COM

267

pointed to the fact that she did not want to stay in too long, but still didn't want to get out too fast. It was important to lock in a profit, and the plan unfolded—to bring the risk exposure to a minimum, when the price rallies from its bull flag pattern, she would raise her stop loss to just under the last low. When the market made a retest of its prior highs, she then would take a profit on the position. Before you enter, do you know your risk level and when to take your profits?

Putting all of these factors together, Mary learned how to play the right game for her personality. Some traders will never look at a bull flag pattern, never consider a 5-minute chart nor use a stochastic or anything less than a 50-period average. Some traders prefer the 5-minute chart as a time frame and love to use a 14-period RSI. There are as many variations as there are traders.

I've taken you through a journey—a journey that puts together a "custom" game plan for someone who lacked one. Mary no longer has to trade 50 times a day and does not need be in the market every waking moment. With help, she was able define a clear, concise trading plan with (1) the financial products she enjoys trading the most; (2) the time frame(s) that fit(s) her comfort level; (3) a solid chart pattern that has endured the test of time, with an indicator to confirm what the price is telling her; (4) a clear concept of risk, and the realization of how much she can reasonably risk; and (5) a profit objective.

Mary now can go in and out of the markets three to five times per day in both stocks and stock index futures. The patterns described above also have taken into consideration the higher time frames for support and resistance levels.

Mission accomplished!

RELAX! THE RIGHT TRADING SYSTEM WORKS FOR YOU! (MAY 2002)

By Scot Hicks

Single stock futures (SSFs) represent a potent new investment vehicle, much the same way that stock index and bond futures did when they were rolled out. To be sure, even if the prerelease estimates are only partially correct, as investors it would be wise to investigate this new tool as a potential component of a diversified portfolio. One avenue to explore would be the use of software programs, also known as computerized futures trading systems, to analyze and in turn make projections. With a broad spectrum of trading systems available, the task of choosing the one that best fits your investment style can be daunting. We will break this search mission down to six easy steps.

SSFs, due to begin trading in the second quarter of 2002, will serve many different purposes to the investing public. Investors, which already hold stock, will be able to hedge their positions. Although this may only apply to the more sophisticated investor, the appeal of efficiently building a balanced and hedged portfolio will help to boost the volume in SSFs.

Those wishing to short a particular stock will now be able to do so without the onerous requirements imposed by brokerage firms. In addition, short positions can be established without having an uptick in price, and without having to borrow the stock from someone and paying the party lending the stock for that right.

This diversity in scope of SSFs has attracted a wide variety of investors. Many are experienced futures traders, but a large group of participants will come from the ranks of those who have never traded futures before. No matter what the background or investment experience one has, many savvy investors will look to acquire some type of tool to use in working with this new vehicle. Especially in the futures arena, those tools have come in the form of software programs, known as trading systems. Investors add historical price data for a particular futures contract to either an off-the-shelf or self-developed trading system for guidance on where to place buy and sell orders. Others rely on input from an advisory service to fine-tune their trading. As with any form of investing, those that devote the time and effort will stand the greatest chance of success.

Trading futures involves a substantially different type of leverage than that experienced by equity traders, even those armed with a margin account. An investor pushing around a position in a stock with five times the leverage will have a whole new appreciation for the impact of a 6 percent, 1-day move in a stock. A 20 percent move may prove to be even more enlightening.

A balanced effort is needed to select any investment vehicle or tool. Choosing a SSF trading system that is right for you is no different. Also, keep in mind that this is a new product. While IBM stock has been around for a long time, the futures version may trade differently. Trading systems are dependent on historical price data to run. The challenge of accurately predicting the direction is hard enough to accomplish, but mix in some spotty data, and chances for success will plunge. What we offer here are some guidelines that may be of help. Investments of any kind must be right for you in light of your risk tolerance and financial situation.

Guidelines to Finding a Trading System to Work for *You*!

1. Determine your Objectives

What exactly are you looking for? Obviously, making money is para-
mount, but trading systems are as diverse as the markets they trade. It is
strongly suggested that you write down, as completely as possible, your
objectives. Determine what it will take to meet your objectives.

Note what is important to you:

- What is your goal for this investment? Will you be using SSFs as
  a hedge against positions you already maintain in the underlying
  stock? Does this represent a portion of your portfolio that you
  have designated for higher-risk ventures? The key here is to define
  which path you are headed down. Another benefit of committing
  this to paper will hopefully be discipline. A downfall of some individuals and corporations who use futures to hedge cash positions
  (example: a farmer who hedges his corn crop with corn futures) is
  that they lack the discipline to stick to their trading plan and then
  in turn subvert the purpose of the hedge. Instead of selling futures
  contracts to protect himself from downward prices, the corn
  farmer instead buys futures contracts to amplify the effect of a
  price rise. If the price of corn does not go up as anticipated, there
  not only is no hedge in place to protect him, but added amounts of
  corn under his belt via the futures contracts.
- What markets are traded? Does the trading system apply to the
  SSF you follow?
- Is the system portfolio-based or "market specific"? Dissecting one
  SSF out of a system's portfolio that was meant to trade a basket of
  SSFs could destabilize the results.
- Long-term, short-term, or day trade? Not only do these various
  systems have different results, but, more importantly, require a
  different temperament of the investor.
- How much money do I have to work with? Speculators (non-
  hedgers) typically allocate 10 percent or less of the value of their
  portfolios to futures investing. As this is highly speculative, only
  risk capital should be used.
- What type of return am I looking for, and is this realistic? While
  the hypothetical performance record is not any sort of guarantee,

it is important to identify what type of returns you are looking to achieve.
- How big of a drawdown can I live with, how big of a risk can I afford with this account? Trading is just like running or, in this case, opening a business. Before you begin, you need to determine what kinds of losses you are willing to live with and then compare that with the hypothetical returns of the trading system.

This is only a partial list. Again, it is important to put it down in writing. Think of it as constructing a business plan. You may have a good picture of it in your head, but committing it to paper will focus your ideas and highlight the potential flaws.

2. Qualitative Analysis

While a good track record is important, researching the background of the system developer is equally significant. Remember, your hard-earned funds are at risk.

Is the developer:

- In good standing with the investment community? Ask the developer if you can speak with other investors who have used the system.
- In good standing with the business community (www.bbb.org)? How long has the developer been selling systems?
- Registered as a Commodity Trading Advisor (CTA) (www.nfa.futures.org)? The National Futures Association can also help you research the compliance and ethics records for a registered member to determine if the system vendor has had complaints or other regulatory issues.
- Trading the system with his or her own money? If so, do they provide brokerage statements?
- Is the trading logic disclosed? Will the developer let you in on how the system works, or is it a black box?

3. Commissions and Slippage

It is critical to determine if the impact of commissions and slippage was taken into account in compiling the performance record. For example, if an IBM SSF day-trading system traded one time a day, every day of the month, that would be 20 trades per month. If slippage (the difference between the price actually entered and that which the system hypothetically posted) was $75 on the entry to the trade and $75 for the exit, then that's $150. Add that to commissions of $40 for a grand total of $190 per trade. $190 times the 20 trades per month equals $3800 in slippage and commissions ($45,600 per year) before any profits have been calculated. This is on top of the sum paid for the use of the system. Most developers factor these figures into their performance, but some grossly understate the impact.

4. Returns and Drawdowns

What types of returns are you looking for? How much risk are you willing to accept? Are these figures realistic? Returns are only one piece of the puzzle. The adage, "If it looks too good to be true, it probably is" was never more accurate. Be wary of systems that show little risk.

Analysis tools such as the reports on trading systems like Trade Center, Inc.'s (www.tradecenterinc.com) SystemTrac or Futures Truth (www.futurestruth.com) can be used to evaluate the performance records in an unbiased and side-by-side fashion.

Further, evaluate the performance history of the system and determine if the track record was built on one trade. If possible, get trade-by-trade historical information. Some hypothetical track records were built on the success of just a few trades. Should you invest with that system, you are in effect banking that lightning will strike again. Ideally, you should look for balanced performance over a long period of time. Slow and steady building of performance and equity is what you should strive for, not to make a killing by having your system guess the correct direction of a move of the decade.

5. What Is Required of the Investor?

How much time, energy, and money will you need to expend to properly execute a trading system? Do you need to be in front of the quote screen during the entire trading session? In addition, you may need data feeds, third-party software, dedicated telephone lines, etc. These all represent significant time and money commitments over and above the purchase of the system.

For those new to using a system to trade a financial instrument, the process is much more labor-intensive than passively investing in a stock or fund. Unless you are using extremely slow-moving indicators, expect to

review or monitor the progress at least daily. You may elect to use the services of a broker that specializes in following trading systems on behalf of clients.
While it is still prudent to follow your account activity closely, having a system broker do all the work will absolve you of the day-to-day legwork.

6. Is the System Tradable?

It is important to find out if the system you are interested in trades in some
fashion that would make it difficult to execute. Obscure rules and trading
logic would fall under this category. Successful systems tend to be simple
in operation and logic. These systems are ones which review history and
attempt to apply that knowledge to the future. Systems with many moving
parts can tend to be a curve fit. Curve fit refers to a system that was
designed using convoluted logic. Such systems are designed around sets
of data (historical prices) that, via computer number bending, create a
result which is almost impossible to duplicate under any set of circumstances. While this is difficult for the novice to evaluate, it is still possible
to inquire as to the complexity of the system. By doing your homework,
your chances of finding viable solutions for implementing these new tools
successfully into your portfolio will be greatly enhanced.

16

Get a Hold of Yourself: Trading Well Under Stress

Once you've developed a trading system or methodology that works for you, you'll have to face the challenge of managing yourself. Novice and experienced traders alike face the same psychological challenges of fear and greed and the stress that can accompany trading, if it is not managed properly. If you wake up one morning and find yourself glued to your computer screen, waiting for prices to move, this chapter is for you. Trading can bring out a variety of emotions. Experienced and successful traders say that managing those emotions and keeping them in check is a critical factor in booking profits at the end of the day.

Sometimes the best way to deal with stress is to have a plan in place before stress exhausts you and blurs the guidelines of your trading strategy. The authors of the articles in this chapter will review some emotional roadblocks that you need to clear before you can walk the path to investment success.

Price Headley gives advice on how to control the main fears with which nearly all traders struggle: the fear of loss, the fear of missing out, the fear of letting a profit turn into a loss, and the fear of not being right. He explains those fears and then explains alternatives to those states of mind.

According to Brett Steenbarger, Linda Bradford Raschke, and Brace Barber, "Successful trading is the result of a learning process." Steenbarger, a psychiatrist and trader, explains that intense practice is what makes any person successful in any field that he or she chooses—including trading. He and Barber, a former Army Ranger, suggest that the Army Ranger training model is a useful model for intense practice in trading. In their training, Rangers rehearse skills so many times that their reactions to challenges become automatic. Similarly, through intensive exposure, traders internalize reactions to common trading challenges. Raschke offers similar advice, but takes her model of training from another branch of the military, the Air Force. She refers to the OODA Loops model developed by Air Force Colonel John R. Boyd. By observing, orienting, deciding, and acting (OODA), she explains, one can become a successful trader.

After you've finished your intense training, you might want to give your life outside of trading some intense thought. Adrienne Laris Toghraie suggests that if you kick life up a notch, you will be more likely to enjoy trading and other areas of your life. To kick your life up a notch, Toghraie advises you to notice and enjoy the smaller things in life, such as eating breakfast or conversing with coworkers. Doing so will enable you to manage the stress that the markets sometimes impose.

MASTER THE FOUR FEARS OF TRADING (NOVEMBER 2002)

BY PRICE HEADLEY

Merriam-Webster's dictionary defines fear as "an unpleasant, often strong emotion caused by anticipation or awareness of danger," going on to explain that fear "implies anxiety and usually the loss of courage." This definition of fear is useful in helping define the issues that traders face when coping with fear. The reality is that all traders feel fear at some level, but the key is how we prepare to address our concerns related to taking on risk as a trader. In this article I will review four major fears experienced by traders, and I'll take it a step further by noting how the outcomes of these fears create undesirable trading behaviors. Basically, my aim is to have you walk away with an understanding of these dangers so you can implement strategies that will address your fears and let you get on with your trading plan.

Mark Douglas, an expert in trading psychology, noted in his book *Trading in the Zone* that most investors believe they know what is going to happen next. This causes traders to put too much weight on the outcome of the current trade, while not assessing their performance as "a probability game" that they are playing over time. This manifests itself in investors getting too high and too low and causes them to react emotionally, with excessive fear or greed after a series of losses or wins.

As the importance of an individual trade increases in the trader's mind, the fear level tends to increase as well. A trader becomes more hesitant and cautious, seeking to avoid a mistake. The risk of choking under pressure increases as the trader feels the pressure build.

All traders have fear, but winning traders manage their fear while losers are controlled by it. When faced with a potentially dangerous situation, the instinctive tendency is to revert to the "fight or flight" response. We can either prepare to do battle against the perceived threat, or we can flee from this danger. When an investor interprets a state of arousal negatively as fear or stress, performance is likely to be impaired. A trader will tend to "freeze." In contrast, when a trader feels the surge of adrenaline but interprets this as excitement or a state of greater alertness before placing a trade, then performance will tend to improve. Many great live performers talk of feeling butterflies just before they go on stage, and how they interpret this as a wake-up call to go out and perform at their highest level. That's clearly a more empowering response than someone who might interpret these butterflies as a reason to run back to his dressing room to get sick! Winners take positive action in spite of their fears.

Fear of Loss

Analysis Paralysis and Its Cousins

The fear of losing when making a trade often has several consequences. Fear of loss tends to make a trader hesitant to execute his trading plan. This can often lead to an inability to pull the trigger on new entries as well as on new exits. As a trader, you know that you need to be decisive in taking action when your approach dictates a new entry or exit, so when fear of loss holds you back from taking action, you also lose confidence in your ability to execute your trading plan. This causes a lack of trust in your method or, more importantly, in your own ability to execute future trades.

Thus, you can see how fear can set in place a vicious cycle of recurring doubt and, in turn, reinforce a trader's lack of confidence in executing new positions. For example, if you doubt you will actually be able to exit your position when your method tells you to get the heck out, then as a self-preservation mechanism you will also choose not to get into new trades. Thus begins the analysis paralysis, where you are merely looking at new trades but not getting the proper reinforcement to pull the trigger. In fact, the reinforcement is negative and actually pulls you away from making a move.

Looking deeper at why a trader cannot pull the trigger, I believe the root stems from a lack of confidence about the trading plan, which then causes the trader to believe that by not trading, he is moving away from potential pain as opposed to moving toward future gain. No one likes losses, but the reality is, of course, that even the best professionals will lose. The key is that they will lose much less, which allows them to remain in the game both financially and psychologically. The longer you can remain in the trading game with a sound method, the more likely you will start to experience a better run of trades that will take you out of any temporary trading slumps.

When you're having trouble pulling the trigger, realize that you are worrying too much about results and are not focused on your execution process. Make sure you have a written plan and then practice executing your plan.

Start with paper trades if you prefer, or consider trading smaller positions to get the fear of losing out of your system and get yourself focused on execution. When in the heat of battle and realizing you need to get in or out of a trade, consider using market orders, especially on the exit. That way you can't beat yourself up for not pulling the trigger on your trade.

Many traders may get too cute with a trade and try to work out of a position at a limit price better than the current market price, hoping they can squeeze more out of a trade. But as famed trader Jesse Livermore advised in the classic book *Reminiscences of a Stock Operator*, by Edwin Lefèvre, "Give up trying to catch the last eighth." Keeping it simple with a market order to exit allows you to bring closure when you need it, which reinforces the confidence-building feelings that come from following your trading plan. In the past when my indicators noted it was time to exit, I have experienced firsthand the pain of not getting filled at my limit, watching the option drop, and then placing a new limit back where I should have exited at the market in the first place! Then I have realized I was not going to get filled there either, so I again kept lowering my limit until, in frustration, I placed a market order to exit much lower than I could have closed the position initially. Not only can you feel the pain of loss financially, but, more important, you can chip away at your internal state of confidence and create frustration by not getting filled.

You should be more concerned about avoiding big losses and less concerned about taking small losses. If you can't bear to take a small loss, you will never give yourself an opportunity to be around when a big winning idea comes along, as every trade you enter has the risk of first turning against you for a loss. You must execute by knowing what your risk is in each trade, and define parameters to make sure you can ride favorable trends correctly as well so that your winners will be larger than your losers. And never get stuck in the mindset of hoping a loser will come back to "breakeven," as that is one of the trader's most deadly mental fantasies. Billions of dollars have been lost by technology investors hoping their stocks would bounce back in recent years to allow them to escape the downtrend. That only led to even greater losses in most cases. That's how a short-term trader can become a long-term investor unintentionally, and that is a position in which you never want to put yourself.

Ask how well you trust yourself to execute your trading plan. You want to judge your effectiveness based on how well you get in and out of the market when your method gives entry and exit signals. You'll need to be decisive, not hesitant, and know in your heart that your method is well tested and that your risk is low compared to your likely reward. In other words, you must be fully prepared before you go into the heat of battle during a trading day. You need to know where you will enter and where you will exit if you are a discretionary trader. Or you need to know what system you are following and be prepared to enter and exit as the system dictates. This keeps you disciplined and focused on following a process that can generate favorable results over time.

Fear of Missing Out

Being a Part of the Crowd Isn't Everything It's Cracked Up to Be

Every trend always has its doubters, but I often notice that many skeptics of a trend will slowly become converts due to the fear of missing out on profits or the pain of losses in betting against that trend. The fear of missing out can also be characterized as greed of sorts, for an investor is not acting based on some desire to own the security—other than the fact that it is going up without him on board. This fear is often fueled during runaway booms like the technology bubble of the late 1990s, as investors heard their friends talking about newfound riches. The fear of missing out came into play for those who wanted to experience the same type of euphoria.

When you think about it, this is a very dangerous situation, as at this stage investors tend essentially to say, "Get me in at any price—I must participate in this hot trend!" The effect of the fear of missing out is a "blindness" to any potential downside risk, as it seems clear to the investor that there can only be gains ahead from such a "promising" and "obviously beneficial" trend. But there's nothing obvious about it.

We remember the stories of the Internet and how it would revolutionize the way business was done. While the Internet has indeed had a significant impact on our lives, the hype and frenzy for these stocks ramped up supply of every possible technology stock that could be brought public and created a situation where the incredibly high expectations could not possibly be met in reality. It is expectation gaps like this that often create serious risks for those who have piled into a trend late, once it has been widely broadcast in the media to all investors.

Fear of Letting a Profit Turn into a Loss

I get many more questions from subscribers asking if it is time to take a profit than I do subscribers asking when they should take their loss. This represents the fact that most traders do the opposite of the "let profits run, cut losses short" motto: They instead like to take quick profits while letting losers get out of control. Why would a trader do this? Too many traders tend to equate their net worth with their self-worth. They want to lock in a quick profit to guarantee that they feel like a winner.

How should you take profits? Should you utilize a fixed target profit objective, or should you only trail your stop on a winning trade until the trend breaks?

Those who can accept more risk should consider trailing a stop on their trending position, while more conservative traders may be more comfortable taking profits at their target objective. There is another alternative as well, which is to merge the two concepts by taking some profits off the table while seeking to ride the trend with a trailing stop on the remaining portion of the position.

When I trade options, I usually recommend taking half of the position off at a double or more, and then following the half position still open with a trailing stop. This allows me to have the opportunity to ride my best trading ideas further, as these are the trades where I am mostly likely to continue being right. Yet, I am also able to get the initial capital at risk back in my pocket, which frees me from worrying about letting a profit turn into a loss; I am guaranteed a breakeven even if the other half position were to go to nothing overnight. My general rule for the remaining half position is to exit if it reaches my trailing stop of half its maximum profit on an end-of-day closing basis, or scale out of the remaining half position every time it doubles again.

I'm also a big fan of moving your stop up to breakeven relatively quickly once the position starts to move in your favor, by about 5 percent on a stock or by roughly 25 percent on the option. It is also critical to recognize the impact of time spent waiting for a position to move. If you are not los- ing—but not yet winning—after several trading days, there are likely better opportunities elsewhere. This is known as a "time stop," and it will get your capital out of nonperformers and free it up for fresher trading ideas.

Fear of Not Being Right—All Too Common

Too many traders care too much about being proven right in their analysis on each trade, as opposed to looking at trading as a probability game in which they will be both right and wrong on individual trades. In other words, their overall method will create positive results.

The desire to focus on being right instead of making money is a func- tion of the individual's ego, and to be successful you must trade without ego at all costs. Ego leads to equating the trader's net worth with his self- worth, which results in the desire to take winners too quickly and sit on losers in often-misguided hopes of exiting at a breakeven.

Trading results are often a mirror for where you are in your life. If you feel any sort of conflict internally with making money or feel the need to be perfect in everything you do, you will experience cognitive disso- nance as you trade. This means that your brain will be insisting that you cannot exit a trade at a loss because it ruins your self-image of perfection. Or if you grew up and feel guilty about having money, your mind and ego will find a way to give up gains and take losses in the markets. The ego's need to protect its version of the self must be let go in order to rid our- selves of the potential for self-sabotage.

If you have a perfectionist mentality when trading, you are really set- ting yourself up for failure, because it is a given that you will experience losses along the way in trading. Again, you have to think of trading as a probability game. You can't be a perfectionist and expect to be a great trader. If you cannot take a loss when it is small because of the need to be perfect, then the loss will oftentimes grow to a much larger loss, causing further pain for the perfectionist. The objective should be excellence in trading, not perfection.

In addition, you should strive for excellence over a sustained period, as opposed to judging that each trade must be excellent. The great traders make mistakes too, but they are able to keep the impact of those mistakes small, while really riding their best ideas fully.

For the trader who is dealing with excessive ego challenges (yet, who wants to admit it?), this is one of the strongest arguments for mechanical systems, as you grade yourself not on whether your trade analysis was right or wrong. Instead you judge yourself based on how effectively you executed your system's entry and exit signals. This is much easier for those traders who want to leave their egos at the door when they start to trade. Additionally, because we are raised in a highly competitive culture, the perception of a contest or competition will also bring out your ego's desire to win and beat others.

You will be better off seeing trading as a series of opportunities that will become apparent to you, and your task is to create a plan that finds opportunities with potential rewards that are several times greater than the risks you incur.

Be sure you are writing down your reasons for entering each trade, as the ego will play tricks and come up with new reasons to hang on to losing positions once the original reasons have evaporated. One of our survival mechanisms is remembering the good and omitting the bad in our minds, but this is dangerous in trading. You must acknowledge the risk and use a stop on every trade to admit when the analysis is no longer timely. This helps prevent undesirable situations where you get stuck in a position because you did not adhere to your original stop. This is a bad use of capital: being tied up in an underperforming position, when there are likely to be many better opportunities elsewhere. Trading without stops is an ego-driven approach that hopes to avoid accountability for a losing trading idea. This is an unacceptable behavior to the successful trader, who knows he must limit risk with stops to stay in the game for the next trading opportunity.

In summary, your trading plan must account for the emotions you will be prone to experience, particularly those related to managing fear. As a trader, you must move from a fearful mindset to a mental state of confidence. You have to believe in your ability as well as the effectiveness of your plan to take profits that are larger than the manageable losses. This builds the confidence of knowing that you are on the right track. It also makes it easier to continue to execute new trades after a string of losing positions. Psychologically, that's the critical point where many individuals will pull the plug, because they are too reactive to emotions as opposed to the longer-term mechanics of their plan. If you're not sure if you can make this leap, know that you can if you start small.

Too many investors have an "all-or-none" mentality. They're either going to get rich quick or blow out trying. You want to take the opposite mentality—one that signals that you are in this for the longer haul. This gives you "permission" to slowly get comfortable and to keep refining your plan as you go. As you focus on execution while managing fear, you realize that giving up is the only way you can truly lose. You will win as you conquer the four major fears, to gain confidence in your trading method and, ultimately, you will gain even more confidence in yourself.

TRADING THE RANGER WAY (SEPTEMBER 2002)

BY BRETT N. STEENBARGER, LINDA BRADFORD RASCHKE, BRACE BARBER

This article is a unique application of trading psychology. It is the product of an unusual collaboration between an Army Ranger and leadership expert (Brace Barber), a master trader and educator of traders (Linda Bradford Raschke), and a professional psychologist/trader/researcher (Brett Steenbarger). In this piece, we are going to challenge a trader's notions about what it takes to become an elite trader of options and futures. Be advised that the goal is not to comfort the traders' afflictions and to reassure them that they will be a great success in the markets. No, in the Ranger tradition, we are here to afflict their comfort. We are going to push traders a bit beyond the boundaries of their normal thinking by introducing a new model for developing trading success. That push is important because, as we shall see, becoming part of any elite requires driving yourself beyond your self-defined boundaries.

Ready to challenge yourself? HOOAH! Let's roll . . .

Lessons from Brett: The Anatomy of Greatness

Psychology is not just the study and treatment of emotional problems. A large body of recent research has focused on individuals who are supernormal: those who have been highly creative, productive, and successful in their fields of endeavor. Summaries of this work can be found on Brett's web page, www.greatspeculations.com/brett.htm, and in his book *The Psychology of Trading* (Wiley; January 2003). Consider some of the more provocative findings:

- Highly successful individuals in sports, science, and the arts are distinguished by the amount of time they spend in intense, deliberative practice. Most have spent multiple hours each day for a number of years refining skills and immersing themselves in their craft. They find pleasure in this immersion and sustain a high degree of concentration during their practice sessions.
- Highly successful individuals across various fields are successful because they are unusually productive. Researcher Dean Keith

Simonton of the University of California, Davis, has found that the greats in any field produce the same ratio of unsuccessful works to successful ones as their less noteworthy peers. They succeed because they produce so many works that at least a few are likely to survive as major contributions.

- The combination of lengthy practice and sustained productivity means that successful individuals are unusually capable of sustaining effort, even under trying conditions. Because a sizable percentage of their works is unlikely to succeed, they require a high degree of emotional resilience to weather disappointment and fatigue.

Research on a phenomenon called implicit learning helps us understand how greatness is cultivated. Suppose subjects are asked to identify complex patterns from a stream of data with no idea of what they are looking for. They are only told whether their guesses are right or wrong. Over repeated trials—and with sufficient concentration and effort—subjects are able to achieve results far beyond what would be expected by chance.

Here, however, is the catch. While the subjects become excellent pattern recognizers, they cannot verbalize the patterns to which they are responding. This is why the learning is called "implicit." After many hours of immersion, people know the patterns they are being exposed to, but they do not know that they know. Experience shapes their intuition.

Savvy traders of options and futures know the "tape feel" that results from long hours spent watching market action. What is less apparent is that the implicit learning studies are actually duplicating the conditions under which greatness thrives. By sustaining intense concentration, practice, and effort, subjects develop the kind of expertise—and confidence—cultivated by highly creative, successful individuals. This immersion is an important psychological element distinguishing futures and options trading from longer-term investing in the stock market (see Table 16.1).

In the Ranger spirit, we challenge traders to examine their own trading practices—especially the ways in which they practice trading. Are they actually practicing trading, or are they merely telling themselves that they will achieve superlative success by finding ever more complex trading formulas or mastering the perfect self-help technique? Research on extraordinary achievement suggests something different: Greatness arises from the continuous posing and surmounting of great challenges. Accomplishment becomes automatic—a natural part of the self—when the repetition of a limited set of core skills becomes an ongoing part of one's daily routine.

Great challenges, tackled routinely, form the basis of Ranger training.

TABLE 16.1

The Psychology of Active Futures/Options Trading vs. Stock Market Investing

	Active Futures/ Options Trading	Stock Market Investing
Speed of required response	Rapid; minute to minute	Slow; month to month
Primary decision-making process	Implicit: intuition supported by analysis	Explicit: analysis supported by intuition
Market decisions based upon	Pattern recognition and money management rules	Fundamental and/or statistical analyses

Traders of very short time frames do not have the luxury to carry out lengthy analyses and thus rely upon internalized patterns for decision making. Their training requires repeated exposure to the patterns they utilize to enter and manage trades so that decision making can become automatic.

Lessons from Brace: Transcending One's Limits

Brace has written extensively about Ranger training, and much valuable information can be found at www.rangerschool.com. For those who need a little background, U.S. Army Ranger School is divided into three phases. The Fort Benning phase is designed to develop basic military skills and physical and mental stamina. The Mountain phase involves immersion in military mountaineering and battle tasks under conditions of severe weather, challenging terrain, and extreme hunger, thirst, and fatigue. The final Florida phase pushes the Ranger to perform against opposing forces in a jungle/swamp environment while under high mental and physical stress. Only when these challenges are successfully met does the student earn the right to wear the coveted Ranger tab.

What is it about forcing individuals to perform complex, challenging tasks under conditions of extreme deprivation and stress that brings out the best in them? Ranger Lance Bagley, speaking of his experience in Ranger School, put it this way:

> *"I learned that there is always something left. When I got to the point where reason said I couldn't continue, there was always something left. . . . It was amazing to learn how far I could push myself, how far down I could go and still function, and what teamwork meant. To me, that was the essence of Ranger School."*

It is difficult to overestimate the confidence that results from successfully tackling the greatest challenges that can be thrown at a person. This confidence, internalized at a deep, emotional level, emerges later in life whenever fresh challenges occur. Ranger W. John Hutt explains,

"My Ranger School experience and learning how to operate under extreme pressure and scrutiny allows me to be cool under pressure now. The discomfort of reduced food and sleep added so much physical distraction to the already intense pressure on us that it makes it easy in the outside world to handle problems when those annoyances are absent."

Trading futures and options is very similar to the challenges faced by the elite infantry soldier. Operating with high degrees of leverage, the trader performs under conditions of high risk where time is of the essence. There is also considerable uncertainty in both trading and combat, with the enemy always ready to take you out of the game. Nothing quite builds the sense of mastery for the beginning trader, for example, as successfully weathering the adversity of an initial drawdown.

The Rangers prepare people for real-life stresses by teaching them basic skills—from land navigation and hand-to-hand combat to teamwork and leadership. Moreover, they review and drill these skills under conditions similar to those found in combat. The goal is to rehearse basic values and skills so thoroughly, under so many challenging circumstances, that they will become automatic. In trading, this means rehearsing all phases of trading: not just entry patterns, but also the all-important exit and money management strategies that maximize opportunity and manage risk.

The Ranger way of training recognizes a fundamental reality: A trader cannot prepare for extraordinary performance by rehearsing under ordinary conditions. Elite troops can only be forged from extraordinary challenges that force them to draw upon emotional and physical reserves they never knew they possessed. So many of the challenges posed by Ranger instructors are unexpected ones that require quick thinking and responding. If a trader has drilled handling his worst-case trading scenario—as in a gap that opens against his position—he will feel confident in handling any situation that arises.

It is commonly heard that the majority of futures and options traders lose money over time. This is not because traders have not yet found the Holy Grail. Rather, it is because traders fail to practice their skills and shape their plans in real-time conditions of stress and uncertainty. Indeed, the majority of traders do not practice their exits and money management disciplines at all!

Traders must push themselves to develop successfully. Trading the Ranger way means conditioning themselves the way infantry soldiers build their conditioning. Experiencing intensive challenges in training allows skills to be so internalized that they emerge naturally in real time. That is how successful traders can experience a "Zen-like" flow state when they are at their best—even in dangerous, volatile market conditions. Extraordinary challenges become normal events when people encounter them repeatedly in training.

Lessons from Linda: Speeding up the "OODA Loops"

When Linda needed a model for guiding her recent training project for traders, she did not turn to the fields of finance or psychology. Rather, she turned to the military and the writings of Colonel John R. Boyd.

Colonel Boyd of the Air Force has an interesting history as a fighter pilot and is known for his challenge to fellow airmen. He allowed himself to be placed in a position of tactical disadvantage in an air fight and promised that, within 40 seconds, he would be on his adversary's tail, ready for the kill. Colonel Boyd was never known to have lost this bet, earning him the nickname "Forty-Second" Boyd.

During his career, Boyd developed his approach to airborne combat into a comprehensive philosophy of military strategy. He described combat decision making as a function of Observing, Orienting, Deciding, and Acting (OODA). These processes form "loops," with new actions providing fresh observations and requiring renewed efforts at orienting and responding. The goal of military training, Boyd stressed, is to accelerate OODA loops, becoming more efficient than the enemy.

Trading futures and options requires especially tight OODA loops. There is always new action to observe across multiple markets and indicators. This requires an ability to rapidly orient and assess whether we are in trending or nontrending markets, volatile conditions or nonvolatile, near support/resistance or away from it, etc. From our orientation, we must rapidly create and update trading decisions and then find the will and clarity to act on these plans.

On this basis, traders might want to ask themselves: "Am I preparing myself to trade like Col. Boyd?" "Am I training myself to observe my market data, size up the action, craft a trading plan, and execute it, all within a matter of seconds?"

A glance through the Ranger Handbook offers some helpful clues as to how this might be accomplished. Much of the book is taken up with

descriptions of drills and procedures, each broken down into easily identifiable components. By breaking complex processes down into clear components that can be reviewed and rehearsed, the Army ensures that they
are "an instinctive and familiar way of thinking for a platoon leader."

Making complex skills instinctive and familiar is the key to tightening
OODA loops. Colonel Boyd could never have overcome his adversaries in
40 seconds if he had to consciously analyze and plan each of his maneuvers.
It was because these maneuvers were overlearned to the point of becoming
automatic that he was able to operate within his opponent's mindset.

Elite traders of futures and options also need to make complex decisions within a time frame measured in seconds. This can only happen if
they have broken their trading down into easily identifiable processes that
can then be rehearsed under pressure until they are second nature. The
process of development being followed in Linda's training project can be
described in three stages: skill, drill, and fulfill. These introduce elements
of trading, then rehearsal and application in real time (see Table 16.2).

In Linda's trading chat room (www.mrci.com/lbr), which trains traders
under real-time conditions, Linda and Brett, working together with a team of
researchers under Andrew Lo, Ph.D., from the Massachusetts Institute
of Technology's Sloan School of Management, are investigating the training of

TABLE 16.2

A Ranger Model of Trader Development

- *Skill*—A trading skill or pattern to trade is taught to the trader or identified by the trader as having profit potential. This corresponds to the Observe phase in Boyd's OODA
loop. If a mentor is involved, the skill will be explained and modeled for the student prior
to any rehearsal.

- *Drill*—The trading skill or pattern is rehearsed, first via walk-throughs (simulated
trades on historical data) and then by paper-trading live markets. The trader learns to
recognize opportunities to utilize the skills and patterns under realistic market conditions, formulating trading plans based upon incoming data. This corresponds to the
Orient and Decide phases of Boyd's loop.

- *Fulfill*—The trader's development culminates in the fulfillment of actual trades in real
time, utilizing the entry, exit, and money management skills that have been rehearsed.
This provides practice in "pulling the trigger" on one's decisions: the Act phase of Boyd's
loop. Such fulfillment may begin with relatively small positions, with traders increasing
size as their results and confidence dictate.

A key to the success of the U.S. Army Rangers is conducting all three phases of training under challenging conditions that mimic the situations they will face in the future. Traders can best internalize
the skills of entering, exiting, and managing trades—and make them automatic—by rehearsing these
in simulated and actual market conditions that pose significant time and performance demands.

traders. Linda assists traders enrolled in the study with their entries and then challenges them to manage the trades on their own, finally reviewing their results at the end of each day. This provides daily experience in skill/drill/fulfill training. Preliminary results suggest that traders can indeed acquire the skills and methods of a veteran trader and improve their performance.

Putting It All Together: The Ranger Way

If the average trader is asked what makes for success, two things generally emerge: good techniques and proper psychology. We are presenting a different perspective: Successful trading is the result of a learning process. It is the same learning process that can be found among great contributors in any field of endeavor, and it is a learning process that can be accelerated through intensive training. Our experience—in psychotherapy, military training, and trading—is that weeks of consistent, hands-on, real-time rehearsal are more valuable than months or even years of leisurely activity.

The Ranger model of training is particularly promising for futures and options traders because it has a long track record of producing high-performance professionals in a relatively short training period. The steepness of the Ranger's learning curve is a function of several factors, including the breaking down of skills into bite-sized components; the relentless rehearsal of those skills in realistic conditions; and the practice of skills in the face of extreme environmental, emotional, and physical challenges.

Our current research will show us whether daily experiences with skills and drills can help traders fulfill their highest aspirations. In future research, we hope to introduce elements of extreme challenge into the training to determine whether or not this will accelerate learning and improve performance. For example, we may have traders rehearse their skills under conditions of high fatigue, distraction, or time pressure as ways of simulating decision making under fire. This truly would train traders the Ranger way!

KICKING LIFE UP A NOTCH: MANAGING THE STRETCH BETWEEN TRADING AND LIVING (DECEMBER 2002)

By Adrienne Laris Toghraie

As we approach the joys that the holidays can bring, it may also be an appropriate time for traders to focus on how to regain their life balance and to cap off what might have been a very difficult year in the markets. By "kicking life up a notch," traders can both manage the stretch they face in the trading arena while appreciating the small things in life that make it worth living.

Recently, a trader named Jack came to me for private consulting. Clearly he needed help, not necessarily solely with his trading, but in his life balance. In his own words, he expressed the problem: "I'm doing okay in my trading, although I could be doing a lot better, but my personal life is not working." Based on my findings from taking him through my Trader's Evaluation, I told him that he needed to "kick his life up a notch" if he wanted to get his trading and his personal life to succeed.

What does it mean to "kick life up a notch"? And more importantly, why is it important to a trader? Yes, I borrowed the expression of "kicking life up a notch" from the famous television chef and restaurateur Emeril Lagasse. He uses this expression on his show as he adds spices to his dishes to make them more appealing. "Kicking life up a notch" to a trader, however, means making choices and taking actions that are beyond the ordinary. These actions and choices are the ones that force you to stretch and stir yourself up. They require that you look beyond the obvious solutions, challenge conventional wisdom, and take the more difficult path when the easy path is comfortable, safe, convenient, and well traveled. The great American poet, Robert Frost, said it best:

"Two roads diverged in a wood and I—
I took the one less traveled by,
And that has made all the difference."

If you are a trader, you have already made the decision to "kick life up a notch" by taking the road less traveled. Trading is not an ordinary profession, and traders do not lead ordinary lives. It is possible to survive as a trader, but you cannot thrive as a trader if you are not willing to stretch. This, of course, was the situation in which Jack found himself. He was merely surviving, not flourishing.

So, how effective is your life as a trader? Do you wake up each morning enthusiastic and excited about the day's activities, or do you live your life simply because you are scheduled to do so? The schedule is your list of responsibilities. To live responsibly to others is to keep your commitments. But, to live responsibly to yourself, you must not only keep your commitments . . . you must also make the effort to enjoy the process. This commitment to enjoying the process requires you to take the road less traveled, add spice to the stew, stretch and grow, try something new, and, as a result, to feel more alive.

Short-Circuiting Aliveness

Every moment of the day is an opportunity to enjoy the experience of life. However, most of us deny ourselves these opportunities to "kick life up a notch" by taking shortcuts.

Instead of sitting down with our family in the morning to have a nutritious breakfast, we eat a Pop-Tart breakfast on the go and forget to acknowledge the people that we love. We deny our bodies the healthy nutrition that we need to sustain an energetic, positive day.

- We time-manage our day so closely that we forget to include the simple joys of interaction with our colleagues.
- We forget that trading was a choice we made to live our passion.
- Workday routines become so mechanical that we fail to notice the nuances that make each day a special experience.
- Exercise becomes a chore or a sentence instead of an experience.
- Dinner digresses to an opened can here and a frozen dinner there instead of an opportunity to enjoy the tastes and smells of great food and the art of preparation.
- And, finally, we spend time with the family in front of the television instead of a time of closeness, playfulness, intimacy, communication, and exploration.

Does any of this sound familiar? Consider the fact that each choice of "nonaliveness" creates more of the same until you are left with no valuable moments. Then, you have nothing from which to draw when you need inspiration, motivation, and support. Every area of life affects every other area of life. So, when you look to improve the bottom line in your trading, you must also look to improve the bottom line of all of the other areas of your life.

Savoring Valued Minutes

Valued moments come from "kicking life up a notch." Some of the widows of the September 11th terrorist attacks have expressed regrets about the last moments they had spent with their spouses on that morning when they left for work. These grieving wives and husbands are wishing that those final goodbyes could have been different. Even with the horrible outcome they have to face, they keep thinking about the importance of those last few moments together with their spouses. If only they had taken more time for breakfast, then the memory of those last spoken words would give them more of a sense of peace.

Today, most people only savor the intense moments of life that mark the significant beginnings and endings. These moments are the extreme high times of celebration and the extreme low times of devastation. These powerful moments tend to completely overshadow the seemingly endless succession of ordinary, forgettable moments that make up the large majority of life. Auntie Mame, the outrageous and larger-than-life character from the play bearing her own name, said it this way, "Life is a banquet, but most poor bastards are starving to death." Without minimizing the deprivations experienced by those in the midst of hard times, it is important to remember that most of us have a great deal for which to be thankful. Each time you recognize the blessings that you do have and express gratitude for them, you are ratcheting up your experience of life.

How Much Is Your Arm Worth?

A prime example of the way that placing value on the blessings in your life can "kick up your life a notch" came from a young trader who was deeply depressed about a lack of money. I asked him if he would sell his right arm for one million dollars. Naturally, he declined the offer. I kept raising the price offered for his arm, and he continued to decline the offer. I pointed out to him that while he valued his right arm at millions of dollars, he placed no value on his entire body, which he was slowly destroying chemically and mentally. This young trader had failed to see the value of his own life and, as a result, was willing to give it up when things were difficult to handle. It requires a willingness to take the road less traveled to continually appreciate the simple, ordinary things that life offers that are so easy to take for granted.

Choice of Focus

You cannot do the extraordinary if you are focused on the negative, the limited, or the impossible. These negative thoughts drain the energy from your life and prevent you from being exceptional. We tend to focus only on the things that justify our feelings about life and, thus, support our position, proving that we are right. Imagine what you could be right about by focusing on the following negative thoughts:

- The markets are a disaster, and there is no way to survive in market conditions like this.

- The people on this planet are the constant victims of weather, fire, and terrorist attacks, as shown on the nightly news.
- Your wife is a constant nag.
- Your children look and act like the cast of a circus freak show.

Because you have chosen to focus only on the parts of the picture that support these negative positions, you conclude that you are right about all of it. However, what does being right about the negative part of this picture give you? It certainly does not "kick life up a notch." However, it does take you down the well-trodden path that leads to complacency and insignificance.

Consider being right about focusing on what you do have, but turning the negatives into positives:

- There are always opportunities in the markets. Someone is always on the positive side of a trade, and I am going to enjoy the process of being the trader who finds that opportunity.
- I live in a free country, in a beautiful neighborhood, with a good family, and I am going to continue to celebrate each day that I have this fortunate life.
- My wife is an incredible homemaker and loving wife and mother. Actively listening to her and letting her know how important and beautiful she is to me enhances both of our lives.
- My children are healthy, creative, and amusing with the choices that they make. I see myself in them when I was their age.

Living Life Artfully

Imagine that you are about to play a board game where you play a character making choices about how he will live his life. Wouldn't you choose to be a character living a dynamic life with lots of adventure, fame, fortune, and exciting challenges? Wouldn't you take more calculated risks, visit more places, and risk more special moments than you do presently in your own life? I think you would.

Well, guess what? You are playing a character in your life, and you do get to make choices! What are the choices that you are making? Do any of these things stop you from living your life as dynamically as you would like it to be?

- Fear of failure or success
- Fear of being wrong and losing what you have

- Routine and bad habits
- Negative interaction and negative influence from those around you
- Living life from the position of "I can't afford to!"

There are lots of good excuses for not living life artfully. Do you want to excuse your way out of living the best you can with what you have?

A trader named Greg told me the story of his life, demonstrating the importance of enjoying what you have while you possess it. While his parents struggled to put meals on the table and a roof over their family's head, they failed to fulfill their family's most basic need for adequate loving and nurturing in the process.

Through hard work and dedication, the family developed a local candy store into a small chain of supermarkets. Greg told me that he could not remember when each step in the process did not come out of sacrifice, worry, and pain. Then, Greg's father had a stroke. The stress of his being in a wheelchair without hiring needed assistance eventually killed both of his parents. Greg's parents lived their lives in the same neighborhood with the same hand-me-down furniture, never taking vacations until the day that they died. The only significant money that his family ever spent was on Greg's education, his wedding, and on a trust fund that was established for the grandchildren's education.

When his parents died, Greg inherited three times the amount of money that he had been told to expect. Now, you would think that money and the ability to spend frivolously after his parents' death would bring Greg some form of pleasure, but it didn't. No matter how much he has had, it has never been enough. Greg could not rid his consciousness of the struggling, poverty-ridden mentality of his youth. No matter how many people he has brought into his life, he has still felt starved for love and attention.

Because Greg was programmed to struggle, he was attracted to trading and the markets. The adage, "You attract what you want out of the markets" applied to Greg. His need to struggle was satisfied in his trading. He wanted to prove himself and to be successful in his own right without his family's money. He thought that if he earned his own money, he would not feel guilty about spending the money that came from their struggle and sacrifice.

In his struggles, Greg managed to make the wrong choices. As a result, he lost a great deal of his fortune along with his wife and children. Before he was able to ask for help, he also became very depressed. He could not give himself permission to appreciate and nurture anything or anyone, especially himself. Greg had to learn the importance of giving before he could learn to live successfully and prosper as a professional trader. The one saving grace for Greg was a resource that he received from his education, and that was his willingness to seek out and pay for help.

Now, Greg lives a much simpler life with a new family. He is happy with an average to good trading career. He has much less monetarily than he had before, but he has said that his life is good. He has learned to savor each moment and does not find it necessary to prove anything. He has also found it unnecessary to continue in his family tradition of struggle and sacrifice. Greg now lives a rich life.

Kicking Aliveness up a Notch

What if, like Emeril Lagasse recommends, you were to spice up the flavor of your life by simply intending to do so?

Recipe for "Kicking Life up a Notch" with Intention

- Recognize what you are thinking and what your actions are when you are depressed. Listen to what you are saying to yourself. Write it down in a notebook and read it aloud so that you can hear your self-talk.
- Take a specific predetermined time to be as miserable as possible until there is nothing left to think about except a repeat of the same self-talk.
- Take a vacation from your negative thinking. Do only what you want to do for a day or two.
- Decide how you would like your life to be. Take into account your present situation.
- Write down what is in the realm of your control and what specific tasks you can take that would make your situation better. Take action on these tasks.
- Check off from your list what you have accomplished at the end of the day.
- Now, think outside of the box of possibilities and consider what you could do if you had the resources and the right frame of mind to accomplish something beyond what is in the realm of possibilities.
- Ask others for help and ideas.

- Decide what you are willing and capable of doing without the resources that you feel you need. Add these tasks to your list of actions.
- Now state your intention out loud. Proceed to stretch yourself just beyond what you thought your limitations were.
- Each day, "Kick your life up a notch."

Conclusion

Each day, you make choices that affect how you play the part of your character in the board game of life. If you are presently in a blessed situation, you can appreciate it more by acknowledging your good fortune and by celebrating each moment. It is important to appreciate each good moment because you never know when life will throw you difficult times.

When you are handed difficulties instead of the bouquet of roses that you were expecting, realize that you still have choices. Sometimes, it is necessary to wallow in depression and worry for a time in order to be able to move on. However, you can either add to the problems by remaining stuck in your misery for too long or you can pick up the pieces as soon as you are able and make the best of the bad situation. By intentionally making better choices, you can free yourself from the role of victim to your need to be right. In good times and in all the other times, always remember to ask yourself, "How can I kick my life up a notch?" Once you ask the question, you will have already taken the first step. The next step is up to you.

CHAPTER 1

The Golden Rules of Trading

Almost any successful trader will tell you that discipline is the key to success. But how do you develop discipline? By following a set of rules for trading. For this portion of the anthology, we've compiled articles that should cover almost every trader's rules. This section will go beyond the old market adage of "let your profits run and cut your losses short." While that is a key rule to remember, there are other golden nuggets of information in this chapter from which all traders can "profit."

In the first article, Larry Pesavento outlines his three keys to avoiding trading mistakes: thinking in terms of probability, having self-discipline, and taking responsibility. Pesavento claims that because all trading depends on probability to a degree, you must think in terms of probability. No one knows to what extent, if at all, a trade will be profitable. Next, to become self-disciplined, you should focus on proper mental, technical, and physical training. Finally, after all is said and done, you should realize that no one is responsible for your trades but you.

David Lerman takes a different approach. According to Lerman, only five things matter when considering a trade: risk, return, costs, taxes, and liquidity. These five considerations can be reworded into questions that many traders will ask themselves when before making a trade: (1) How much could I lose? (2) How much could I make? (3) How much is this going to cost me? (4) How much will I owe the government? (5) How easily can I get out of this trade if necessary? These five considerations must then be analyzed in light of your trading strategy and your trading objectives.

Finally, we'll give you 21 more rules to consider. Russ Wasendorf developed a comprehensive list of trading rules to guide you through your trading days. These rules range from common advice, such as diversify your portfolio, to more personal advice, such as be well aware of who you are. And, in addition to these rules, he has also sketched some brief notes for all traders to consider. In these notes, he emphasizes the importance of remaining calm while trading and preparing a trading plan.

KNOW WHEN TO HOLD THEM AND WHEN TO FOLD THEM (AUGUST 2002)

BY LARRY PESAVENTO

It is a given that traders cannot win 100 percent of the time, because with reward comes risk, and losses are as much a fact of life as taxes and death. But there are highly valuable lessons to be learned about the trading process that go far beyond the dollar signs. How traders put reliable steps in place to ensure that their performance may be enhanced on the road to success is critical. And, for most, success is dependent not only on what is done correctly, but also on what potentially havoc-wreaking mistakes can be avoided.

The three practical principles that can aid in anticipating and, possibly, avoiding mistakes are probability, self-discipline, and responsibility—simple enough to write, but harder to carry out.

No successful trader would deny that mental preparation is just as necessary as charts and market signals. Trading is all about probabilities and, while every trader encounters a losing streak or drawdown of equity, success as a trader is measured by how well losses are handled mentally.

A "sure" sign of potential disaster is holding large losses in open positions while at the same time taking many small profits. This is contrary to the market adage by a wise trader/mentor from Commodity Corporation, Amos Barr Hostetter, who said, "Take care of your losses and your profits will take care of themselves." A trader who mentally dupes himself into believing that the small profits will offset the large losses is taking a dangerous ostrich approach.

Most losing streaks are the result of probability distribution. In 100 trades, a system should encounter a losing streak of up to eight trades in a row, and this is the time when the trader begins to question the validity of the system. It also normally is the worst time to stop trading as long as the trader has followed his methodology, because it's been shown that winning streaks generally follow losing streaks.

Examining daily trading logs enables the trader to spot some common trading mistakes, such as lack of discipline, sloppiness in trade preparation, impulse trading, impatience, and all of the other cousins and uncles in the "mistake family." One of the big advantages of the pattern recognition method of swing trading is the probability associated with each pattern. Winning is a matter of executing all of the trades as the patterns develop.

Traders must train themselves to think in terms of probability for three very important reasons:

1. No one knows with 100 percent certainty whether the trade will be profitable or not.
2. No one knows how much money will be made or lost on a trade.
3. If the trader does not control the profit outcome and does not know with 100 percent certainty which trades will work, then the trader should spend 100 percent of his time concentrating on the only element of the trade he can control—the risk of the trade.

Key to success is the ability to pinpoint how much one can afford to lose. Winners think, "How much can I lose?" while losers think, "How much can I win?" This fact is easy to demonstrate. Anyone visiting Las Vegas has been greeted by brightly colored, flashing slot machines that beckon the full-pocketed tourist with the promise "Win One Million Dollars!" However, no visitor has ever seen a sign that reads, "This machine has taken in three million dollars this year." When the trader truly learns how to think like the "house," the probability of winning is increased.

Thinking about losing requires discipline. By focusing acutely on a trading plan, the probabilities for profits or losses and streaks of each, and risk control, risk taking becomes more manageable and can give traders the ultimate gift—freedom. In fact, making discipline a daily habit allows traders "to weave a habit of a strand a day of discipline until the cable of discipline is almost unbelievable."

Discipline in trading presents itself in several parts. First, there is preparation. Trading is simple, but it takes time. Many hours of preparation occur long before any trade is entered. These steps include:

Mental. Traders must think through what risks are present in the trade, and know in advance how to get out of the trade and at what point. Mental preparation, from my experience, also assumes eliminating or limiting alcohol consumption from Sunday through Thursday of the trading week, because it typically takes up to 24 hours to completely leave the blood system. It's best to have the brain working at an optimal level.

Technical. Methodologies vary by the individual trader. All trading opportunities should be explored. A daily ritual of scanning charts will present many good opportunities. This is the time-consuming part of trading. Opportunities, however, do not guarantee profits.

Physical. Traders need to release tension in a positive way. Take time to do some type of exercise like golf, tennis, or walking.

Discipline is also necessary on the execution side of trading. Risk control is the most critical element of the trading process. Never forget how a devastating loss can destroy the psyche. It damages the trader's soul.

Monitoring a profitable trade in progress also requires discipline— follow the trading plan. Do not be concerned about minuscule fluctuations if your goal is higher. There are two questions that every trader should ask: "Has the market changed since I placed the trade? Can I afford the risk on this trade?" If the answer to both of these questions is "yes," the trader should stay in the trade.

Along with discipline, responsibility plays a significant role in the trading game. Once in the market, the trader alone has responsibility for his or her trading decisions—no one else. Not assuming personal responsibility is like jumping into a fast-moving river without a life jacket in the hopes that there is a lifeguard somewhere on the shore. The trader can keep afloat only if he is responsible for his own destiny. Take joy in the good decisions and learn from the bad ones. Place the orders, close the orders, and take the profits. Or, swallow hard and take the loss if that's the responsible thing to do and your plan points in that direction.

Traders can and do fall into the habit of making excuses about why something went wrong. Again quoting Hostetter, "Forget your profits, but forget your losses faster."

Taking responsibility can be improved by including a few steps or reminders in the trading plan. What works for one trader might not work for another. The way to handle this is to place a written statement on the computer. The statement says:

> *Has the pattern in the trade changed from the original pattern? Has the initial price objective been reached?*

If the answer to both of these questions is "yes," it's time to exit the trade. If the answer is "no," then the trade must continue; trading is a business of dealing with probabilities, not certainties. Hostetter held that, "We never know which trades will work; the problem arises when we only 'think' we know."

Probability, discipline, and responsibility are traits that every trader should strive to attain. Probability assures that losing streaks will develop, just as winning streaks will. What matters is how to recover from those losses. Discipline and responsibility help to prevent devastating losses and aid in recovery. Have the discipline to exit or stay in a trade, and take responsibility for the actions. Again, losses are not 100 percent preventable; however, with the right trading strategies and mental focus, many may be avoided.

THE FIVE DIMENSIONS OF SUCCESSFUL TRADING (AUGUST 2002)

By David Lerman

I used to teach an investment management class at the college level, and, invariably, students would approach me about a particular investment. They wished to determine if it was appropriate and if I thought it was a good "bet." I would always respond with five questions:

1. What are the risks?
2. What is the return potential over the short, medium, and long haul?
3. What are the costs associated with making the investment?
4. What are the tax implications of making the investment?
5. How liquid is the investment (although technically, this falls under risks and costs)?

When you cut through all the headlines, all the hype, written material, web sites and analysis, only five things matter: risk, return, costs, taxes, and liquidity. We will address risk and return together and the others individually, using case studies/illustrations.

Investment Risk/Return: Just as in Life, There Is a Relationship

According to Gary Gastineau in his *Dictionary of Financial Risk Management,* risk is the exposure to change. It is usually viewed in terms of adverse change, i.e., "How much money can I lose?"

In many financial circles, risk is defined mathematically as the annualized standard deviation of returns. Higher-standard-deviation instruments have higher risk, and vice versa. For example, the NASDAQ 100 index has a standard deviation or risk measurement of more than 55 percent. Compare this to the S&P 500 index, which has a standard deviation of around 22 percent (in calendar year 2001). The NASDAQ 100 index is one of the more volatile financial instruments (*risk* and *volatility* are used interchangeably in the markets) in the world. As a further comparison, Canadian dollars, which have a standard deviation of less than 5 percent, are one of the least volatile instruments. Instruments with higher risk obviously fluctuate more than those with low-risk gauges. So, if you had to remove your money sooner than expected and the instrument was on a volatile downswing, you might lose money (an adverse change per Gastineau's definition).

All Returns Are Not Created Equal

Risk is not a bad thing, but most investors ignore it or fail to try to understand its implications. This is mainly because novices tend to look primarily at returns and ask questions such as, "How much can I make on this trade or investment?" without taking into account the risks involved in obtaining that given return. Let's look at an example using two investors.

- Investor A trades pork belly futures and obtains a 3-year annualized rate of return of 5 percent.
- Investor B invests in U.S. Treasury notes and obtains a 3-year annualized return of 5 percent.

So, which investor would you rather be? Many people would indicate it doesn't matter—both earned the same return. Smarter investors that analyze risk in terms of return would answer differently. Pork bellies are similar to the NASDAQ 100 index in that they are extremely volatile. In other words, they are typically much riskier than U.S. Treasury notes (actually, more than twice as risky). In this case, investor B is getting the same returns as investor A, but is taking much less risk. Now, what if investor A obtained a 7 percent return? A 10 percent return? Again, the investor must ask what is an adequate return relative to the risk that he/she is taking.

It stands to reason that someone trading a risky or volatile commodity should expect to be compensated for that added risk. When risk is reduced, returns typically also should come down. There are money managers in finance who have perfected the art of obtaining very good returns while taking less risk. Too often, though, investors take huge risks and fail to be compensated with higher returns. We have to look no further than the NASDAQ 100 and S&P 500 index examples. Risk in the NASDAQ 100 index far outweighs the risk of the S&P 500, yet the higher risk did not provide higher returns recently, as the NASDAQ 100 slid 80 percent from its high mark in March of 2000. The S&P 500 has "only" declined by 30 percent. In this case, more risk did not provide greater relative returns.

These principles apply to futures trading or, for that matter, any kind of trading. Similarly, when investors are comparing managed futures funds or hedge funds, they often will look at risk-adjusted returns to see which managers are obtaining the best possible returns while taking the least amount of risk. The overall lesson to be learned: The riskiest path might not be the most profitable! Turn the other way when you see promises of triple-digit returns every month. To obtain those returns, you would have to subject yourself to enormous risks . . . risks which most people really should avoid. After all, the greatest investors achieve returns (over a two- to three-decade horizon) in the area of 25 to 30 percent. These notables include Michael Steinhardt, George Soros, and Warren Buffett, none of whom would ever expect to double their money each year for 30 years.

Watch Costs like a Hawk

The next consideration, after getting a handle on risk and reward, is the various costs incurred by investors. These come in the form of commissions, bid-offer spreads, and additional fees such as management or incentive fees, as well as margin requirements. One of the reasons futures contracts have enjoyed such popularity over the years is because of their low-cost nature. However, some investors have not learned to mitigate these various costs, and their trading suffers as a result. Believe it or not, there are some firms (name and location not to be revealed) that have exorbitant commission and fee structures. One investor confessed to me that he paid $295 commission to get into a futures contract. I was floored. Even a full-service top-of-the-line firm is dramatically less than $295. Discounters can be as much as one-tenth as cheap or even cheaper. Fortunately, many firms are reasonable, and with the advent of discount commissions and electronic trading, commissions have really dropped dramatically in the last 5 years.

Bid-offer spreads also contribute to costs. The tighter the spread, the better in terms of slippage, especially if you are an active trader. Wide spreads make consistent profits harder to achieve, and the combination of high spreads and large commissions can be a real drag on profitability.

With mutual funds, the cost comparisons are particularly interesting because most Americans own mutual funds via their 401(k) plans. (See Table 17.1). The average fund's expense ratio is about 143 basis points per annum (1.43 percent). However, some of the lower-cost funds, such as index funds, have expense ratios of less than 20 basis points.

At the end of 2002, the investment community will witness the launch of single stock futures. One of the advantages of these investments will be the up-front margin relative to securities margin. Currently, securities that are margined require 50 percent of the value of the security (Regulation T). Single stock futures will be margined at considerably less, probably around 25 percent. Futures, in general, have a tremendous advantage in that the up-front capital costs are a fraction of the Federal Reserve's Regulation T margins.

The lesson to be learned: Focus on keeping costs and capital outlays to a minimum, and your results will be dramatically better. Often the difference between a successful trader and an unsuccessful trader is costs.

Uncle Sam Collects

The Internal Revenue Code of the United States applies to 280 million Americans, and, to the dismay of some investors, the IRS is one intermediary that always gets its due. One way of avoiding paying higher taxes is to hold stocks or mutual funds for a longer period of time, allowing investors to qualify for long-term capital gain status. But for those who trade more actively, the best solution is to trade futures, as they fall under the IRS's "section 1256 contracts" and are usually taxed more favorably (Section 1256 of the Internal Revenue code is the area that deals with taxation of futures contracts). Section 1256 contracts are treated at the favorable 60/40 rate. Hence, 60 percent of the gain is taxed at favorable rates

TABLE 17.1

Greatest Risk Not Always Greatest Return

To further our understanding of risk and return, let's examine three popular mutual funds and their risk/return profiles over the last few years.

Fund	10-Year Compounded Return*	Standard Deviation (Risk)
Mutual Qualified	15.12%	13.39
Fidelity Magellan	11.77%	16.91
Fidelity Growth Co.	12.77%	37.70

*10 years ending 5/31/02.

As the table above clearly illustrates, higher risk doesn't always translate into higher returns. Mutual Qualified had the best 10-year returns of the group, yet did it with less risk than the Fidelity Magellan fund and significantly less risk than the Fidelity Growth Co. fund.
Source: Morningstar.

and 40 percent is taxed at ordinary income rates . . . for a blended rate of about 28 percent (for someone in the 39.6 percent bracket).

Lesson to be learned: Paying taxes means you are profiting from your trades. Pay them with joy! Or trade futures and minimize the bite.

Get Involved in Liquid Markets

In the United States, we are fortunate in that we enjoy regulated exchanges that provide excellent liquidity, which enables us to get in and out of most of our investments. Unfortunately, there are some investments that don't fall under the "liquid" category. In the 1980s, there were some real estate limited partnerships that had no liquidity. If the investor wanted to exit, it was next to impossible to sell some of these partnerships (they also had very high fees—approaching 10 percent). Ditto with an arcane insurance product called viatical settlements; they were interesting instruments but had no secondary market on which to trade out of them. In addition, there are some OTC deals in structured products that do not enjoy good liquidity.

On the other hand, Eurodollar futures (and options) are the most liquid futures contracts in the world. You can do a $5 billion notional value trade (5000 contracts) in these markets and not move the bid/offer spread on a typical day. The E-mini S&P 500 is less than 5 years old, yet large trades of up to 300 to 500 contracts regularly are traded on the Globex system. However, there are some contracts that don't share the same liquidity. If you are a novice, you must tread carefully and avoid illiquid markets. If you need to get out of (or into) a trade in a hurry, you want deep, liquid markets. Make sure there is adequate open interest and average daily volume to affect your trading plan.

THE 21 GOLDEN RULES OF TRADING (SEPTEMBER 2002)

BY RUSSELL WASENDORF, SR.

Rules inspire discipline, which is the single most important characteristic any trader can possess. And the trader that doesn't have a written set of trading rules for himself would be wise to prepare one. Writing stimulates thought, and it helps traders refine and define their thinking.

Like any profession, a body of rules has evolved over the years for futures traders. Why learn the rules? There are two reasons. First, they give a trader a good insight into what other traders can be expected to do when faced with similar situations. Futures trading, by its very nature, deals with the unknown. But because no one really knows what will happen next, many tend to stick with the rules and move with the crowd. If a trader can sense the direction of the herd and move with it, he can potentially make a good living as a commodity trader. This is how a trend-following system works. The only caveat is that the market must be trending, which is not always the case.

The second reason to learn the rules is to know when to break them. This is the essence of contrarian trading. These traders zig when everyone else is zagging. They look to short bull rallies, going south when everyone else is headed north. These traders often do well in choppy, trendless markets. Plus, if they are right, they can catch trends just as they begin and exit before they crash. Trend followers, on the other hand, often miss or lose a portion of each move.

Let's take the example of a long silver position that has been trending slowly higher for the last 6 weeks, moving from $5.00 an ounce to $5.25. That's a gain of $1250.00 (5000 oz. × $0.25) per contract. When the move stalls, trend followers must wait to see if the trend has actually changed or if silver is going to head higher after some sideways movement. If the trend has changed, it may drop a nickel or so before the trend change is confirmed. In other words, they give up $250.00 (5000 oz. × $0.05) waiting for confirmation. They probably lost approximately the same amount at the beginning of this move, as they waited for confirmation that the move had begun.

The life of the contrarian isn't any easier. The classic contrarian can catch moves early but, in the process, often trades a false start or move. The market moves his direction temporarily, only to move violently against his position. In other words, contrarians are prey for false moves. They may also get out of moves too soon, if they misread the market or get another false signal.

There is no simple, sure-fire route to trading success. But knowing and understanding the following rules, even if the trader chooses to ignore one or more of them from time to time, can help. At least he'll have an idea of what other professional traders are considering as they face the same situation. Let's begin with some very general, almost philosophical principles and then get more specific.

Rule #1: Contradicts All the Ones That Follow. Be a Doubting Thomas!

Don't believe everything you hear about trading. Use advice as a guide and find out what works for you. This frame of mind spills over into those things your broker and fellow traders tell you are going to happen in a particular market—or their advice in general. A lot of people make a lot of money in the futures market, but there are few, if any, who have made money consistently by simply listening to someone else. The basic rules, combined with your education, experience, and understanding of the markets, blend into a unique approach. This is your trading system, and it includes money management and psychological restraints, as well as your trade entry and exit decisions.

Rule #2: Be Open to New Ideas, New Strategies, New Markets, New Information and New Forms of Trading and Communicating

Never forget that you are attempting to predict what will occur at some point in the future. Most traders assume that price patterns repeat, but exactly when and how closely the patterns mirror past ones is unknown. Look for the old, but trade the new. Your approach to the markets should include the flexibility to change your mind.

- Trade the short side of a market as well as the long.
- Make adjustments in your money management or trading system.
- Consider markets you haven't previously traded.

A successful trader is aware of the most options or alternative paths. He has the flexibility of a master chess player and can adjust to anticipate the unexpected.

Rule #3: Be Well Aware of Who You Are

Trading futures is 90 percent mental, and, to paraphrase a famous baseball saying, the rest is knowledge and experience. Know your level of risk tolerance. You won't make sound decisions when you are over your head financially, when you are too tired or ill, or if you are not prepared to trade. Don't be afraid of missing an opportunity by taking a day off. Believe it or not, there are always great new trades in the offing. Learn to be patient, and pick and choose your trades carefully.

Also, be sure to match your personality and temperament to your trading system. If you're not a detailed person, use a system that doesn't require any. If you're very excitable, avoid day trading. Consider being a position trader and, once you put a position on, let it alone until you're ready to offset it or you've been stopped out.

Rule #4: Diversify!

Think about diversification on many levels. To begin with, futures trading should represent only a portion of your risk capital. Allocate 10 percent to

20 percent of what you consider risk capital. This is money that, if you were to lose all of it, would not affect your lifestyle.

Next, you need enough trading equity to give yourself a better-than-average opportunity to be in the right market on the right side at the right time. Having the resources to trade only one market at a time limits your odds substantially. Additionally, you need enough reserves to withstand setbacks and losses. Some very serious traders even like to further diversify by investing in some type of professionally managed futures trading program, besides the account they personally trade.

There is also the concept of negative correlation to consider. This is the backbone of the Modern Portfolio Theory. Negative correlation occurs when one market or investment class (stock, futures, real estate, etc.) moves up compared with another that is moving down.

Rule #5: Place Your Markets in Their Historical Perspectives

Even if you don't use them as signals or indicators, you should know the historical highs and lows of the markets you trade. Additionally, you must have a good understanding of the seasonal patterns and major cycles. Why? Simply because a large number of technical traders will trade based on these patterns. You must take their anticipated reactions into account as part of your overall trading analysis. If, for example, you go long corn into what are the normal seasonal lows (at harvest), you better have good reasons or deep pockets.

Rule #6: Develop a Sound Knowledge of Technical Analysis

The same reasoning expostulated in #5 applies to developing a sound knowledge of technical analysis. It is often called a "self-fulfilling prophecy" because so many traders see the same technical signal and react in unison. For example, an uptrend line is broken, alerting technical traders that the current uptrend is now a downtrend. Just like a herd of longhorns heading for water, they stampede to the short side of the market.

Rule #7: Don't Spit into the Wind, Trust a Junkyard Dog or Trade Contrary to the Trend

There are good psychological reasons why trends are created and maintained. For instance, would you pay more for something you intended to resell if you didn't think it was going to increase in value? Of course not. You go long a market because you believe you'll be able to sell the futures contract for more in the future. The same is true of a downtrending market. You sell them because you think you'll be able to buy or offset your positions at a lower price. This is nothing but human nature. Just about all traders feel this way, causing markets to trend.

Therefore, you need to know the trend of the market you are about to enter before you open a position. You can either go with or against the trend. If you go against the trend, you need a good reason. Is it about to enter an area of resistance you feel it cannot penetrate, or are you becoming aware of some fundamental information that is not yet in the market, but has the potential of turning it around? Either way, you want to know what the herd is thinking.

Rule #8: Develop a Definite Plan or Strategy for Entering and Exiting Trades

For example, you might enter a market with limit orders and exit by continually moving your trailing stops closer to the trading range, until they are hit. There is a danger in not carefully planning entry and exit points. All too often, traders get into markets too late and exit too early. Also, novice traders may get filled "unexpectedly" and have no idea what to do next or when to get out.

Rule #9: Your Trading Plan Should Include a Risk-Array Analysis

Part of your trading plan should include a risk-array analysis. This makes you aware of the downside risk you are facing. The first part of this array is locating areas of support for long positions and resistance for short positions. Next, you need to evaluate how strong or dependable these support or resistance points are.

For example, let's say you are planning to take a long position in the silver market at $6, and your analysis leads you to believe that silver will move to the $6.50 area. This would be a gain of $2500 per contract ($0.50 × 5000 oz.) before transaction costs, over the next 3 to 4 weeks.

But what if you're wrong? What if it moves lower? By studying the long, mid, and/or daily price charts (or using some other type of analysis), you pinpoint areas of support at $5.95, $5.86, and $5.84. This simply means that past downward movements in this market have slowed, stalled, or stopped at these prices. Therefore, you assume they may do the same again. If you assume that this analysis highlights $5.86 as the most reliable of the support areas, you'll calculate your downside risk at 14 cents, or $700. Your expectations (or best estimates) are a $2500 gain versus

$700.00 loss, or 31/2:1 reward-to-risk ratio. This is an acceptable range.

One last consideration you need to be aware of is daily trading limits. For silver, it is 50 cents. This means that, in the case of a 5000-ounce silver futures contract, your position can move against you to the tune of 50 cents per ounce on a given day—or $2500.00. And, a futures contract can make limit moves for more than one day in a row. Limit days occur when there is a lot of volatility in a market, caused by uncertainty, fast-breaking news, rumors, or other unexpected events! To complete your risk-array analysis, you must factor in the possibility of limit moves for or against your positions. Calculating this unknown is a value judgment you make from experience.

Rule #10: Guard Against Overtrading

There are two situations in which traders are particularly vulnerable—either right after they have just made a big gain or a big loss. If they have just pocketed a major gain, they feel omnipotent, invulnerable, and can't make a mistake. They believe every trade they pick will be a winner. On the other hand, following a substantial loss, some traders become desperate to earn back their loss. Their trading becomes wild and erratic. This is called the "double-or-nothing" syndrome.

In either case, the trader has lost the discipline needed to rationally trade. The best thing to do is to take a "trading holiday." In other words, just stop trading for a day or two (longer if necessary) until the warm glow of success or the pain of failure passes. Then, go back to the markets as if the event never occurred.

Rule #11: Don't Let Profits Become Losses

This may sound obvious, but it is a common problem for many traders. Variations of this axiom are (1) never hold positions too long and (2) avoid the temptation to pick tops or bottoms. What often happens is that traders become greedy once their positions become profitable. Instead of taking profits when available, they cling to trades. Eventually, as all markets do, trends change direction. Since bear moves tend to be faster than bull moves, prices can plunge. Before traders with profitable long positions realize it, the profits disappear and the positions are losers. The same can happen to traders holding out to close long positions at the top or shorts at the bottom.

So, if you wait too long to take profits, you'll often regret it, and it can play havoc with your nervous system. An approach mentioned earlier—that of following profitable positions with protective trailing stops—can help resolve this character flaw. Remember, "Bears win and bulls win, but hogs always lose in the end!"

Rule #12: Avoid Closing Positions Prematurely

A corollary to the previous rule is to avoid closing positions prematurely. Traders have been known to frequently open a position and close it precisely when their price objective is hit. No one, of course, can tell just how far a market is going up (or down) by how far it has gone already. The only true way of knowing is when it changes direction and is no longer going up or down. Following positions with protective stops also helps to correct this downfall.

Rule #13: Learn the Art of Placing Protective Stops

While it is easy to tell you to place stops, it is not as easy to tell you how or where. It requires a great deal of experience with the specific markets traded and a good feel for the current and expected volatility. You need to place your stops close enough to where your position is trading to protect yourself from losing what you've gained so far, yet not so close as to get prematurely stopped out. In other words, if the futures contract you are trading has had a day range over the past few weeks of 4 cents, you would place a stop at least outside of this range (above for short positions and below for long). Additionally, you'll need to know where the support and resistance levels are and if there are any technical signals that could influence other traders.

For example, if your market has been trending upward along a 45-degree angle for the past 3 weeks, many traders will be following it. If this trend line is broken, these traders will probably react to it by going short, driving the market down further. Therefore, your stop should follow this trend line. If you get stopped out and are still bullish, look for a point to reenter. Where would this be? It can often be found at the next support or resistance level.

Your objective in placing stops is to protect yourself if your analysis is wrong and/or to avoid giving any profit back to the market once it is earned. At the same time, you want to avoid being whipsawed.

Rule #14: Try Not to Overtax Your Resources, Particularly Time

Carefully evaluate how much of a commitment in time, money, and mental resources you can make. Most part-time traders should avoid day trading because they can't sit in front of a quote screen during trading hours.

Also, day trading takes a lot out of one emotionally, and there's nothing left some days for your regular job.

Part-timers should limit themselves to tracking three to five markets and actually trading only two to three. The markets should be ones for which you have a special knowledge or a special interest. Trading markets of which you're particularly fond makes the research easier.

Rule #15: Plan and Develop Rules for Taking Profits

For example, don't exit a market just because you've become bored with a trade. On the other hand, if a market moves dramatically in your direction and you have no idea why, take your windfall profit, or at least put a tight stop behind the position. Part-time traders should never buy or sell to get scalping profits (these are small, short-term profits); it takes too much time to follow the markets closely enough to be successful on a regular basis.

Rule #16: Learn How to Short the Market

The majority of new and part-time traders go long. Most of us are just more comfortable buying a futures contract at a given price and selling it for a profit at a higher price. We seem to find it foreign to our thought process to sell something we don't have and to buy it back later. But futures trading is a zero-based business, meaning that for every gain there is a loss. The short side of the markets can be just as rewarding as the long. Keep in mind that bear moves last about half as long as bull moves and the use of stops is just as important.

Rule #17: Never Hedge "Trade" or Try to Spread out of Losses

True hedging occurs when you are on both sides of a market. The correct way to do this is to be on the cash market on one side and the futures side on the other. The rationale for hedging is to pass the risk of ownership to a speculator and lock in an acceptable profit.

Some futures traders, when faced with a losing long position, sell a short. They call it hedging, but it is not. It's more like a spread. This is poor trading. When faced with a losing position, offset it and take your loss. If you wish to trade spreads, do so. Look for spread opportunities when the relationship between two related contracts is misaligned. If you decide to reverse your position, do it. But do it as a completely new trade.

Rule #18: Never Go Long Just because a Futures Price Is "Low" or, Conversely, Short because a Futures Price Seems "High"

The logic that if a commodity is below the cost of production, it must go higher often traps traders. This may be true in the long run, but it isn't true in the short to medium term. The old onion contract once went below the cost of the bags in which they were packaged. Silver is often a by-product of lead and other base-metal mining. Its production can continue after its price drops below production costs. Even the livestock market can continue to produce when it is in the red. For example, it takes 21/2 years from the time a cow is bred until a steak is produced from its offspring. This process can't be turned on and off at will.

Consequently, if you shorted the silver market in early 1980 because it was "too high" at $30.00 an ounce, you would have regretted your move, as silver futures shot up over $10.00 more an ounce.

Rule #19: Never Leg out of a Spread Unless This Was Your Original Strategy

Legging out of a spread means selling off one side and continuing to hold the other. For example, let's say you notice the gold-to-silver ratio is over 90 to 1. It takes 90 ounces of silver to buy 1 ounce of gold. You think this is "high" and should return to a level of 60 or 70 to 1, so you decide to enter a spread. Your analysis indicates silver should gain on gold, reducing the spread. Therefore you go long silver and short gold. To get a better balance dollarwise between the two metals, you decide to go long two silver contracts and short one gold contract per spread.

You are in a legitimate spread for legitimate reasons. Therefore, when you close out this position, you should offset both legs. Sometimes inexperienced traders see both gold and silver increasing in value. They adjust by offsetting the short gold and holding the long silver, or even reversing the short gold to a long gold. Remember that the purpose of a spread is to profit from the changing relationship between the two commodities. In this case, the trader expects silver to move farther and faster than gold, while being protected from adverse bearish moves in metals by being short gold. It is generally considered a more conservative play than that of holding net long positions in both commodities.

There is nothing wrong with being net long or net short. It is just a completely different trade than a spread and should be entered that way. You can get yourself in trouble by making changes and adjustments mid-stream. Most of the time, you are better off backing out of any trades that are not working, taking your losses, and beginning new trades.

Rule #20: Learn the Risks and Rewards of "Pyramiding"

Learn the risks and rewards of "pyramiding," or using unrealized profits on current futures positions as margin for more positions, usually in successively smaller increments. For example, let's say you are long 10 IBM single stock futures positions. The price goes up $0.25 per share, and your research indicates it is going even higher. You add 5 new positions with your paper profits. Your analysis is correct, and you add 2 more positions with additional new profits. It moves still higher, so you add 1 more. You build a pyramid with a base of 10 contracts, then 5, 2, and 1. Ergo, the name "pyramiding."

The risk is, of course, giving in to greed and holding the positions too long. You're buying new positions with unrealized (paper) profits. If the market turns against you, you now have 18 contracts, not the initial 10. The last 8 were purchased at prices substantially higher than the initial 10. These are more vulnerable to negative price activity.

On the other hand, the reward is that you are increasing your leverage. The initial leverage required to purchase 10 contracts, now controls 18. If you exit with a profit on all contracts, your reward-to-equity ratio will be spectacular.

Rule #21: Self-Discipline Is the Ultimate Key to Successful Futures Trading

If you learn nothing else from this material, this is the most important single aspect.

- Create a comprehensive trading strategy. This includes money management as well as a trading system. Money management is the more important of the two.
- Never trade when you are sick, physically or psychologically.
- Follow your own trading system. Avoid the advice of others. If you want someone else to make your trading decisions, give them the discretion (limited power of attorney) to do it.
- Set break periods. For example, if you have several losses in a row, it's time to back off for a while.
- Keep a written journal explaining why you entered each trade, why you exited, the results, and a critique of your performance. Compare what you actually do to your initial money management and trading strategy.

- Try not to procrastinate. If you select a trade, do it. If you're hesitant, don't do it.

Futures traders are working for themselves. Trading is a business at best, an investment at the least. It requires the same attention and devotion your employer expects from you on the job.

And if you're serious, there is a definite need to keep permanent, preferably written, records of your trading activity. If for some reason you just can't put it into writing, at least dictate it into a recorder. This process will help you clarify your thinking. As you play it back, ask yourself: "Do I believe what I'm hearing?" "Is this trader (me) rationalizing away his (my) errors?" If you can, have your recording transcribed.

A paper trail is better. It takes more thought to put something into writing, and thinking helps trading. Detail notes written on the pages of a charting service. They explain why the trades were put on; your feelings of the trader before, after, and during the trade; and why the positions were exited. After a period of time, go back and review each trade. Write a line or two recording what you learned from each trade. Eventually, this casual trading history will become an extremely valuable guide. Having a written account also will allow you to refer back to it from time to time when you run into similar markets, problems, or areas of uncertainty. Some day, it will make an excellent textbook on trading.

Don't do another thing, particularly a trade, until you have at least a rough draft of your trading rules. Procrastination could be very costly. It's your future you're creating, so do it right!

TRADER'S NOTE: DON'T PANIC—#1 IN THE SERIES (FEBRUARY 2003)

By Russell Wasendorf, Sr.

I became involved in the futures industry about 30 years ago. The industry and trading has held my interest for all these years, perhaps because I never really mastered the futures markets. No matter how much I think I know about the markets, myself, and trading strategies, I still learn something new every day. The futures markets are a quintessential example of the axiom that the only thing in life that is constant is change.

As a personal trader, despite constant variability, or perhaps because of it, I have been able to eke out a consistent trading profit. With Trader's Notes, I intend to offer *SFO* readers a few trading tidbits, ideas, or even some "war stories." I make no claim to be a market guru or trading genius; I am just a guy that makes money trading in the futures markets.

During the last 30 years I have been exposed to nearly every trading strategy, concept, technique, and misadventure in the futures industry. Yet, I use no technique religiously. With all that I have learned, I still make mistakes, miscalculations, and fail to follow proven rules of trading. Basically, I'm much like most traders. To extend that analogy even further, I am a part-time trader like most personal traders. I don't trade every day, and I don't even maintain constant attention to my open positions. I do, after all, have a "real job," like most of you.

Also like most of you, when it comes to trading, I am left to my own devices. Regardless of the fact that I head a large futures brokerage firm, I do not tap the resources of my firm for trading ideas or strategies. My trading decisions are my own decisions. I firmly believe for any personal trader to be successful in the long run, they need to make their own decisions.

With that said, I'll begin with what I feel is the single most important trading advice—Don't Panic! Like revenge, trading ideas are best served cold. Trading is the worst place to express passion, fear, greed, joy, hope, or, for that matter, any kind of emotion. If it feels good, don't do it.

The opposite of panic is patience. Joe Gressel told *SFO* readers in my January interview with him that patience is his most important trading virtue. Patience is important in every aspect of trading: market entry, market exit, position building, taking profits, and even cutting losses. Patience is passive, while panic is aggressive and active. Simply put, to be a successful trader, you can't become emotionally involved with your decision making or with your trades.

As I continue this series of Trader's Notes, you will discover the consistent thread in the advice is to take emotions out of futures trading. Yet, I'll be the first to admit that it is not entirely possible to fully extract emotions. No matter how often I remind myself, I occasionally panic, and I pay dearly for it! It does help that I have a sign on my trading screen, in large friendly letters, "Don't Panic."

TRADER'S NOTE: TRADING WITH A PLAN—#2 IN THE SERIES (MARCH 2003)

By Russell Wasendorf, Sr.

Last month, I emphasized the significance of having patience in your trading tactics and underscored the calamities of panicking. To panic is to abandon your plan. Trading without a plan is seldom profitable, even on a short-term basis and never for the long-term. I can offer you some general advice on constructing a plan, but, ultimately, you'll have to construct your own trading plan. You need a trading plan that fits your personality and is matched to your personal idiosyncrasies and style. The three essential elements of a trading plan are:

1. A call to action. Many traders feel this is the entire plan, or at least their overemphasis on this point would lead one to believe this is the most critical element. The fact is that market analysis and trading signals are worthless without the two points that follow. A call to action is the event or series of events that you select as your indication that it is time to buy or sell a market. Volumes have been written on this subject. Analysis techniques are abundant, and some actually do a great job of giving market entry recommendations, but giving a buy or sell indication is only part of a good plan. A good trading plan also tells you when to get out of the market—when to take profits and when to cut losses. You need to determine in advance what to do if you are right in your market analysis and, conversely, what you need to do if you are wrong.

2. A plan for what to do if you are right. OK, so you have selected the right direction—how far will the market go or, more important, how far do you expect it to go? This is where a lot of trading plans fall apart. Most trading advice and advisers leave you out in the cold on this issue; they tell you what markets to get into but don't tell you when and how to get out. Will you get out too soon and leave profit potential "on the table," or will you wait too long and have your profits disappear? Perhaps the statesman and financier Bernard M. Baruch should influence your plan; he once said, "I made my money by selling too soon."

3. A plan for what you will do if you are wrong. Everyone has heard the adage, "Cut your losses short and let your profits run," but cutting losses forces you to admit that you are wrong, and many people have a real problem doing that. Some of the best traders I know are humble; some of the worst are doctors and lawyers. But, the willingness to actually admit being wrong is essential to surviving—remember, to be a successful trader, you must first be a market survivor!

Clearly, two-thirds of a successful trading plan falls into the category of money or position management, and only one-third relies on market analysis.

Glossary

A

Amex: The American Stock Exchange, located in New York City. Its lines of business include stocks, stock options, and exchange-traded funds (ETFs). This exchange, which offers many products through its trading floor, is the only echange that is not wholly electronic that announced intention to offer security futures. As of press time, it has not released contract specifications or a list of possible security futures products.

Arbitrage: The simultaneous purchase of an asset in one market and the sale of a comparable asset in another market in order to profit from discrepancies in usual price relationships. See also *Spread*.

Ask price: The price at which a seller will sell.

Associated person (AP): One who solicits orders, customers, or customer funds for a futures commission merchant, an introducing broker, a commodity trading adviser, or a commodity pool operator and who is registered with the Commodity Futures Trading Commission.

At the money: An option whose strike price equals, or approximately equals, the current market price of the underlying asset.

B

Back month: Traded contract month of a futures contract that is furthest from expiration. Also referred to as deferred months. See also *Contract month, Front month*.

Basis: The difference between the price of the futures contract and the cash or spot price. (Unless otherwise specified, the price of the nearest contract month is used to calculate basis.)

Bear market/bear/bearish: A market in which prices are declining. A market participant who expects prices to move lower is called a bear. An event is considered bearish if it is expected to produce lower prices.

Best execution: A requirement that brokers and others execute customer orders at the best available price in the shortest amount of time.

Bid: An offer to buy a financial instrument at a stated price.

Bid/ask spread: The price difference between the current highest offer to buy and the current lowest offer to sell.

Break: A quick and steep price decline.

Breakaway gap: A gap in prices that indicates the end of a trend and the beginning of a critical market move.

Broad-based index futures: Futures contracts whose underlying asset is a broad-based index generally consisting of ten or more securities and does not fall under the definition of a narrow-based index. They are not considered to be security futures products, so they are regulated soley by the Commodity Futures Trading Commission. See also *Stock index*, *Narrow-based index futures*.

Broker: A person who is paid a fee or commission for acting as an agent in making contracts or sales. More specifically, the term may refer to (1) a floor broker, who executes orders on the trading floor of an exchange, (2) an associated person account executive, who deals with customers and their orders at a broker/dealer, futures commission merchant, or introducing broker, or (3) a broker/dealer, futures commission merchant, or introducing broker.

Broker/dealer (B/D): An individual or firm, paid a fee or commission, that acts as an agent between buyer and seller, and may also be in the business of buying and selling securities for his or her own or the firm's account.

Brokerage fee: The charge for executing a transaction. The charge may be per transaction or a percentage of the total value of the transaction. Also known as a commission fee.

Browser-based systems: Trading systems that provide a series of web pages that allow you to enter orders, view working orders, get quotes, and so on.

Bull market/bull/bullish: A market in which prices are rising. A market participant who expects prices to move higher is called a bull. An event is considered bullish if it is expected to move prices higher.

Buy or sell on open or close: To buy or sell at the beginning or end of the trading day.

C

Calendar spread: The simultaneous purchase of one contract month and sale of another contract month for the same instrument on the same exchange.

Call (option): In options, a contract that gives a buyer the right, but not the obligation, to purchase a particular futures contract or security at a stated price on or before a stated date. Buyers of call options generally hope to profit from an increase in the price of the underlying asset.

Carrying charges: Costs incurred in holding a physical commodity or financial instrument; these generally include interest, insurance, and storage.

Cash commodity: The physical commodity, as distinguished from futures contracts. Also known as actuals.

Cash settlement: The receipt of money instead of the underlying commodity to fulfill the delivery requirements of the futures contract. The amount of money is based on the daily settlement price of the underlying commodity.

Charting: In technical analysis, the use of charts and graphs to plot price trends, average movements of price and volume, and open interest. See *Technical analysis*.

Clearing: The method by which trades are reviewed for accuracy. After trades are validated, the clearinghouse or association becomes the buyer to each seller and the seller to each buyer. Through this procedure, a clearinghouse keeps records of all trades and resulting positions, ensures performance on those positions, and facilitates the daily passthrough of profits and losses via a mark-to-market process.

Clearing member: A member of a clearinghouse or an association. All trades of a nonclearing member must be settled through a clearing member.

Clearinghouse: An agency connected with an exchange through which all futures contracts are made, offset, and fulfilled by physical delivery or cash settlement.

Close: The end of the trading session designated by the exchange, during which all transactions are considered to be made "at the close."

Commission: The fee a broker charges a customer for completion of a certain duty, such as the buying or selling of futures contracts.

Commodity: A unit of trade or commerce, services, or rights on which futures contracts may be traded. Commodities may include, but are not limited to, agricultural products, financial instruments, foreign currencies, indexes, and metals.

Commodity Exchange Act: The federal act that provides for federal regulation of futures trading and is the mandate for the Commodity Futures Trading Commission.

Commodity Futures Modernization Act (CFMA): The act, passed in December 2000, that amends the Commodity Exchange Act and legalizes the trading of security futures products, including single stock futures.

Commodity Futures Trading Commission (CFTC): A commission set up by Congress through the Commodity Exchange Act to oversee the futures industry.

Commodity pool: A venture in which assets contributed by a number of persons are collected for the purpose of trading futures contracts and/or options on futures. Not the same as a joint account.

Commodity pool operator (CPO): An individual or firm, generally required to be registered with the Commodity Futures Trading Commission, that operates or solicits funds, securities, or property for a commodity pool. According to the NFA, registration is required unless the total gross capital contributions to all pools are less than $200,000 and there are no more than 15 participants in any one pool.

Commodity trading adviser (CTA): An individual or firm that trades for commodity pools and/or individual clients. A CTA may also issue analysis or reports on commodities and advise others on trading in commodity futures, options, or leverage contracts.

Common stock: A class of securities representing ownership in a company whose value may appreciate or depreciate. Owners of this type of stock may also receive dividends, but only after preferred stockholders, if any, receive them. See *Preferred stock*.

Consolidation: A break in trading activity during which prices move sideways. Traders often assess their positions during periods of consolidation.

Contract: A term describing a unit of trading for a commodity.

Contract month: The month in which a contract is to be settled, either physically or monetarily, in accordance with the futures contract.

Contract size: The quantity of the underlying asset represented by a futures contract.

Corporate actions/events: Changes in the structure of a corporation or in the price and/or quantity of a corporation's stock. These changes may be caused by stock splits, stock consolidation, special dividends, and spin-offs. Exchanges adjust security futures contracts to reflect these changes.

Cover: See *Offset*.

Current delivery (month): The futures contract that will expire and must be settled during the current month; also called spot month.

Customer segregated funds: See *Segregated account*.

D

Day order: An order that expires automatically at the end of the trading session on the day it was entered if it is not executed.

Day traders: Traders who establish and liquidate positions in one trading day, leaving them with no open positions. They are generally members of the exchange and active on the trading floor.

Debit balance: The state of a customer's account when the trading losses exceed the amount of equity.

Default: In futures markets, the failure to carry out a futures contract as required by exchange rules, such as a failure to meet a margin call or to make or take delivery.

Deferred months: The more distant delivery months in which futures trading is taking place, as distinguished from the nearby delivery months.

Delivery: In settlement of a futures contract, the tender and receipt of an actual commodity or other negotiable instrument covering that commodity.

Delivery month: The calendar month during which a futures contract may be settled and becomes deliverable. See *Contract month.*

Delivery notice: A clearinghouse notice of a seller's intention to deliver the physical commodity against a short futures position.

Delivery price: The official settlement price of the trading session during which the buyer of futures contracts receives delivery notice of the seller's intention to deliver and the price the buyer must pay for the contract's underlying commodity.

Derivative: A financial instrument whose value is determined in part by the value and characteristics of another instrument, the underlying asset. For example, a single stock futures contract is a derivative of the underlying stock on which it is based.

Discount: (1) A description of the futures contract price when it is less than the cash price of the underlying asset. For example, this single stock futures contract trades at a discount to its underlying stock. See also *Parity, Premium.* (2) A reduction in the expected price of a financial instrument produced by various factors.

Discretionary account: An arrangement by which an account holder authorizes another person, often a broker, to make buying and selling decisions without notification to the holder; often referred to as a managed account or controlled account.

Dividend: A corporation's payment to its stockholders.

Downtick: A situation in which a financial instrument sells for less than its previous transaction price. In securities markets, the "uptick rule" currently prevents the short sale of stock on a downtick. See *Uptick.*

Downtrend: A price trend involving a series of lower highs and lower lows.

E

Electronic trading: Computerized trading through an automated order entry and matching system.

Equity: (1) In a futures account, the dollar value if all open positions were offset at the current market price. (2) In a securities margin account, the excess of the market value of securities over debit balances. (3) The ownership interest of a company's stockholders.

Euronext.liffe: The derivatives business of Euronext, which also trades universal stock futures, the exchange's name for single stock futures.

Exchange: An association engaged in the business of buying and selling financial instruments.

Exchange-traded fund (ETF): A basket of securities designed to track an index while trading like a stock. For example, OneChicago's DIAMONDS contract is a future on the DIAMONDS ETF, which tracks the Dow Jones Industrial Average.

Exercise: In options trading, choosing to accept the underlying asset at the strike price.

Exercise price: The price at which the buyer of a call (put) option may choose to exercise his or her right to buy (sell) the underlying asset. Also called strike price.

Expiration cycle: A term describing the quarterly expiration dates applicable to derivatives. Three commonly used cycles are January/April/July/October, February/May/August/November, and March/June/September/December.

Expiration date: (1) The last date on which an option may be exercised. (2) A term used for the last trading day of a futures contract, although futures contracts technically do not expire because they must be either offset or performed.

F

Fair market value: For single stock futures, the theoretical value of the futures contract on a stock. In theory, the price of a single stock futures contract should equal the value of the underlying stock plus the interest rate less dividends, calculated over the life of the futures contract.

Fibonacci number or sequence of numbers: A sequence of numbers identified by the Italian mathematician Leonardo de Pise in the thirteenth century. It is the mathematical basis of the Elliott wave theory, where the first two numbers of the sequence are 0 and 1 and each successive number is the sum of the previous two numbers (0, 1, 2, 3, 5, 8, 13, 21, 34, 55, 89, 144, 233 . . .).

Fill or kill order (FOK): A limit order that must be either filled right away or canceled.

First notice day: The first day on which sellers can notify buyers, via the clearinghouse, of their intention to deliver cash commodities against futures contracts and on which buyers can receive notification.

Floor broker: One who executes orders on an exchange's trading floor for someone else.

Floor trader: Exchange members who are personally present on the trading floors to make trades for themselves and their customers. Also referred to as scalpers or locals.

Forward contract: A privately negotiated agreement, common in many industries, to complete a transaction at a time in the future, at a price often negotiated in the present.

Forward curve: The price of a series of futures contracts throughout several months.

Front month: The traded contract month of a futures contract that is closest to maturity. Also referred to as the nearby month or nearby. See also *Back months* and *Contract month.*

Fundamental analysis: The examination of the underlying factors that will affect the supply of and demand for the underlying assets. See also *Technical analysis.*

Futures commission merchant (FCM): An individual or organization that solicits or accepts orders to buy or sell futures contracts or options on futures and accepts money or other assets from customers to pay for such orders. The individual or organization must be registered with the Commodity Futures Trading Commission.

Futures contract: A standardized agreement to buy or sell a specified quantity of a commodity or financial instrument during a specified month in the future that can be traded only by public auction on designated exchanges.

G

Gap: A price range on a chart where no trading takes place from one day to the next.

Good till canceled: An order that stands until it is canceled or filled or until the contract expires.

Guided account: An account that is part of a program directed by a commodity trading adviser (CTA) or futures commission merchant (FCM). The CTA or FCM advises the customer to enter and/or liquidate specific positions, but the customer must give final approval to enter the order. These programs generally require a minimum initial investment and may include a trading strategy that will draw on only a part of the investment at any given time.

H

Head and shoulders: A chart formation representing three successive rallies and reactions, where the second rally, or head, reaches a higher point than the other two rallies. It usually indicates a major market reversal.

Hedging: The sale (purchase) of futures contracts in anticipation of future sales (purchases) of the underlying asset as a protection against possible price declines (increases).

I

Index: A group of securities whose calculated price is intended to represent economic trends. An index may be designed to track changes in the overall economy, the stock market, or a sector of the stock market, such as pharmaceuticals or technology.

Indexation: An investment strategy designed to mimic the price movement of an index or of a particular basket of securities.

Initial margin: A customer's funds required at the time a futures position is established or an option is sold to ensure that the customer carries out the contractual obligations. Margin in futures is not a down payment, as it is in securities. See also *Margin*.

In the money: A call option with a strike price below, or a put option with a strike price above, the current market price of the underlying asset.

Intrinsic value: The value of an option if it were to expire immediately.

Introducing broker (IB): A firm or individual that solicits and accepts commodity futures orders from customers but does not accept money or other assets from customers. An IB must be registered with the Commodity Futures Trading Commission and must carry all of its accounts through a FCM on a fully disclosed basis.

Inverted curve: A market state in which the price of a security futures contract is below the price of the security, or at a discount to the security.

Inverted market: A futures market in which the nearby months sell at a premium to the more distant months; generally occurs in a market where there is a supply shortage.

Island Futures Exchange (Recently renamed INET Futures Exchange): An affiliate of INET, that has been approved to offer security futures products. As of press time the exchange had not released contract specifications or a list of security futures products to be offered.

L

Lagging indicators: Market indicators that confirm or deny the trend indicated by the leading indicators. Also referred to as concurrent indicators.

Last trading day: The day on which trading for the current delivery month ends.

Leading indicators: Major market indicators that suggest the economic state for the coming months. Some leading indicators include index of consumer expectations, change in material prices, prices of stocks, and change in the money supply.

Leverage: A characteristic of a financial instrument that allows an investor to establish a position with funds that are less than the value of the financial instrument.

Life of contract: The time during which a contract trades, from the day it begins trading to the expiration of trading in the delivery month.

Limit: See *Position limit, Price limit, Reporting limit, Variable limit.*

Limit move: The maximum price movement allowed during one trading session, as designated by the rules of a contract market.

Limit order: An order in which the customer sets a limit on either price, time of execution, or both, unlike a market order, which should be filled at the most favorable price as soon as possible.

Liquidation: The purchase or sale of futures contracts, of the same quantity and delivery month as contracts sold or purchased earlier, to offset the obligation to make or take delivery.

Liquidity: A characteristic of a market in which buying and selling can be accomplished without dramatically affecting prices and in which bid/offer price spreads are narrow.

Long: An individual who has purchased a financial instrument, in contrast to a short, who has sold a financial instrument.

Long hedge: The act of buying futures contracts to protect against possible price increases in the underlying asset. See also *Hedging.*

Lot: A term for one futures contract. Also describes a number of futures contracts—for example, a 5-lot purchase of Microsoft single stock futures contracts.

M

Maintenance margin: The amount of money that must be maintained in an account while a futures position is open. If the equity in a customer's account drops under the maintenance margin level, the broker must issue a margin call to the customer, asking for money to restore the customer's equity in the account to the required minimum level. See also *Margin.*

Margin: (1) In the futures industry, an amount of money deposited by futures traders to ensure performance against the contract; it is not a down payment. Also referred to as a performance bond. (2) In the securities industry, a deposit made to a broker/dealer by a securities trader to buy or sell securities. When traders are buying securities, the margin is considered a down payment.

Margin call: A call from a brokerage firm to a customer asking the customer to deposit additional funds so that the equity returns to the minimum level required by exchange regulations; similarly, a call from a clearinghouse to a clearing member firm asking the firm to make additional deposits to return clearing margins to the minimum level required by clearinghouse rules.

Mark to market: The daily adjustment of accounts and margin requirements to settle daily gains and losses in each open position at the end of each trading day.

Market if touched: A price order that becomes a market order when the financial instrument trades at a designated price at least once.

Market maker: An exchange member who improves market liquidity by placing bids and offers for his or her own account in the absence of or in addition to public buy and sell orders.

Market order: An order that is to be filled at the best possible price and as soon as possible, unlike a limit order, which may specify requirements for price or time of execution. See also *Limit order*.

Matched-pair trade: A strategy in which one would purchase and sell two different stocks within the same industry, but generally in the same contract month. For example, one could buy the strong stock, sell the weak stock, and profit from the difference.

Maturity: The time between the first notice day and the last trading day of a commodity futures contract. During this time, the contract must be settled either by delivery or by cash.

Maximum Price Fluctuation: See *Limit move*.

MEFF: The Spanish futures and options exchange that trades single stock futures.

Minimum Price Fluctuation: See *Point*.

Misrepresentation: An untrue or misleading statement about a material fact upon which a customer based an investment.

Momentum indicator: A line plotted to show the difference between today's price and the price a fixed number of days ago. For example, momentum can be measured as the difference between today's price and the current value of a moving average. Often referred to as a momentum oscillator.

Moving average: A form of technical analysis that smoothes price and volume by averaging selected prices. It emphasizes the direction of a trend and confirms trend reversals.

N

Narrow-based index futures: Security futures products whose underlying asset is a narrow-based index, which has any one of the four following characteristics, in general, and subject to certain exclusions: (1) it has nine or fewer component securities; (2) any one of its component securities comprises more than 30% of its weighting; (3) the five highest weighted component securities together comprise more than 60% of its weighting; or (4) the lowest weighted component securities comprising, in the aggregate, 25% of the index's weighting have an aggregate dollar value of average daily trading volume of less than $50 million (or in the case of an index with 15 or more component securities, $30 million). Also commonly referred to as narrow-based indexes or NBIs.

NQLX: A wholly electronic security futures exchange that was originally a joint-venture operated by NASDAQ and Euronext.liffe, until NASDAQ pulled out in June 2003, leaving its stake to Euronext.liffe. It is located in the United States.

National Association of Securities Dealers (NASD): The self-regulatory organization of the securities industry.

National Futures Association (NFA): The self-regulatory organization of the futures industry.

Nearby month: See *Front month*.

Net position: The difference between the open long (buy) contracts and the open short (sell) contracts in any one futures contract month or in all months combined.

Nominal price: Declared price, usually an average of bid and ask prices, for a futures month. It is sometimes used in place of a closing price when no recent trading has taken place in that delivery month.

Notice day: See *First notice day*.

Notice of delivery: See *Delivery notice*.

Notional value: The face value, normally expressed is U.S. dollars, of the underlying asset of a futures contract.

O

Offer: A sign of willingness to sell at a stated price—the opposite of bid.

Offset: Closing an open position through the purchase (sale) of an equal number of futures contracts of the same delivery months. This turns over the contractual obligations to someone else.

OneChicago: The joint-venture security futures exchange operated by Chicago Mercantile Exchange, Chicago Board of Trade, and Chicago Board Options Exchange.

Open: The time at the beginning of the trading session officially defined by the exchange during which all trades are considered to be made "at the open."

Open interest: The sum of futures contracts that have not yet been offset or carried out by delivery.

Open outcry: A system of public auction for making bids and offers on trading floors.

Open trade equity: The potential gain or loss on open positions.

Option (option contract): A one-sided contract that gives the buyer the right, but not the obligation, to buy or sell a stated quantity of the underlying asset at a stated price within a designated time period, no matter what the market price of the underlying asset may be. The seller of the option has the obligation to buy the stated quantity of the underlying asset from the option buyer or to sell it to the option buyer at the exercise price if the option is exercised. See also *Call (option), Put (option)*.

Option premium: The price of an options contract.

Option seller: See *Writer*.

Options Clearing Corporation: A clearinghouse for several U.S. markets and an issuer of all listed option contracts that are trading on national option exchanges.

Order execution: The management of a customer's order by a broker, including receiving the order, transmitting it to the trading floor or trading platform of the appropriate exchange, and returning confirmation (fill price) of the completed order to the customer.

Orders: See *Limit order, Market order, Stop order*.

Original margin: The initial deposit of margin money required of clearing member firms by clearinghouse rules, similar to the initial margin deposit required of customers.

Out of the money: A put option with a strike price below or a call option with a strike price above the current market value of the underlying asset.

Overbought: A view that the market price has risen too sharply and too quickly relative to underlying fundamental factors.

Oversold: A view that the market price has declined too sharply and too quickly relative to underlying fundamental factors.

P

Par: The face value of a security.

Parity: A description of the price relationship between a futures contract and its underlying asset when they are trading at the same price.

Performance bond: See *Margin*.

Physical settlement: The process of fulfilling a futures contract at the expiration date by delivering the underlying asset. A single stock futures contract's underlying asset is usually 100 shares of the stock.

Pit: A recessed area on the trading floor of some exchanges in which open-outcry futures or options trading takes place. Some exchanges have rings instead of pits.

Point: The minimum price movement for a futures contract.

Point-and-figure chart: A graph of prices charted with x's for rising prices and o's for declining prices; used to reveal buy and sell signals.

Point balance: A computation of official closing or settlement prices provided in a statement prepared by futures commission merchants to show profit or loss on all open contracts.

Position: An individual's standing in a market. For example, a buyer has a long position and, conversely, a seller has a short position.

Position limit: The maximum number of security futures contracts any trader can hold in a position as designated by the Commodity Futures Trading Commission.

Position trader: A securities, futures, or options trader who maintains positions for an extended time period, in contrast to a day trader, who will normally initiate and close positions within a single trading session.

Preferred stock: A security that generally pays a fixed dividend and that gives the holder claims to corporate earnings and assets that surpass those of the holders of common stock. See also *Common stock*.

Premium: (1) In price relationships between different delivery months of futures contracts or between a futures contract and its underlying asset, one trades at a premium over another when its price is greater than that of the other. (2) The price paid for an option.

Price discovery: The economic function provided by futures markets in determining cash market prices.

Price limit: The maximum price fluctuation, up or down, from the previous day's settlement price that is allowed for a commodity during one trading session. This limit is set by exchange rules.

Purchase and sale statement (P&S): A statement that a customer receives when a position has been liquidated or offset. The statement lists the quantity of contracts traded, the gross profit or loss, the commission charges, and the net profit or loss.

Put (option): In options, a contract that gives a buyer the right, but not the obligation, to sell the underlying asset at a certain price on or before a certain date.

Q

Quotation: The actual price or the bid or ask price of cash commodities, stocks, futures contracts, or options contracts at a specific time.

R

Rally: An upward movement of prices after a downward movement.

Rally top: The price at which a rally stops. A bull move will usually hit many rally tops over its market span.

Range: The difference between the high and low price, generally during a single trading session.

Reaction: A short-term price movement against a current trend.

Recovery: See *Rally*.

Registered commodity representative: See *Associated person (AP), Broker*.

Registered representative: An employee of a broker/dealer who solicits its business, gives securities trading advice, and receives a percentage of commissions.

Regulation T: A rule of the Federal Reserve Board that limits the amount of credit that broker/dealers can extend to customers to enable them to purchase and carry securities.

Reporting limit: Sizes of positions for which commodity traders are required to make daily reports to the exchange and/or the CFTC. The sizes of reportable positions are designated by the exchange and/or by the CFTC. Daily reports include the size of the position by commodity, delivery month, and the purpose of trading, i.e., speculative or hedging.

Resistance: The price level at which bullish prices stop rising. It is the opposite of support.

Retender: The right of the holders of futures contracts who have received a delivery notice from the clearinghouse to offer the notice for sale on the open market, voiding their contractual obligation to take delivery; the opportunity to retender is restricted to certain commodities and periods of time.

Retracement: A price movement in the opposite direction from the main trend.

Return: The percentage profit that one gains, or might gain, on an investment.

Ring: A round space on an exchange trading floor in which traders and brokers stand and execute futures or options trades. Some exchanges have pits instead of rings.

Risk disclosure statement: A statement sent out to potential futures traders that they must read and sign; by doing so, they acknowledge that they understand the risks involved in trading futures.

Roll forward: Liquidation of a position in a nearby month, followed by the purchase or sale of a distant contract month to transfer the long or short position. Also called a rollover.

Round turn: The combination of a purchase (sale) of futures contracts and the offsetting sale (purchase) of an equal amount of futures contracts with the same delivery month. Also known as a round trip.

S

Scalper: A speculator on an exchange trading floor who buys and sells rapidly for small profits and losses and holds positions for only a short time during a trading session.

Securities: Common stocks, preferred stocks, corporate bonds, and government bonds.

Security deposit: See *Margin*.

Securities and Exchange Commission (SEC): The government-created commission that oversees the entire securities industry, including self-regulatory organizations like the NASD. It regulates security futures jointly with the CFTC.

Security futures principal: The designated supervisor accountable for the security futures business at a broker/dealer, futures commission merchant, or introducing broker.

Security futures product: A futures contract based on a single security or a narrow-based group of securities. See *Narrow-based index futures, Single stock future*.

Segregated account: An account that holds a customer's assets and separates them from the broker's or firm's assets.

Settlement: See *Cash settlement, Physical settlement*.

Settlement day: The designated day on which buyer and seller fulfill their contract through either final cash settlement or physical delivery.

Settlement price: The closing price or a price within the range of closing prices, as determined by the exchange, that is used to calculate net gains or losses at the official end of each trading day.

Shad-Johnson accord: An agreement between the CFTC and the SEC to ban the trading of narrow-based stock index futures and single stock futures.

Short: An individual who has sold a security or a futures contract; a long, in contrast, has purchased a security or futures contract.

Short hedge: The sale of futures to protect against a possible decline in the price of the underlying asset. See also *Hedging*.

Short sales: In stocks, borrowing shares and then selling them, with the requirement to repurchase them at a later date. Selling short is a bearish strategy.

Short-term capital gains rate: The tax rate applied to trading profits on assets held for a year or less.

Side: Each contract has two sides—the buy action and the sell action. Two sides equal one round turn.

Sideways trend: A movement in price that does not go above or below certain levels.

Single stock future: A security futures contract based on an individual stock.

Speculator: A market participant who tries to forecast price changes and make profits through the sale and/or purchase of futures contracts. A speculator with a bullish price forecast tries to profit by purchasing futures contracts and then closing his or her long position with a later sale of an equal number of futures of the same delivery month at a higher price. A speculator with a bearish price forecast tries to profit by selling futures contracts and then covering his or her short position with a later purchase of futures at a lower price.

Spot: Usually, the cash price for a product available for immediate delivery. Also refers to the nearest contract month for delivery.

Spot commodity: See *Cash Commodity*.

Spread: (1) The simultaneous purchase of one futures contract and sale of another in order to profit from the variations in price relationships between the two contracts. Several versions of a spread include the purchase of one contract month and the sale of another contract month of the same commodity; the purchase of one contract month of one commodity and the sale of the same contract month of a similar, but different, commodity; or the purchase of a commodity in one market and the sale of the same commodity in another market. (2) The price difference between two similar markets or trading instruments. See also *Arbitrage*.

Stand-alone system: A trading program that you download directly onto your computer.

Stock: A percentage of ownership in a company. Stock ownership entitles one to be involved in the company's growth and decline, to receive dividends as declared by the company's board of directors, to choose members of the board of directors, and to participate in corporate actions as determined by law.

Stock index: An indicator that measures price changes in a specific group of stocks or tracks the overall market. Indexes vary based on their composition, the sampling of stocks, the weighting of individual stocks, and the method of averaging used to establish the index.

Stock future: See *Security futures product*.

Stock split: The division of stock into a larger number of shares that are worth less. For example, a 2-for-1 stock split would create twice the number of shares, but these shares would be worth half the price. A reverse split creates a smaller number of shares that are worth more.

Stop loss: A risk management strategy to liquidate a losing position at a given point. See *Stop order*.

Stop limit order: Similar to a stop order, except that the trade must be executed at the *exact* price or better. If the order cannot be fulfilled at the exact price, it is held until the exact price or better is reached again.

Stop order: An order to buy or sell that becomes a market order when the market hits a designated price. A buy stop is placed above market price, and a sell stop is placed below market price. Also known as a stop-loss order.

Strike price: See *Exercise price*.

Suitability requirement: An NASD and NFA rule that requires a security futures principal to ascertain whether customers' financial means and investment objectives are appropriate to security futures trading.

Suitable: An assessment of an investor who trades in accordance with his or her financial means and investment objectives.

Support: A price level at which bearish prices have stopped falling. It is the opposite of resistance. Once this level is reached, prices consolidate for a period of time.

Synthetic future: A combination of a put and a call with the same strike price. If both are bullish, it is a synthetic long future; if both are bearish, it is a synthetic short future. Such combinations mimic the purchase or sale of a single stock futures contract, and thus the risk/return characteristics of trading a single stock futures contract.

T

Technical analysis: The examination of technical indicators, such as price range patterns, rates of change, volume changes, and open interest, in order to forecast future prices.

Tender: The notice that a seller of futures contracts gives to the clearinghouse to inform it that he or she intends to deliver the underlying asset to fulfill the contract. The clearinghouse then sends the notice to the oldest recorded buyer in that delivery month. See also *Retender*.

Tick size: The minimum change in price, up or down, for a security or a futures or options contract. See also *Point*.

Time value: Any amount by which an option premium is above the option's intrinsic value, usually relative to the time left to expiration.

Trader: (1) One who trades for his or her own account. (2) An employee of a broker/dealer (B/D), futures commission merchant (FCM), or other type of institution who trades for her or his employer's account.

Trading range: An established set of high and low price limits within which a market will spend a distinct period of time.

Transaction costs: The expenses associated with buying or selling a financial instrument, such as brokerage commissions, regulatory fees, taxes, and the spread between the bid and offer prices.

Transferable Notice: See *Retender*.

Trend: The general direction of price movement in a market. See *Downtrend, Uptrend*.

Trend line: A line that connects a series of either highs or lows in price movement. An uptrend line represents support, whereas a downtrend line represents resistance. Horizontal trend lines mark periods of consolidation.

U

Unauthorized trading: Buying or selling financial instruments for a customer's account without the customer's permission.

Underlying: (1) The cash commodity, index, or security on which futures contracts are based. (2) The futures contract, index, or security on which options are based.

Unit of trading: The quantity of the underlying asset that a futures contract represents. The unit of trading for a single stock futures contract is generally 100 shares of the stock for 1 contract. Each security futures exchange sets the size of its own contracts. Also, the minimum quantity required when trading.

Uptick: A situation in which a financial instrument sells for more than its previous transaction price. See *Downtick*.

Uptrend: The tendency for a market's price movements to create a series of higher highs and higher lows.

V

Variable limit: A price system that permits greater-than-normal price movements under certain conditions, such as extreme volatility.

Volatility: A calculation of a futures contract's tendency for price fluctuation based on its daily price history over a period of time.

Volume: On a futures exchange, the number of contracts, usually round turn, traded during a specified period of time.

W

Wirehouse: See *futures commission merchant (FCM)*.

Writer: The seller of an option. The seller *is obligated* to buy (in the case of a put) or sell (in the case of a call) the underlying asset. The buyer has the right, *but is not obligated*, to buy (in the case of a call) or sell (in the case of a put) the underlying asset.

Note: This glossary is included only to assist the reader and should not be construed as a set of legal definitions.

Bibliography

Abbott Gidel, Susan. "100 Years of Futures Trading: From Domestic Agricultural to World Financial." *Futures Industry*, December/January 2000, <http://www.futuresindustry.org/fimagazi-1929.asp?v=p&iss=93&a=607> (June 2002).

Abbott Gidel, Susan. "Stock Indexes Roar Into the Next Century." *Futures Industry*, October/November 1999 <http://www.futuresindustry.org/fimagazi-1929.asp?v=p&iss=89&a=598> (June 2002).

Bozworth, Carole G. "Investment Basics: Stocks." 15 December 1999 <http://muextension.missouri.edu/xplor/hesguide/famecon/gh3522.htm> (August 2002).

Burghardt, Galen. "Off the Charts: Futures Volume Soars to Record Highs," *Futures Industry,* January/February 2002, <http://www.futuresindustry.org/fimagazi-1929.asp?v=p&iss=121&a=756> (June 2002).

Butler, Chad. "Discover Another Asset for Your Trading Toolbox." *Stock Futures and Options*, August 2002: 52-56.

Chicago Board Options Exchange. "Learning Center: The Basics" <http://www.cboe.com/LearnCenter/basics.asp> (July 2002).

Clary, Isabelle. "Slow Start Seen for Single Stock Futures." *E-Securities*, August/ September 2001.

Commodity Futures Trading Commission and Securities and Exchange Commission. "Customer Margin Rules Relating to Security Futures" August 2002.

Commodity Futures Trading Commission. "CFTC Recognizes New Joint Venture Exchange for Single-Stock Futures," <http://www.cftc.gov/opa/press01/opa4559-01.htm> (August 2002).

Commodity Futures Trading Commission. "CFTC Recognizes New Exchange for Single-Stock Futures," <http://www.cftc.gov/opa/press02/opa4656-02.htm> (June 2002).

Commodity Futures Trading Commission. "CFTC Recognizes New Exchange for Single-Stock Futures," <http://www.cftc.gov/opa/press02/opa4608-02.htm> (August 2002).

Commodity Futures Trading Commission, "Economic Purposes of Futures Trading" <http://www.cftc.gov/opa/brochures/opaeconpurp.htm> (June 2002).

Commodity Futures Trading Commission. "Synopsis: CFTC/SEC Agreement to Reform Shad-Johnson Accord," <http://www.cftc.gov/opa/press00/opaysnopsis.htm> (August 2002).

Earnest, Debra. "Who is This Broker Anyway?" *Stock Futures and Options*, August 2002: 65-68.

Euronext.liffe. "About Euronext.liffe — The Exchange" <http://www.liffe.com> (October 2003).

Euronext.liffe. "Accessing LIFFE" <http://www.liffe.com> (July 2002).

Euronext.liffe. "Euronext.liffe Announces a Further 25 Universal Stock Futures" <http://www.liffe.com/press/releases/030923.htm> (October 2003).

Euronext.liffe. "Universal Stock Futures Volume 2003" <http://www.liffe.com/liffedata/contracts/liffe/usf/volumes_usf2003.csv> (October 2003).

Euronext.liffe. "Universal Stock Futures Contract Summary Specification" <http://www.liffe.com> (October 2003).

Euronext.liffe. "Universal Stock Futures (physical delivery) List" <http://www.liffe.com> (July 2002).

Foley, Kevin M. "Foreign Products Still Off Limits to U.S. Investors." *Futures Industry*, December 2001

Commodity Futures Trading Commision "Congress Passes Commodity Futures Modernization Act" <http://www.cftc.gov/opa/press00/opa4479-00.htm> (October 2003).

Hill, Patrice. "Roaring Twenties Redux" <http://www.findarticles.com/cf_dls/m1571/10_16/60130265/print.jhtml> (July 2002).

Hong Kong Exchanges and Clearing Limited. "History of the Hong Kong Securities Market" <http://www.hkex.com.hk/exchange/history/history.htm> (August 2002).

Island Futures Exchange, LLC. "Trading Single Stock Futures on Island" <http://www.island.com/futures/index.asp> (August 2002).

Leitner, Anthony (moderator) and Onnig Dombalagian, Ira Krulik, Alan Lawhead, John Lawton, and Thomas Sexton (speakers). "Customer Accounts and Reporting." Presentation at the Futures Industry Association's meeting, *Security Futures: Are You Ready?* 25 September 2002.

Lerman, David. "Fair Value: Myth v. Reality." *Stock Futures and Options*, July 2002: 10-13.

Lerman, David. "Reading Between the Lines of Single Stock Futures Pricing." *Stock Futures and Options*, October 2002: 76-78.

"Looking Back at the Crash of '29: Then, as Now, a New Era." *New York Times*, 15 October 1999 <http:www.nytimes.com/library/financial/index-1929-crash-2.html> (July 2002).

McCoy, William (moderator) and Michael Foley, Alan Lawhead, William Pomicrski, and Regina Thoele (speakers). "Getting Your Staff and Customers Ready to Trade." Presentation at the Futures Industry Association's meeting, *Security Futures: Are You Ready?* 25 September 2002.

MEFF. "Equity Statistics" <http://www.meff.com/estadown.html> (October 2003).

National Association of Securities Dealers. *Letter and enclosures to the Securities and Exchange Commission; Re: Security Futures Rules.* 21 March 2002.

National Association of Securities Dealers. "SEC Approves New Rules and Rule Amendments Concerning Security Futures; Effective Date: October 15, 2002." *Notice to Members*, November 2002.

National Futures Association and National Association of Securities Dealers, "Security Futures Risk Disclosure Statement," September 2002.

National Futures Association. "Security Futures Regulatory Update" <http://www.nfa.futures.org> (August 2002).

National Futures Association. "Approved Rules and Interpretive Notices" <http://www.nfa.futures.org/member_education/archive/approved_rules.html> (August 2002).

Newsome, James. "Testimony of James E. Newsome, Chairman of the Commodity Futures Trading Commission, before the U.S. Senate Committee on Energy and Natural Resources" <http://www.cftc.gov/opa/speeches02/opanewsm-23.htm> (March 2003).

NQLX. "Euronext.liffe to Take Over Ownership of NQLX" <http://www.nqlx.com/aboutnqlx/LIFFE%20to%20take%20over%20NQLX%201.pdf> (October 2003).

NQLX. "Full Product Listing" <http://www.nqlx.com/products/Product%20List.xls> (October 2003).

OneChicago "OneChicago Reports Record Volume for September 2003" <http://www.onechicago.com/060000_press_news/press_news_2003/10012003.html> (October 2002).

Osten, Gail. "And...They're Off!" *Stock Futures and Options*, September 2002: 18-24.

Pratt, Sereno Stansbury. *The Work of Wall Street.* Reprint: Arno Press, Inc., 1975.

Securities and Exchange Commission. "The Laws That Govern the Securities Industry" <http://www.sec.gov/about/laws.shtml> (June 2002).

Securities and Exchange Commission. "Reporting Obligations Because of Securities Act Registration" <http://www.sec.gov/info/small-bus/qasbsec.htm#eod5> (August 2002).

Simons, Howard. "Single Stock Futures: Considerations for Technicians," PowerPoint presentation, 2002.

Simons, Howard. "Single Stock Futures: Hedging Applications," PowerPoint presentation, 2002.

Singapore Exchange "SGX to Launch Six More Single Stock Futures on 15 August 2002"

<http://info.sgx.com/webnewscentre.nsf/bc.../48256838002f07b148256c 1300356edd?OpenDocument> (August 2002).

"Single Stock Futures Are Set to Debut on August 21: Is Anyone Ready to Trade?" *Securities Week*, August 20, 2001.

"Stock Valuation" <http://www.stockworm.com/tours/stock-value.html?coupon=overture_v1> (October 2002).

Tait, Nikki. "Americans Poised to Be Offered Contracts." *Financial Times*, 21 June 2001.

Tan, Kopin. "As U.S. Finalizes Rule for Single-Stock Futures, Brokerage Firm Offers Flat Rate of $1 a Contract." Dow Jones Newswires, 2002.

Walker-Daniels, Kimberly et al., ed. *PassTrak Series 24: Principles and Practices*, 10th ed. Dearborn Financial Publishing, 1996.

Wasendorf, Russell Jr. "Single Stock Futures: Success at Spain's MEFF Exchange."
Stock Futures and Options, July 2002: 48-52; 97-100.

Wasendorf, Russell Sr. "Global-Minded and Connected: Interview with Hugh Freedburg, Chief Executive of LIFFE." *Stock Futures and Options*, May 2002: 34-39; 68-72.

Wasendorf, Russell Sr. "You as an Analyst." *Stock Futures and Options*, July 2002.

Wasendorf, Russell Sr. "Technical Analysis 101: Significant Chart Patterns." *Stock Futures and Options*, August 2002.

Wasendorf, Russell Sr. "Profiting From Options on Futures: Part 1." *Stock Futures and Options*, Fall 2001.

Wasendorf, Russell Sr. "Profiting From Options on Futures: Part 2." *Stock Futures and Options*, March 2002.

Wasendorf, Russell Sr. "Single Stock Futures: The New Generation" *Futures and Options Week*, March 2002.

Wasendorf, Russell Sr. *All About Futures*, 2nd ed. McGraw-Hill, 2001.

Contributors

Brace Barber graduated from the United States Military Academy at West Point in May 1987. The thought process and principles that he learned at the academy and at U.S. Army Ranger School have guided his personal achievement and decisions as a leader. In more than 11 years of military experience, Brace studied leadership as the head of three platoons and two companies. He is the co-founder and president of Tax Recovery Group, Inc.

Linda Bradford Raschke has been a full-time professional trader since 1981. She began as a floor trader and later started LBR Group, a professional money management firm. In addition to running successful programs as a CTA, she has been a principal trader for several hedge funds and has run commercial hedging programs. Raschke was recognized in Jack Schwager's book *The New Market Wizards* (HarperBusiness, 1994) and is well known for her book *Street Smarts* (M. Gordon Publishing Group, 1996). Numerous educational articles are available on her web site, www.LBRgroup.com.

Chad Butler has been involved in the markets as both a futures broker and a trader for the past 6 years and a market analyst for nearly 15 years. His expertise in technical analysis and advanced option strategies has enabled him to become involved in creating arbitrage and program trading models in stock index futures and security futures. He has also worked on several successful financial web sites, including pfgbest.com, sfomag.com, tradethedow.com, themarketvushow.com, kwiktrading.com, and tradespotter.com.

Clif Droke is the editor of the three-times-weekly *Bear Market Report* and the monthly *Gold Strategies Review* newsletter. He is the author of several books on trading and technical analysis, including the recently published book *Moving Averages Simplified* (Traders Library/Marketplace Books, 2001).

David Floyd is the president of Aspen Trading Group and a columnist with TradingMarkets.com. Trading professionally since 1994, he specializes in NYSE stocks and is an active investor in the foreign exchange markets.

Marc H. Gerstein, director of investment research for Reuters, is the author of *Screening the Market: A Four-Step Method to Find, Analyze, Buy and Sell Stocks* (Wiley, 2002) and *The Value Connection: A Four-Step Market Screening Method to Match Good Companies With Good Stocks* (Wiley, 2003). He regularly shares his views in the financial media, having appeared periodically on Bloomberg TV's *Money Cast* and CNNfn's *Street Sweep*. He has also been quoted in *USA Today*, CBSMarketWatch, the *Wall Street Journal*, *Money Online*, and the *New York Daily News*, as well as in *Lessons from the Legends of Wall Street* (Dearborn Trade Publishing, 2000), by Nikki Ross, and *The Value Reporting Revolution* (Wiley, 2001), by Robert Eccles, Robert H. Hertz, E. Mary Keegan, and David M. H. Phillips. Gerstein has created a collection of screens catering to a variety of investment goals and a layered screening technique known as Reuters Select.

Price Headley is the founder and chief analyst at www.BigTrends.com, which provides daily trading education and recommendations on stocks and options.

Scot R. Hicks, senior vice president for Trade Center, Inc., has been with the firm since 1995. Trade Center, Inc., is a futures brokerage firm specializing in the administration of futures trading systems on behalf of clients worldwide.

Christopher Krohn is the managing director for strategy and marketing for OneChicago, an electronic exchange committed to being the global leader in futures on individual stocks and narrow-based indexes. OneChicago is a joint venture between the Chicago Board of Options Exchange, the Chicago Mercantile Exchange, Inc., and the Chicago Board of Trade. In his role at OneChicago, he has delivered numerous educational presentations to brokers and investors throughout the U.S. , focusing on equity derivatives and their applications.

David Lerman is the associate director of equity products at the Chicago Mercantile Exchange, Inc., and the author of *Exchange Traded Funds and E-Mini Stock Index Futures* (Wiley, 2001).

Kira McCaffrey Brecht is associate editor of *SFO* magazine. A Chicago-based financial writer, she has been writing about the futures markets for more than 12 years. Posts during her career include Chicago bureau chief at Futures World News, derivatives reporter and market analyst at Bridge News, and technical analyst at MMS International.

Lawrence G. McMillan, author of the best-selling options book *Options as a Strategic Investment, 4th ed.* (Prentice Hall, 2002), is president of McMillan Analysis Corp. (www.optionstrategist.com). McMillan Analysis Corp. publishes several option trading newsletters, has a wide array of educational material and seminars available, and manages individual accounts in the option markets. The company also sells software, such as a stand-alone version of the Black-Scholes model.

Larry Pesavento has more than 40 years of trading experience, including 3 years as a local S&P 500 futures trader at the Chicago Mercantile Exchange. He managed the commodity department at Drexel Burnham Lambert for 6 years and traded at Commodity Corporation for 2 years. Pesavento has written a cycles-based newsletter and since 1994 has traded for a private hedge fund in Tucson, Arizona.

Barbara Rockefeller is an economist and international market fore-caster, using both macro and technical indicators. She is the author of *CNBC 24/7—Trading around the Clock, around the World* (2000); *The Global Trader* (2001); and, most recently, *Technical Analysis for Dummies* (to be released February 2004), all published by Wiley. She prepares custom technical chart reports for private clients. Her web site is www.rts-forex.com.

Brett N. Steenbarger, Ph.D., is an associate professor of psychiatry and behavioral sciences at SUNY Upstate Medical University in Syracuse, New York. He is also an active trader and writes occasional feature articles on market psychology for MSN Money (www.moneycentral.com). The author of *The Psychology of Trading* (Wiley, 2003), Dr. Steenbarger has published more than 50 peer-reviewed articles and book chapters on short-term approaches to behavioral change. Many of his articles and trading strategies are linked on www.greatspeculations.com.

Christopher Terry is a full-time stock and index futures trader. He has spoken at a number of conferences and written articles for various magazines. In addition to trading, Terry and his partner, Linda Bradford Raschke, provide a wealth of free educational information for both stock and futures traders at www.LBRgroup.com.

Adrienne Laris Toghraie, a trader's coach, is an internationally recognized authority in the field of human development for the financial community. Her eight books on the psychology of trading including, *Traders' Secrets* (Target Press, 1999), coauthored with Murray Ruggiero, have been highly praised by financial magazines. Toghraie's public seminars and private counseling, as well as her television appearances and keynote addresses at major industry conferences, have achieved a wide level of recognition and popularity. Her web site is www.TradingOnTarget.com.

Russell Wasendorf, Sr., is chairman and CEO of PFG, Inc., a futures commission merchant. He also heads Wasendorf & Associates, Inc., a research firm devoted to trader education. He is the author of six books.

INDEX

About the Authors

Russell Wasendorf, Sr. is chairman and CEO of Peregrine Financial Group, a pioneering and still powerful firm in the trading of single stock futures. He is the founder and head of Wasendorf and Associates, which publishes *Stocks, Futures, & Options* magazine. Wasendorf is also the author or coauthor of a number of higher-level trading books including *All About Futures*, *Foreign Currency Trading*, and others.

Elizabeth Thompson is on the editorial staff of *Stocks, Futures, & Options*, where she is also a regular contributor and researcher.